Marketin

The M & E Handbook Series

Marketing Ov

Alan West
*Course director of International Marketing,
Thames Polytechnic*

Pitman Publish
128 Long Acre,

© Longman G

First published 7

British Library Cataloguing in Publication Data

West, Alan
　Marketing overseas.—(M & E handbooks)
　1. Export marketing
　I. Title
　658.8'48　　　HF1009.5

ISBN 0 7121 1547 1

Dedicated to all students of international marketing

All rights reserved. No part of this publication may be reproduced, stored in a retrieval system, or transmitted, in any form or by any means, electronic, mechanical, photocopying, recording and/or otherwise, without the prior written permission of the publishers. This book may not be lent, resold, hired out or otherwise disposed of by way of trade in any form of binding or cover other than that in which it is published, without the prior consent of the publishers.

Typeset by Avocet Marketing Services, Bicester, Oxon.
Printed and bound in Great Britain.

Contents

Preface ix

1 Concepts 1
   The role of marketing; The international environment; The development of international activity

2 The international environment 10
   Trends in international trade; The nature of international trade; The international trade of the United Kingdom

3 Concentration in international trade 22
   The concept of globalization; Market sectors and international concentration; Reasons for industrial concentration

4 Multinationals 32
   Introduction; The development of multinationals; The impact of multinationals; Controls on multinational development

5 Differences and similarities in overseas markets 39
   Segmentation; Avoiding the pitfalls of segmentation; Segmenting markets at home and overseas

6 International strategic development 49
   Determining an international strategy; International strategic constraints

Contents

7 International marketing strategy and market investment 61
The level of investment; Assessing the risk; Other factors

8 Information systems for initial development overseas 69
The need for information; Information systems; Collecting information; Using existing sources of information; Conducting specific market research

9 Information systems for controlling international markets 81
Information needs in established markets; Identifying trends

10 International product management 91
The product and the market; Product options; The issue of standardization

11 Further aspects of international product policy 101
Factors affected by nature of product; Packaging; Branding; Service warranties

12 Distribution channels: design and management 111
Distribution channels; Using intermediaries; Strategic implications; Maintaining a competitive distribution channel

13 Factors in physical distribution 121
Physical distribution implications; Total distribution cost; Export packing; Transport; Other factors

14 Indirect exporting opportunities 131
Indirect export; Export agencies; Other intermediaries; The importance of indirect export

15 Direct exporting opportunities 139
Direct exports; Agents; Distributors; Choosing an agent or distributor; Contact with agents and distributors; Agency and distributor agreements; Motivating agents and distributors; Direct sales; Direct mail

Contents vii

16 Overseas investment 155
   Establishing subsidiary activities; Industrial co-operation ventures; Licensing; Franchising overseas; Management contracts; Joint venture operations; Establishing a local sales or marketing office; Contract manufacture overseas; Local assembly operations; Buying overseas companies; Creating a fully owned overseas manufacturing plant

17 International communications 173
   The nature of communication; Communicating with an international market; Strategic factors affecting promotion; Standardization; Agencies

18 Sales promotion and public relations 188
   Defining sales promotion; In-store promotions; Couponing and direct mail; The international exhibition; Public relations; Access to media available for public relations activity; Public relations for local subsidiaries

19 Overseas sales management 199
   The nature of international sales management; The role of the sales manager; The national and international sales manager; Sales strategy and sales management overseas

20 Pricing factors in overseas marketing 207
   The pricing environment; Strategic issues; Factors affecting pricing; Setting a price; Legal and governmental aspects of pricing; Currency implications; Cash flow implications

21 Implementing pricing policy – export terms and conditions 219
   Introduction; The overseas contract of sale; Documentation; Terms of trade in exporting; Methods of payment in overseas export sales; Minimizing risk of default in payments; Financing overseas sales; Multinational financing; Financing overseas investment

viii Contents

22 Organizing for overseas marketing 232
   The importance of organization design; Organizational development for overseas markets; Training; Multinational organization; Management

23 Staffing the international firm 242
   Introduction; Employing expatriates; Employing local nationals; Employing third-country nationals; Creating an international management team; Factors influencing the choice of staffing system

24 Marketing overseas for the service company 251
   Introduction; Factors affecting the development of international service companies; Problems for service companies; Solutions for service companies

Appendices 260
1 Case studies; 2 Examination technique; 3 Examination questions; 4 GNP

Index 281

Preface

The face of the world is changing rapidly in the 1980s and with it the task of the marketing executive. This book attempts to introduce the student to the main principles and issues that drive markets worldwide and to discuss what the company wishing to develop in the international sector will need to consider.

For many countries international trade is vital to economic success. For the United Kingdom the decline in share of world trade is a particularly worrying trend relying as the UK has on the sale of manufactured goods overseas to maintain a favourable balance of trade.

The importance of long-term issues has often been minimized in marketing texts with their concentration on short-term tactical issues such as pricing and promotion in the market. As development overseas must be viewed as a long-term commitment this book deals with major market issues that face the firm in other countries, particularly long-term strategic factors that will need to be considered. Marketing is concerned with the use of all company resources, and so the book also considers personnel issues in the international environment, and the mechanics of international existence which are often considered not to be the preserve of the international marketing textbook.

The three Case Studies in Appendix 1 have been prepared with the help of Mark Cullinane (BIS in Scandinavia), Caroline Woodstock (DLW and the USA) and Debbie Merrens (A tale of two companies); to whom I am most grateful. I should also like to thank David Palfreman whose hints on examination technique have been reproduced in Appendix 2.

I hope that the reader will find the book stimulating and enjoyable as an introduction to the international business environment which the author enjoyed during years of working in international marketing.

Alan West

1
Concepts

The role of marketing

1. Definition of marketing. Marketing can be defined in a number of ways. Most commonly it is considered as the fulfilling of consumer needs at a profit to the organisation. More specifically it demands an understanding of the market – factors such as how the law, government, competition or structure of the market will affect what the firm is trying to achieve, what is preferred by potential customers and the implications of producing and selling the item that is involved.

2. The role of marketing within the firm. Efficient application of marketing principles provides the firm with a competitive advantage. In other words it is able to use its resources more effectively than other firms, thereby becoming more profitable and growing more rapidly. Marketing helps the firm in the following ways:

(*a*) By producing an integrated view of the entire market, which allows the development of an effective long-term strategy: *What can the firm achieve?*

(*b*) By defining medium-term investment criteria from the long-term strategy to invest in new products or services: *Where are the greatest opportunities?*

(*c*) By positioning both new and old products to achieve the best result consistent with the long-term strategy: *How can the firm take advantage of those opportunities?* This positioning process involves the

2 Marketing Overseas

interaction of a number of factors, called the 'marketing mix'. They are:

(*i*) *product factors* – including packaging;

(*ii*) *distribution factors* – how the product should reach the consumer and how the interaction with intermediaries, wholesalers, or retailers, for example, should be handled;

(*iii*) *pricing factors* – including credit terms;

(*iv*) *promotional factors* – how the product should be promoted, including advertising, sales promotion and public relations.

These four elements have become known as the 'four Ps': price, product, place, and promotion. Recently, with the increase in the competitive environment and with the growth in importance of the service sector, other elements have been added:

(*v*) *competition* (or parity) – how the competition will react and what competitive factors will be important;

(*vi*) *people* – employee involvement is very important in the majority of service organisations;

(*vii*) *physical* – the environment in which the service takes place is also often crucial;

(*viii*) *process* – the way in which the service is carried out (*see* Fig. 1.1).

The international environment

3. The importance of the international environment. Access to the international environment provides a number of advantages to any organisation.

(*a*) *Growth*. A firm with a new concept can grow rapidly in the home market but it will find that each increase in market share becomes progressively harder – from 5 to 10 per cent, for example, may be easy, but from 30 to 60 per cent may be impossible. For the innovative firm, the international environment creates opportunities for maintaining sales and profitable growth.

Elders IXL, the Australian conglomerate with interests including Fosters Beer, reached the stage of having its growth potential limited by the size of the Australian market. In 1985 it approached Allied Lyons, the UK food and drink firm, with an attempt to take it over to provide additional growth opportunities.

1. Concepts

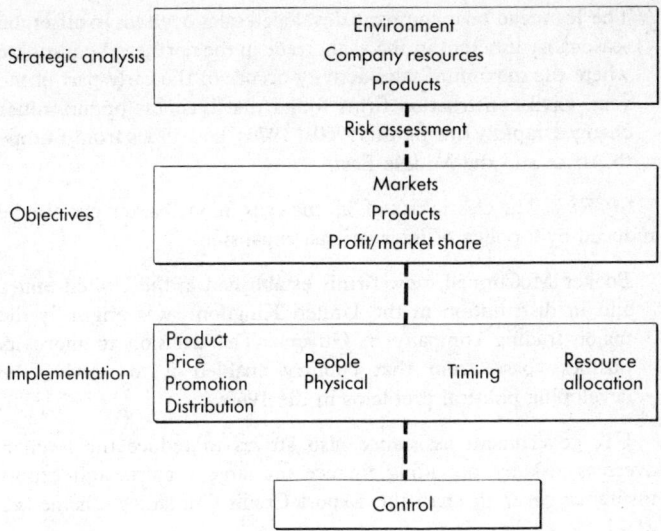

Figure 1.1 *Marketing mix process*

The level of economic growth has also varied considerably throughout the world since 1945 – growth in South East Asia has been considerably more rapid than in the United States which has experienced a higher rate of growth than Europe.

(*b*) *Profit.* Some overseas markets may be substantially more profitable than the home territory either because of competition or price control. Expansion overseas may offer major opportunities to achieve high levels of profit.

Inchcape is one of the major alcoholic drinks distributors in the Arabian Gulf and maintains retail margins that are substantially higher than those that would be possible in European alcohol retailing.

(*c*) *Trade fluctuations.* Each country will experience different short- and long-term trade fluctuations. Overseas development will help the organisation to smooth out such fluctuations.

The Jeanneau boat company developed sales overseas to offset the seasonality inherent in the yacht trade in the northern hemisphere where the maximum sales activity occurs in the early part of the year. Civil construction firms found that business opportunities changed rapidly during the 1960s, 1970s, and 1980s from Europe to Africa and the Middle East.

(d) *Risk.* The classic risk of 'all the eggs in one basket' can also be reduced by a policy of international expansion.

Booker McConnell, now firmly established in the United States and in distribution in the United Kingdom, was originally the major trading company in Guyana. The decision to move its business base from that country enabled it to survive the developing political problems in the 1960s.

UK government assistance also strives to reduce the level of overseas risk by providing finance for large projects and export insurance cover through the Export Credit Guarantee scheme (*see* 21:**21**).

(e) *Product life cycle.* It has been shown that for many product fields there will be a steady progress of introduction, growth in acceptability, a period of stable sales followed by decline. This process is known as the product life cycle, and will vary in length according to the nature of the industry, from very short (especially fashion and high technology products, for example) to very long. (*See* Fig. 1.2.)

Different countries will often be at different stages in the cycle, and an international company can take advantage of this by selling overseas products which are no longer competitive in the home market.

The introduction of wide scale electrification varied from country to country after the Second World War. A manufacturer of paraffin lamps such as Aladdin in the United Kingdom found that a market that had ceased to exist in the United Kingdom would still be thriving overseas, and that expertise in the manufacture and distribution of paraffin lamps continued to be profitable for the organisation.

(f) *Competition.* Involvement overseas will provide the company

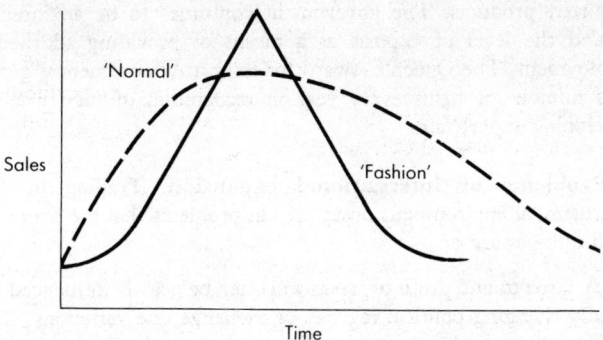

Figure 1.2 Product life cycle

with contact with competitive products that may not yet be present in the core home market. This will allow the company to develop policies to cope effectively with competition in regions of the world which have lower levels of risk than the home market.

(g) *Finance.* Development overseas allows the company greater access to international finance. Analysis of international companies also reveals that the tax burden on companies with substantial overseas earnings is lower than that for nationally based companies – the former companies with large overseas earnings can choose to an extent where and when profits are achieved whereas this is not possible for the latter.

(h) *Economies of scale.* International manufacture can substantially increase the manufacturing volumes that a company can achieve, thus improving its production efficiency and lowering cost both at home and abroad. International exposure can therefore have a substantial advantage in the home market.

(i) *New product development.* Companies operating in the international environment have greater opportunities of encountering new product ideas, and also have access to markets in which they can test new product concepts away from the cost and difficulty of operating in the core market (*see also (f) above*).

(j) *Social value.* In the UK, the export of goods and services maintains the balance of payments against the high volume of

6 Marketing Overseas

imported products. The government continues to be anxious to expand the level of exports as a means of providing additional employment. The Queen's Award for Export Achievement is given to a number of firms every year in recognition of their role in developing export sales.

4. Problems of international expansion. Trading in the international environment poses certain problems that the firm will need to be aware of:

(*a*) Growth and profit overseas will often be heavily influenced by rapidly changing political regimes or exchange rate variations.

(*b*) Exporting obscolescent products may stop the firm seeing the need for product development at home.

(*c*) Product modifications necessary for the overseas markets may be such that there are no economies of scale.

(*d*) The establishment of overseas trade may be extremely resource intensive, and the payback longer than the firm can allow.

(*e*) The length of credit and amount of risk involved in overseas trade is substantially higher than in trading in the home market.

(*f*) The administration and development of international business may be extremely costly.

5. Definitions of international marketing. There is no broadly accepted definition, but the following elements are important:

(*a*) the marketing of goods and services across national boundaries;

(*b*) the development of overseas subsidiaries or associates which market products developed and controlled by the parent company.

This broad definition however hides the fact that companies exist on a continuum of the development of export activity. As the degree of international exposure increases the nature of the business naturally changes and though there is no clear cut point from which a firm will change, a number of stages can be identified.

The development of international activity

6. Nationally based firms with no export activity. This category includes many small UK businesses. It has been estimated that it costs in the region of £60,000 to set up an effective in-house export department, and in consequence many firms tend to ignore the possibilities of exporting using indirect methods such as export houses (*see* Chapter 14).

7. Nationally based firms with some export activity. Such firms do little actively to develop business overseas but service enquiries obtained through national exhibitions from overseas buyers. A survey of small businesses in the UK shows that on average 1.5 per cent of their profits are obtained from overseas sales. This stage is often defined as export marketing. The key feature of export marketing is that the firm is neither actively seeking business overseas nor is it attempting to define overseas market requirements.

8. Nationally based firms with substantial export activity. Such firms will be achieving at least 20 per cent of their profits from overseas sales though their production may still be concentrated in one country. These firms can be defined as being engaged in international marketing as they attempt to develop overseas sales actively by understanding the international environment.

9. Firms with more than one country as a production source. These firms will tend to obtain a larger percentage of profitability from overseas markets and will have assets in overseas territories. Though similar in many respects to the international company, the local base of these operations will tend to mean that they will need to take a longer-term view of business development. These companies can be defined as multinationals.

10. Firms that have substantial assets overseas and receive no more than 50 per cent of their profit from any one market. Such companies will move away from purely national considerations in their operations towards a much more global approach towards investment and activity as the firm becomes increasingly free of relying on a single market for the bulk of its profits. Such firms can be termed transnational.

11. Success in international development. There is no single

8 Marketing Overseas

factor that produces success in the international environment. However the following have all been identified as key elements in the success of UK and European firms in overseas development:

(*a*) The commitment throughout the firm, especially at senior levels, to a world-wide development policy. This will involve defining and solving problems in terms of how both the key home market operations and the larger overseas potential operations will be affected.

(*b*) A continuing high level of research and development to maintain a competitive position in world markets.

(*c*) Continually re-evaluating and re-defining market approaches to achieve high levels of profitability and market share.

12. The development of an international philosophy. The attitude of the firm will be crucial to its growth. Those firms that view all development proposals in an international context are those most likely to survive; the firms that place activities in compartments (e.g. home trade, export) will fail.

The Airfix group was one of the first companies to produce ranges of plastic construction kits. Though by the late 1970s they were achieving 50 per cent of overall group profitability from overseas sales, development in the range of products was concentrated into products that could only be sold in the United Kingdom, such as trains with specific British Rail styles and preschool toys aimed at the British market. The failure to capitalise on a world market presence was one of the factors that led to eventual bankruptcy and takeover by an American group.

Progress test 1

1. What is marketing? (**1**)
2. What has marketing to offer the company? (**2**)
3. What are the elements of the marketing mix? (**2**)
4. Explain the advantages of exporting. (**3**)
5. What are the problems of international expansion? (**4**)
6. List the important features of international marketing. (**5**)
7. Describe the different types of export activity. (**6–10**)

1. Concepts 9

8. List the key elements in the development of overseas markets. (**11**)

9. What is the relevance of an international philosophy to successful marketing overseas? (**12**)

2
The international environment

Trends in international trade

1. The increasing importance of international trade. International trade has increased fifteen fold in value since 1950. Though a major part of this increase has been caused by the rising world price inflation levels between 1970 and 1980 the underlying trend has been for a steadily increasing percentage of world GNP (gross national product) to be exported.

	1950 $m	1960 $m	1970 $m	1980 $m
Total exports $m	78300	128660	313100	1180000
% Total GNP	3	4	5.5	6

Much of this trade has expanded between what is termed the 'developed' world: North America, the EEC (the current eleven members of the European Community), EFTA (the five members of the European Free Trade Association), Australasia (Australia and New Zealand) and Japan. These countries have dominated world trade since the 1950s.

2. The increasing role of the developing countries. The creation of OPEC (Organization of Petroleum Exporting Countries) in the 1970s did have an effect on the balance of world trade affecting the growth of exports particularly in what are termed 'developing' countries, LDCs (lesser developed countries) or the 'Third World'.

2. The international environment

	Share of world trade			
	1950 %	1960 %	1970 %	1980 %
Developed world	63	67	72	63
OPEC			6	14
Developing countries	27	22	18	27
Centrally planned economies	10	12	10	6

Most rapid growth has recently been achieved by this group, especially LDCs in the Far East such as Hong Kong, Taiwan, Singapore, South Korea, Thailand and Malaysia. Their achievements have steadily increased the overall percentage of world trade contributed by the developing world partially at the expense of the major trading blocks, but also eroding the share of world trade held by centrally planned economies: Comecon, Albania, China, Cuba, Mongolia, North Korea, Vietnam, Laos, Kampuchea.

3. Trade within the developed world. As might be expected from these figures more than 75 per cent of exports from the developed world are to other developed countries. In consequence major trading partners of developed countries will always be other developed countries. This will have important consequences on the level of competition in the provision of goods and services that companies face in the international environment. As well as having to compete within an often highly sophisticated home market, exported items will also face pressure from the industries of the other developed economies which will also be attempting to gain a share of markets overseas.

4. Relationships with GNP. Countries with high levels of export growth have also shown substantially higher per capita increases in overall GNP than countries with slower export growth, and this would argue that the Pacific basin countries will be steadily more important in world trade in the 1990s (*see* Fig. 2.1).

5. The impact of foreign investment overseas. One feature of the statistics is that they increasingly understate the level of international involvement. This is because the amount of foreign

12 Marketing Overseas

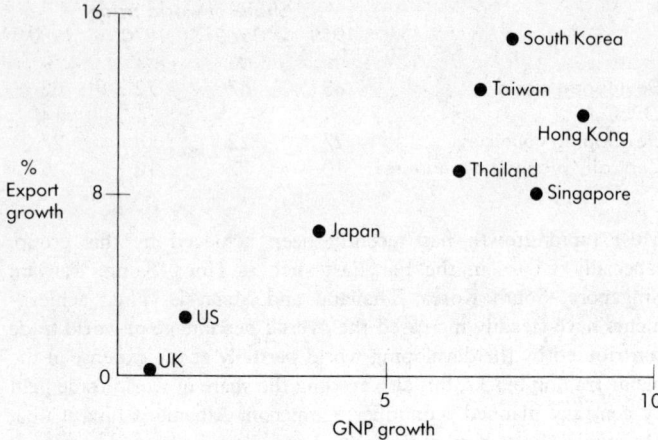

Figure 2.1 GNP growth 1973-83

investment overseas by all the major trading areas is steadily increasing. In 1946 the total level of overseas investment was estimated at around £12 000 million. By 1980 this had increased to £120 000 million, about 60 per cent of which originated in the United States. Direct investment in overseas markets obviously reduces direct physical trade flows, though there is an inevitable substantial increase in the level of invisible trade – the movement of revenue from one country to another. As the level of trade investment increases the accuracy of the trade statistics in providing a good measure of the amount of international trade become in consequence less and less reliable.

The nature of international trade

6. The products. As might be expected, the nature of the products exported shows considerable variation between the various trading sectors within world economies. The developed world shows a far lower reliance on food or other raw materials (iron ore, oil, coal, other minerals) as a percentage of total trade. For example, there are 58 countries in the world dependent on three or fewer crops for 50 per

2. The international environment

cent or more of export earnings; an additional 22 are dependent on minerals for more than 40 per cent of their export earnings. For countries within the developed world the reliance on manufactured goods is much greater, a trend also shown in the LDCs of the Pacific basin such as Hong Kong - with 90 per cent of earnings from manufacture; South Korea - 80 per cent; and Taiwan with 60 per cent.

Barriers to trade

7. Tariff barriers. Many countries maintain high tariff barriers to reduce either the entire level of imports; or to protect specific areas of industry. These can be imposed in a number of ways.

(*a*) Controlling the issue of foreign exchange.
(*b*) Totally banning the import of particular items.
(*c*) Imposing a strict quota on the number of items that are imported.
(*d*) Developing a system of import licences which are restricted and/or expensive to obtain.

8. Non-tariff barriers. These also exist in many countries. They can operate in a number of ways, including:

(*a*) extremely lengthy customs clearance procedures;
(*b*) complex safety clearance regulations.

Japan introduced new regulations for the ski industry in 1986. These regulations were necessary, it was claimed, because of the 'different' type of snow in Japan. They set standards for flexibility and width of skis which foreign ski manufacturers, who dominate the £250 million Japanese ski industry, would have to meet to achieve the seal of approval. Although not obligatory, the imported skis' ability, or inability, to meet the new standards would obviously become a major selling point in the Japanese market.

Structure of trade

9. Commodity agreements. A number of trade agreements exist

14 Marketing Overseas

to promote the interests of commodity producers by attempting to iron out fluctuations in demand and to maintain pricing in what is often a highly volatile international environment. The most well known, OPEC, had been very successful in maintaining control over oil production and pricing until early 1986, substantially increasing the OPEC countries' share of world trade (see above).

The International Tin Agreement, set up in 1956, maintained a 'buffer' stock of the metal for many years, with upper and lower price bands. Tin would be bought into stock when the price fell below the minimum price levels. This agreement worked until 1986 when high buffer stocks caused its collapse.

An International Coffee Agreement was established in 1959. It attempted to set quotas on a country by country basis to maintain prices and smooth out demand. This has continued to operate though the effects of the weather on the producing areas of the main supplier, Brazil, has prevented an entirely consistent approach being adopted.

The International Cocoa Agreement, signed in 1973, has faced a series of severe problems and has never functioned effectively; similar problems have faced attempts to establish sugar and wheat agreements.

In addition there are a number of formal or informal restrictions placed upon supplier nations to limit their share of the market. The MFA or multi-fibre agreement limits the amount of cloth that supplier nations, mainly in the Pacific basin, can export to Western Europe. Similarly, Japanese car and video manufacturers have been asked to adhere to undertakings to limit similarly the volume of exports to the EEC.

10. Dumping. A number of agreements exist between governments on what is a fair pricing structure for international trade. Products sold below production cost in overseas markets are considered to be 'dumped'. Areas of special concern include steel, textiles and raw materials for industry.

11. Regional agreements. Within the overall pattern of world trade development, there are inevitably strong regional biases, often reinforced by government to government (bilateral) trading agreements or regional trade associations. An example of the first is the

2. The international environment

strong trading links between Russia and India on the exchange of machinery and agricultural production.

The EEC or European Economic Community is the most important regional trading agreement for the UK economy. Established in 1962 under the Treaty of Rome, membership has steadily expanded and by early 1986 it included West Germany, Belgium, Holland, Denmark, Ireland, Spain, Portugal, Greece, Italy, France, and the United Kingdom. Its aim has been to reduce barriers to trade between the member countries and create a single trading entity, with preference given to members of the Community. Provisions in the original Treaty of Rome have also led to the establishment of the Common Agricultural Policy or CAP with controls on the levels of production and pricing of a wide range of agricultural commodities (milk, meat, sugar, butter, wine, cereals and olive oil), and co-ordinating bodies for iron, steel and coal production. Long-term plans exist for greater economic and fiscal integration. Preferential terms for certain non-EEC countries have also been established especially for former colonial territories in Africa, the Carribean, and the Pacific. Agreements also exist with the European Free Trade Association or EFTA.

EFTA, like ASEAN (Association of South East Asian Nations) has a much simpler aim than the EEC; the reduction of custom and tariff barriers between its members. More recently established is the Central American Common Market which also plans the development of a single customs and trading system.

COMECON, the Council for Mutual Economic Aid, is the major trading block in Eastern Europe, with substantial trading preference between the partners in Eastern Europe.

There are other trading areas established by treaties such as that for the Caribbean region.

ANCOM	– Andean Common Market
ASEAN	– Association of South East Asian Nations
CACM	– Central American Common Market
CARICOM	– Caribbean Common Market
CMEA	– Council for Mutual Economic Assistance
EEC	– European Economic Community
EFTA	– European Free Trade Association

16 Marketing Overseas

LAIA — Latin American Integration Association
NC — Nordic Council
OCAM — Organization Commune Africaine et Malagache

International institutions

12. GATT. GATT, the General Agreement on Tariffs and Trade is a treaty which tries to lay down rules on the level and structure of import duties, non-tariff barriers, and export subsidies. Currently there are 83 members.

GATT attempts to equalize duties and terms of trade between all member states, though there are a number of exclusions to this general statement of intent – for example Commonwealth preference whereby goods were traded between Commonwealth member countries at reduced tariffs was allowed under the GATT rules. Though enforcement of GATT rulings is difficult, it has allowed countries to more easily move towards reciprocal lowering of customs duties and tariff barriers. It is not unusual for members of trading blocks, like the EEC, to adopt a common stance at GATT negotiations.

13. UNCTAD. UNCTAD – the United Nations Conference on Trade and Development – deals with broader issues than those of GATT. Its membership is open to any member of the United Nations. It is especially concerned with issues of international financing and development aid but has been involved in seeking to provide support for price stabilization arrangements for individual international commodity agreements. As with GATT, trading block members negotiate as single units.

14. OECD. The OECD – the Organization for Economic Co-Operation and Development – comprises the 25 member states of Western Europe, North America, Japan, Australasia, Turkey and Yugoslavia. It serves as a forum for international trade development and research.

15. The IMF. The IMF – the International Monetary Fund – was set up in 1947 to aid the orderly expansion of world trade. Members

2. The international environment

have access to loans from the fund based on the size of their contributions, provided they meet the frequently stringent rules on exchange rates and government spending that are preconditions of the loan. The IMF has had an important role in providing short- and medium-term bridging finance to many countries, and has been a major influence in maintaining economic growth.

16. The World Bank (full title the International Bank for Reconstruction and Development or IBRD). Funded in the same fashion as the IMF, the World Bank makes available finance for government-supported projects at full commercial rates to member countries, who must also be members of the IMF. Concessional or 'soft' loans are made available to developing countries through two subsidiary organizations, the International Development Association, and the International Finance Corporation. Total lending in 1980 was $12 billion.

17. Regional development banks. There are a number of independent banks that operate on the same principles as the World Bank, and often co-operate on financing particular projects. Currently there are four of these development banks in existence:
   Inter-American Bank,
   African Development Bank,
   Asian Bank,
   Arab Fund for Social and Economic Development.
By 1980, the total funds at their disposal were in the region of $15 billion.

Other features of international trade

18. Illegal trade. Where there are major barriers to trade between countries there will often be a substantial level of illegal trade or smuggling.

> The smuggling of gold and other products into India was, for many years, a major industry in the lower Arabian Gulf.
> The high duties on foreign tobacco in Italy meant that sales of tobacco in Tangier were substantially in excess of the local population needs.

Togo has on the surface one of the highest per capita consumptions of scotch whisky in the world. The reality is that its neighbours, Ghana and Nigeria, have limited the import of foreign consumer goods due to foreign exchange shortages.

19. Development aid. Many countries provide official aid to developing countries. By 1982 this was estimated at around $20 billion per annum.

It is divided into two categories.

(*a*) Bilateral aid of which 'tied' aid is the most important, making the major proportion. It is aid for specific projects involving an agreement between donor and recipient including the obligation to purchase most of the equipment from the donor government. It can therefore be an important method of boosting exports and in the 1980s the award of a number of substantial construction contracts in the Third World has depended upon the terms of the tied aid offered by the national governments of the competing British, American and Japanese companies.

(*b*) Multilateral aid channeled through international organizations, the United Nations Development Programme being the most important. Spending is determined by the priorities of each organization some of which – like the World Health Organization and its attempts to reduce the cost of drugs to governments – have an influential role in world trade.

The international trade of the United Kingdom

20. The United Kingdom's position in the international trading environment. Overseas trade has been central to the development of British industry since the early 19th century. Total exports in 1984 were £45,000 million or 25 per cent of the gross domestic product.

As a small island, the UK is heavily dependent on the import of food and raw materials for manufacturing purposes. The level of imported, manufactured goods has been steadily rising and during 1985 the United Kingdom imported more manufactured goods than it exported (*see* Table 2.1).

As a member of the EEC, the United Kingdom has developed

2. The international environment

Table 2.1 Composition of UK Trade

Item	Exports %	Imports %
Food	8	15
Basic materials/chemicals	13	35
Fuel	7	4
Manufactures	56	35
Textiles	1	3
Others	3	9

steadily stronger links with the other members of the Community, and this shows in the trading pattern on a country basis which became established in the 1980s (*see* Table 2.2).

Table 2.2 UK Trading partners in the 1980s

Country	Exports %	Imports %
United States	10	10.5
West Germany	9	11.2
France	7	8
Netherlands	6	6
Belgium	6	5
Ireland	6	4
Italy	2	5
Switzerland	5	5
Sweden	3	3
Canada	2	2
Japan	–	3

These 11 countries take 56 per cent of UK exports and provide 63 per cent of all imported products. The developing countries in total (other than the oil producing states) provide markets for 14 per cent of British exports, and 11 per cent of imports. The balance of trade has since the 1980s been improved by oil exports; for the previous 15 years the United Kingdom had tended to run a deficit on visible trade (that is the physical movement of goods) while earning money from invisible trade (tourism, banking and insurance) to offset this short fall, a sum running at around £5000 million per annum.

The relaxation of exchange control has made overseas investment by British firms considerably easier and direct foreign investment has risen from an estimated £29,000 million in 1978 to £52,000 million in 1985.

21. Trends in United Kingdom international trade. Table 2.3 shows that the UK's share of the world market for manufactured goods has declined since 1953 with Japan showing the major increase in percentage share, and Pacific basin countries increasing their share of world trade rapidly.

Table 2.3 Percentage share of world trade, 1953 and 1984

	1953	1984
US	19	12
UK	9	5
West Germany	6	9
Canada	5	5
France	5	5
Soviet Union	4	4.5
Belgium	3	3
Japan	2	9
Switzerland	2	2
Singapore	1.5	1.5

Progress test 2

1. Describe the main trends in international trade since 1950. (**1**)
2. What are the limitations of international trade statistics? (**5**)
3. What is the connection between a country's level of development and the type of goods it exports? (**6**)
4. Describe the mechanisms for restricting the entry of goods into a market. (**7–8**)

2. The international environment

5. Explain the role of international agreements in world trade. (**9–11**)

6. What is GATT, UNCTAD, OECD, IMF, the World Bank? (**12–16**)

7. How does development aid contribute to world trade? (**19**)

8. What type of goods are (*a*) imported into Britain; (*b*) exported from Britain in the 1980s? (**8**)

9. Who are Britain's main trading partners? (**20**)

10. How had the pattern of UK exports altered by the mid-1980s? (**21**)

3
Concentration in international trade

The concept of globalization

1. Introduction. The steady growth in international trade has strengthened the view, increasingly held by large businesses, that effort must be directed towards international dominance in order to become as strongly established in as many world markets as possible.

2. Globalization. This development within internationally based businesses has led to the application of common strategies and marketing mixes in all world markets by some companies, a concept which has become known as globalization.

There is some controversy attached to the concept. On the one hand is the view that companies will increasingly adopt global approaches to world-wide markets. Critics however say that few companies use exactly the same positioning or marketing mix in all overseas markets. But this comment can be applied equally to companies operating within national boundaries, where different marketing mixes are developed to service key customer groups.

The key issue is the degree of application of a standard body of experience to developing world markets. Where this occurs, the process of globalization is underway.

Lux, the beauty soap, is in some ways a classic example of the original idea of a global product. Although the product differs in different markets in respect of soap formulation, perfume and packaging, it is clear that a common body of experience is devoted to modifying Lux world wide on a country-by-country basis. This

3. Concentration in international trade

is achieved through the Unilever head office group called Detergents Coordination.

3. The nature of international investment. Since 1945 there has been a continuing increase in overseas investment by all the major, industrialized economies. Initially, the major investment was by the United States, though by the mid 1980s there had been a substantial expansion of Japanese investment.

Cumulative Overseas Investment (book value)

	1967 $ bill	1977 $ bill	1985 $ bill
United States	50	100	180
United Kingdom	20	30	40
West Germany	3	20	32
Japan	1	20	27

The growth rate of Japanese investment has been most marked in the United Kingdom during the 1980s. Nissan established a car assembly plant, Toshiba and Mitsubishi have established electronic assembly plants.

The effect of the growth in overseas investment has been to steadily change the nature of the ownership of manufacturing industry in many countries.

% Foreign Owned Manufacturing Production by Country

Country	% Foreign owned manufacturing production
Australia	23
Canada	57
France	28
West Germany	22
Italy	24
Japan	4
United Kingdom	21
USA	1
Brazil	44
Singapore	83
India	13

24 Marketing Overseas

These statistics reveal two interesting facts. The first is that the amount of overseas investment does not greatly affect the level of economic growth. West Germany with a relatively high level of inward investment has nevertheless achieved a level of economic growth similar to that of the United States. However high levels of investment in certain sectors of the economy can make the manufacturing sector face problems when labour costs rise, as happened in Singapore in the early 1980s.

Market sectors and international concentration

4. Concentration of industrial activity by market. One facet of increasing global activity is increased concentration of industrial activity exemplified by the dominance of a few, major, companies in specific, international market sectors. For the student or business executive interested in trends of international marketing, this is probably the key factor in the 1970s and 1980s and one which has important implications in a number of key areas.

The list of areas of industry in which activity is dominated by a few major companies is a long one, underlining the strength of the trend. The sectors include:

(a) *Large civil aircraft.* Two companies dominate the civil aircraft market – Boeing of the United States has around 70 per cent of the world market of wide-bodied jets, with Airbus Industries providing the sole current competition. Lockheed and McDonnell Douglas have effectively withdrawn to concentrate on the military market. It has been estimated that the cost of producing a successor to the 747 is in excess of $3 billion.

(b) *Mainframe computers.* IBM and Fujistu of Japan control around 80 per cent of the world mainframe market, and IBM also dominates the world minicomputer market with approximately 30 per cent of the total market. The amount of investment in R & D by IBM annually is greater than the total turnover of the main British computer company, ICL. IBM's annual turnover is also almost equal to the sum of its five main American competitors: Burroughs, Sperry-Univac, NCR, Control Data and Honeywell. Collectively known as the BUNCH.

3. Concentration in international trade

(c) *Heavy construction equipment.* Komatsu and Caterpillar dominate the world market for heavy construction equipment. The other manufacturers, Deere and Clark, have tended to continue to lose market share in the heavy construction market against this world-wide competition.

(d) *Oil.* The world oil market continues to be dominated by the 'Seven Sisters': BP, Shell, Texaco, Exxon, Mobil, Amoco and Gulf, with the vast investments in refining and exploration that is required. It is interesting to note that the small independent oil companies spawned by the North Sea discoveries have been rapidly taken over by larger groups.

(e) *Motor cars.* Around three quarters of total world car sales are achieved by 9 manufacturers.

Company	Unit sales (mill)	%Total production (cum)
General Motors	4.9	18
Ford	2.9	29
Toyota	2.4	38
Nissan	2.0	46
VW	2.0	53
Renault	1.9	60
Peugeot	1.5	66
Fiat	1.4	71
Honda	0.9	74

The inability of British Leyland to achieve sufficient volume (during the early 1980s BL maintained an annual volume around the 400,000 mark) has continued to prevent it from achieving adequate profitability.

(f) *Tractors.* The rapid decline in the size of the market in the mid 1980s has further reduced the number of manufacturers of large tractors in the market.

Company	Unit sales (000s)	%Total production (cum)
Massey Ferguson	142	18
Fiat	106	31
Case	90	42
Ford	90	53
Deere	80	63

26 Marketing Overseas

(g) *Integrated circuit manufacture.* There has been a steady increase in the investment required to produce integrated circuits, semiconductors, and microprocessors, which has accelerated the concentration of production in a limited number of companies.

Company	Total sales ($bill)	%World share (cum)
Texas Instruments	1.3	12
Motorola	0.8	20
IBM	0.8	27
NEC	0.6	33
Philips	0.5	38
Hitachi	0.5	42
Fairchild	0.4	46

(h) *Drugs and biotechnology.* The greatly increased length of time that is required to provide some return on new drug research and development will almost certainly mean that the numbers of firms active in the market will decline over the next ten to fifteen years. A recent estimate by ICI stated that if they were now taking the decision to enter the pharmaceutical market instead of in 1959, investment costs would have to be of the order of £1500 million, with a repayment period of around 23 years.

Currently 70 per cent of the world pharmaceutical market is supplied by 15 companies, with the major groups accounting for a steadily higher proportion.

Company	Total sales ($bill)	%World share (cum)
Merck	2.66	6.3
AHP	2.42	12.5
Hoechst	2.38	18.8
Bayer	2.19	24.6
Ciba Geigy	2.16	30.2
Pfizer	1.89	35.7

(i) *Television manufacture.* The degree of investment required for the cost-efficient manufacture of television sets has also had its effect on a steadily increasing concentration in a smaller number of producers.

3. Concentration in international trade

Company	Total sales (mill units)	% World share (cum)
Philips	4.9	17
Matushista	3.6	29.5
RCA	2.0	36.5
Zenith	2.0	43.5
Sanyo	2.0	50.5
Sony	1.7	56
Toshiba	1.5	61

The recent growth in the video market has also been dominated by the main Japanese manufacturing companies such as Sony and Sanyo, being able to maintain impressive world market shares.

(*j*) *Detergents.* The dominance of the three main detergent companies, Unilever, Procter and Gamble, and Colgate Palmolive, is maintained throughout the world with combined market shares in most markets exceeding 65 per cent. Within Europe, only Henkel of Germany offers substantial competition with market shares in Germany and Austria of around 25 per cent.

(*k*) *Photographic film.* The market continues to be dominated by Kodak, with other major companies including Agfa, Polaroid and Fuji.

(*l*) *Steel.* Though the manufacture of steel has been the centre of much governmental involvement in many countries the concentration of production has also occurred on an international basis; the main ten companies producing around 40 per cent of the total world production (outside Comecon and China).

Company	Total production (m tons)	% World production (cum)
Nippon Steel	27	9
US Steel	13	14
British Steel	13	19
Finsider	12	23
Nippon Kokan	11	26
Kawasaki	10	29
Sumimoto	10	32
Thyssen	10	35
Bethlehem Steel	10	38
Usinor	9	40

28 Marketing Overseas

(m) Paint. The international market for paint is also showing a trend towards domination by a small number of large international units.

Company	Total production (m litres)	% World production (cum est)
ICI	720	17
PPG	450	28
BASF	440	38
Hoechst	320	45
Sherwin Williams	300	52
Azko	270	58

There are many other examples of concentration of manufacture in other sectors:

Accountancy: Arthur Anderson, Peat Marwick Mitchell, Price Waterhouse.

Advertising: Young and Rubicam, Saatchi & Saatchi, John Walter Thompson, Interpublic (McCann Erikson, Lintas), Ogilvy and Mather.

Aluminium: Alcoa, Alcan.

Breakfast cereals: Kelloggs, Nabisco, Quaker, Weetabix.

Charge cards: American Express, Diners Club.

Chocolate: Nestle, Mars.

Cigarettes: Reynolds, Philip Morris, American Brands (which includes Gallaher), British American Tobacco.

Coffee: Nestle, General Foods.

Cola drinks: Coca Cola, Pepsi Cola.

Cooking oil: Unilever, CPC, Proctor and Gamble.

Evaporated and powdered milk: Nestle (including Carnation).

Flavours and fragrances: Unilever (PPF), IFF, Givaudan.

Hamburger outlets: McDonalds, Burger King.

Motor tyres: Goodyear, Firestone, Michelin.

Motorcycles: Yamaha, Suzuki, Honda.

Petfood: Mars, Nestle.

Razors: Gillette, Bic.

Sauces: Heinz, CPC, Nestle, Kraft.

Single lens reflex cameras: Canon, Minolta, Nikon, Asahi.

Soups: CPC (Knorr), Heinz, Campbell's, Nestle.

Spirits: Seagram, Allied Lyons (now including Hiram Walker), Guinness (now including Distillers and Bells), International Distillers and Vintners, Bacardi (a special case controlling ⅔ of the world rum market).

Sporting accessories: Nike, Adidas.

Toilet paper and tissues: Scott, Kimberly Clark.

Toys: Hasbro, Fisher Price, Palitoy, Mattel.

Trucks: Volvo, Daimler Benz, Renault, Ford.

From such an analysis it is clear that a much larger proportion of each market sector is in fact dominated by international companies, be they American, European or Japanese.

Reasons for industrial concentration

5. Factors favouring industrial concentration. These examples illustrate what appear to be the common factors that encourage the development of a global business sector.

(*a*) *Level of investment.* The size of investment required to produce effective products will have an effect on the nature of the industrial unit. The level of required investment in a new drug, aircraft or mainframe computer will prevent any but the largest companies competing in these particular market sectors.

General Motors has effectively decided to withdraw from the heavy truck market which is dominated by European firms because of the substantial investment that is required to maintain a competitive product. Volvo alone spends over £100 million per annum on research and development.

In contrast, the level of investment required to create a new microcomputer is relatively small with the result that this sector of the market is relatively fragmented with over 400 IBM compatibles available in the UK market by the mid-1980s. In the consumer goods sector the development of a consumer franchise can also be seen as a similar investment. Part of the formula of McDonalds' success in the United Kingdom can be seen in their high level of investment in promotion. In 1985 the group, which is concentrated in the South East, spent a total of £6.5 million on promotion, which would perhaps nationally be equivalent to £15 million or the same expenditure as Unilever on soaps and detergents.

(b) *The length of investment payback.* Only the largest companies are able to absorb the financing costs of a long term investment in a major product or development of a major market which is unlikely to repay the investment over many years.

(c) *The degree of regulation.* High levels of regulation in a particular sector will inevitably mean that the development of international business will be hampered. Banking is an example of this factor at work. Many countries still maintain strict control over the development of overseas banks in their countries: many countries also will restrict foreign ownership of property, preventing hotel groups from creating a world wide network other than on the basis of management contracts with physical ownership of the building being held by local nationals (examples include the Intercontinental and Hilton Hotel groups).

From such considerations one would expect it to remain difficult for global companies to become firmly established in mass market clothing (though not in fashion) and basic non-processed food, home construction, printing.

6. Implications for UK companies developing international trade.

(a) *Currency movements.* The increasing development of global companies has lead to steadily increasing transfers of money between head offices and subsidiaries. This has had the effect of making currencies far more volatile which affects the way in which companies trading internationally need to plan their pricing and internal dividend policy should they own overseas subsidiaries.

(b) *Product planning.* As many of the world's mass markets are dominated by a few companies with vast resources, the successful competitor will need to concentrate increasingly on specialization to maintain growth.

(c) *Market development.* However, with a more specialized product, the home market is unlikely to provide sufficient volume for the growing company, which will need increasingly to look overseas for the maintenance of progress.

3. Concentration in international trade

(*d*) *Main competitive factor.* As the concentration of industrial activity continues the most important single factor in the market for the majority of UK companies will be what the competition is achieving or what it is planning to do. A greater and more detailed knowledge of competitive activity will therefore become essential.

(*e*) *Research and development.* High levels of research and development expenditure will need to be maintained to achieve high added value products which can compete effectively in the international arena.

(*f*) *Distinctiveness.* It will be important for any company operating in the international environment to be able to demonstrate product benefits and quality clearly. This makes international branding a very important part of international sales development.

(*g*) *Quality control.* Continuing emphasis on quality control will be an essential part of effective market control in international trade.

JCB, the world market leader of what are technically known as backhoe loaders, is a good example of these factors. Specializing in a narrow sector of the market it sells in 50 overseas countries and is the leading product in many.

Jaguar, once part of British Leyland, has also shown how a specialized approach to world markets can be effective even in a highly competitive market sector.

Progress test 3

1. What is globalization? (**2**)
2. Give two outcomes of the growth in overseas investment. (**3**)
3. Show how industrial activity has become more concentrated. (**4**)
4. Explain the factors favouring international concentration. (**5**)
5. Given the concentration of power in the hands of a few companies, how can the newcomer to export survive? (**6**)

4
Multinationals

Introduction

1. Defining multinationals. A multinational, as described in Chapter 1, is a company which maintains assets in an overseas territory and is actively involved in sale of product or service in overseas markets.

2. Types of multinationals. Multinationals operate in a number of different industrial areas. They differ considerably in the nature of their complexity of sourcing and variety of products or services that they are involved in. The following divisions can be made:

(*a*) *Extractive industries.* Many of the largest multinationals including the oil companies are based in the extractive industries, obtaining raw material from wherever available and processing it into an intermediate product which is acceptable for industrial or consumer use. This category includes some of the largest multinationals in the world. Examples are Shell, Exxon, Rio Tinto Zinc (RTZ).

(*b*) *Manufacturing industries.* The range of manufacturing industry can be divided into a number of sub-components.

(*i*) *Single product concept, single manufacturing centre* – Boeing.

(*ii*) *Multiple product concepts, single manufacturing centre* – Sony.

(*iii*) *Single product concept, multiple manufacturing sites* – Caterpillar.

(*iv*) *Multiple product concepts, multiple sourced* – Unilever.

4. Multinationals 33

(*c*) *Financial conglomerates.* There has been an increase in the number of companies that are essentially involved in financial management rather than the development of clearly identified core businesses. A recent successful example is Hanson Trust, with a clearly identified financial strategy in both the UK and the US.

(*d*) *Trading companies.* Much of the growth of Japanese overseas trade has resulted from the activities of the large trading firms, such as Mitsui, Mitsubishi, and Sumimoto; it is estimated that around 50 per cent of Japanese import and export activity is channeled through these organizations. Because of their large size they are particularly suited to provide low cost entry for small Japanese firms into overseas markets and have the financial resources to handle large barter deals (*see* 21:**26**). Additional services that they provide include:

(*i*) market identification for exporting companies;

(*ii*) providing overseas sales offices to co-ordinate sales development;

(*iii*) shipping, finance and insurance for overseas trade.

Smaller trading companies such as Lonhro, Inchape, Jardine and Swire remain part of the multinational development in other countries; companies such as the Tata group in India provide valuable export expertise in some developing countries.

(*e*) *Service.* Though the development of multinational service organizations has been slower than that of other groups (*see* Chapter 24), the following types of service organizations have become established world wide:

(*i*) *single concept, with all the outlets owned by the parent company* – advertising agencies; banks;

(*ii*) *a single concept with a large element of franchising or management contracts* – hotels, food outlets;

(*iii*) *multiple concept service operations such as retailing* – Marks and Spencer has substantial investments in a chain of discount stores in Canada.

The development of multinationals

3. The origins of multinationals. Multinational trading has been a feature of all organized societies. Archaeology reveals that burial sites in Ancient Britain contained artifacts manufactured throughout

34 Marketing Overseas

the Mediterranean basin, and similar finds are reported in other countries.

Even before the Industrial Revolution trading companies such as the East India and Hudson Bay companies had been extremely profitable enterprises; much of the excitement surrounding the episode of the South Sea Bubble in the early eighteenth century had to do with the enormous expectations surrounding the profits of international trading.

4. Development of the modern multinational. The introduction of mass production techniques by many American firms from the 1920s meant that many were already established overseas by 1939. Since 1945 the growth has been far more rapid, fuelled in part by the increasing influence of the international regulatory bodies such as GATT (*see* **2.12**) which have had a major impact on reducing inter-country barriers.

5. Trends in multinational development.

(*a*) *Numbers.* The total number of firms that can be termed 'multinational' is estimated in the mid-1980s to be well over 12,000.

(*b*) *Overseas involvement.* Most multinationals maintain assets in only one overseas country, but there is a steadily growing number that are involved in five or more countries and are moving towards a 'transnational' status.

(*c*) *Industrial co-operation.* In areas of high research and development costs, there is an increasing number of companies that are entering into 'shared technology' arrangements or contractual joint ventures. Philips and Sony have undertaken joint research in particular areas of compact discs and digital audio tapes.

The impact of multinationals

6. The importance of multinationals.

(*a*) *Employment.* By 1985 it was estimated that 50 million people in the industrialized world were employed by multinationals.

(*b*) *Size.* Of the top 100 economic units in the world, 50 are countries and 50 are multinationals (*see* Appendix 4).

4. Multinationals

(c) *Effect on trade flows.* Increasing amounts of international trade in manufactured goods now consist of the transfer of goods between subsidiaries of multinationals. It is thought that this now accounts for 40–50 per cent of the international trade in manufactured goods.

(d) *Political influence.*

(i) *Taxation.* Multinationals appear to manage their tax affairs more efficiently than nationally based companies.

(ii) *Effect on the level of employment.* Governments actively court inward investment by multinationals. Closure of overseas manufacture plants on head office decisions may have dramatic effects on local employment.

(iii) *Effect on the style of employment – attitude towards unions.* Many Japanese companies investing in Europe have insisted on no-strike agreements with trade unions as a pre-requisite of investment.

(iv) *Effect on currency stability.* The way in which local subsidiaries remit money will affect currency stability considerably. A study of payments around devaluations has shown that local subsidiaries of multinationals dramatically increase their payments at times of financial crisis in both France and the United Kingdom.

(v) *Effect on political stability.* Multinationals have often been accused of involvement in political activity. One clear example was the actions of ITT in Chile during the Allende regime, another the actions of the oil companies in the Middle East after the Second World War.

(e) *Control over technology.* American governmental controls, implemented with the agreement of Western European governments, over the export of technology to both COMECON and countries such as Libya effectively prevent European firms supplying these markets because of the components that are supplied from American multinationals.

(f) *Cultural effects.* The impact of multinationals has been criticized by many writers as causing an international convergence in culture. Wabenzi has become a new word in Swahili. Its meaning (wa = people, Benzi = Mercedes Benz car) underlines the internationalization of status symbols.

7. Factors encouraging the growth of multinationals.

(a) *The steady increase in the speed of communications.* In 1800, it

36 Marketing Overseas

would have taken two weeks to cross the Atlantic and three months to travel from Hong Kong to Europe; modern jet travel and telecommunications enable the firm to maintain continuous information flows about what is happening to overseas subsidiaries thus enabling the company to be effectively integrated.

Combined with this rapid communication is the ability of the head office to deal effectively with steadily increasing quantities of information via the use of more and more sophisticated computer systems.

(b) *Relaxation of trading barriers.* The action of GATT, the development of the EEC and other trading areas has meant that the size of markets accessible to the firm has substantially grown.

(c) *Growth in the world economy.* In addition to the relaxation of trading barriers, population growth and real (i.e. adjusted for inflation) increases in per capita GNP have added to the market potential.

(d) *Improvement in regulatory systems.* It has become easier to register and defend patents and trade marks on a world-wide basis.

(e) *Reduction in cultural differences.* The advent of world-wide television has tended to encourage multinational development by standardizing cultural values. Satellite television systems envisaged for the 1990s will further develop this trend. In the 1980s Dallas was the most popular programme on Italian television.

(f) *Growth in international finance.* The increase in such investment sources as the Eurodollar market have made it progressively easier for the multinational to gain access to finance which is independent of national boundaries. By the mid-1980s the 24 hour financial market had become a reality with trading occurring in London, New York and Tokyo.

Controls on multinational development

8. Governmental. National governments have a variety of laws regulating the freedom of action for multinationals in their own country; the way in which multinationals can move funds (*see* 21:28) makes enforcement difficult. Tax authorities in individual countries are gradually increasing their links with others to exchange information on multinationals. The IRS (Internal Revenue Service)

4. Multinationals

of the United States and the British Tax Inspectorate for example are closely involved in the maintenance of double taxation agreements.

9. Regional. The EEC has established a limited legal framework for mergers and takeovers within the Community, slowly establishing the European Court as the controlling body for transnational corporations.

10. Employees. International trade unions such as the International Metalworkers' Federation and the International Federation of Chemical and General Workers' Unions provide a forum within which national employees of multinationals can formulate and instigate action with support from the multinationals' employees in other countries. The recession in the 1970s prevented a further growth of such attempts at concerted action. In some countries such as Holland and Sweden employees must agree to takeovers from foreign-owned companies, and there is a trend towards introducing such employee rights on a wider base.

11. Management. Senior management of multinationals will tend to be of one national group, even though this requirement is changing. The loyalty of the mangement will however tend to be towards the company rather than national interest.

In the words of one senior multinational executive, the manager of the multinational enterprise must: 'set aside any nationalistic attitude and appreciate that in the last resort his loyalty must be to the shareholders of the parent company, and he must protect their interests even if it might appear that it is not in the national interest of the country in which he is operating'.

12. Shareholdings. Many companies in their Articles of Association lay down guidelines as to share ownership. The nature and size of large multinationals will mean that no one individual or organization will be able to build up a major stake in the company without access to enormous resources. Shareholdings tend to be diffuse and power of shareholders limited.

13. Public opinion. Multinationals because of their size and

38 Marketing Overseas

international spread are particularly vulnerable to the effects of public opinion. Their activities in one overseas country can have significant effects on their acceptability in another. In consequence, multinationals need to pay close attention to the effects of their investment decisions and spend extensively on building good international public relations images.

IBM emphasises its contribution to the local economy in a range of press material. Shell stresses the minimum damage to the environment. McDonalds emphasizes commitment to local activities, so much so that in Japan the company is often regarded as a Japanese rather than an American company.

14. The future of multinationals. The current economic and political climate emphasizes the reduction of trade barriers and the encouragement of international trade. This implies that the importance of the multinational will continue to grow. The following trends will probably continue.

(*a*) Movement towards transnational corporations. More companies will become transnational reducing the dependency on a single country for the majority of their earnings.

(*b*) Specialization versus generalization. The increasing domination of mass markets by a smaller and smaller number of companies (*see* 3:4) will mean that new multinationals will tend to develop in small specialized segments of the market (*see* 3:6).

(*c*) Regional controls on the activities of multinationals will perhaps become more important with the EEC for example taking a more active role in the policing of multinational activity.

Progress test 4

1. What is a multinational? (**1**)
2. Describe the different types of multinational. (**2**)
3. Why are multinationals important? (**5, 6**)
4. Explain the spread of multinationals. (**7**)
5. What constraints are there on the growth of multinationals? (**8–13**)
6. What trends are likely to influence the future of the multinational? (**14**)

5
Differences and similarities in overseas markets

Segmentation

1. Introduction. Overseas markets differ from each other in some way. Companies developing overseas must develop approaches or mechanisms to review market potential and market conditions in order to decide which market is most appropriate for company development. This process is known as segmentation, and is essential in understanding the differences and similarities in overseas markets so that resources can be properly and effectively allocated to the markets that are most likely to provide the greatest return to the company.

2. A definition of segmentation. Segmentation involves the division of a total market into a number of subdivisions. Each subdivision will exhibit a different type of demand pattern.

> The car-buying market can be divided into a number of different categories. These include the small economy sector, the family car, the executive car sector, the sports car market, the four wheel drive market and so on. Each of these particular segments will show a large degree of common requirements – price, performance, styling and comfort, for example.

3. Importance of segmentation. Segmentation is essential to the successful implementation of marketing strategies. Each market or market sector will have a series of subdivisions or segments which have different types of demand. Ascertaining these demand patterns, and developing combinations of product, price, promotion, dis-

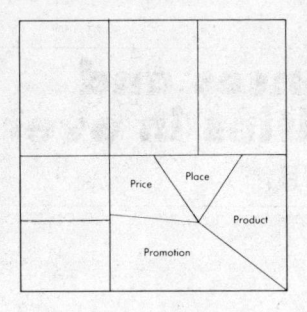

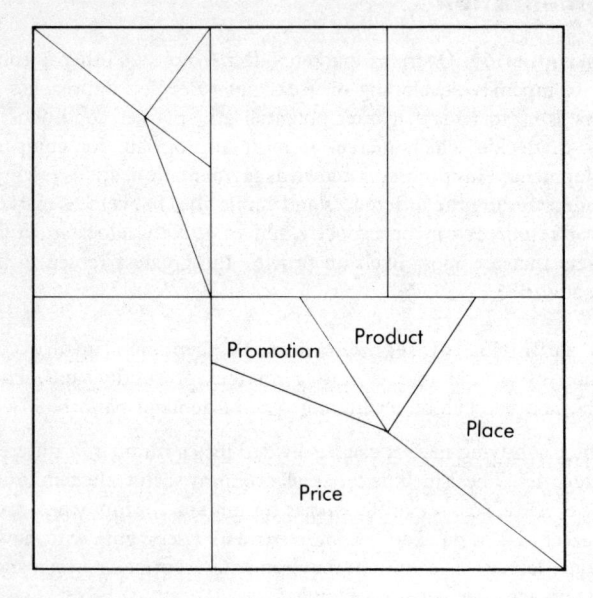

Figure 5.1 *Segmentation*

tribution and other elements of the 'marketing mix' (discussed in Chapter 1) to meet them will give the firm a competitive advantage over other firms that are less astute in accurately matching marketing mix to market segment (*see* Fig. 5.1). Alterations in segments served will demand changes in marketing mix.

5. Differences and similarities 41

CPC, the large American food company, adapts Helmanns' mayonnaise for each country in which it is sold, to match consumer taste and maximize potential sales.

The nature of the segment which the company can successfully exploit will vary according to the resources of the company and the degree of competition in the market. There are three options open, each of which has strategic and tactical implications.

(*a*) *Niche segmentation.* Developing expertise for one small area of the market.

Morgan Cars of Wales produce a single model sports car for a specialized market sector, individuals seeking an old-style convertible model. The company continues to be successful.

(*b*) *Selective segmentation.* Broadening the appeal to cover a wider range of opportunities.

ICL, the British computer firm market a mini computer – the ICL system 25 – and software specifically written for a range of applications which require significant data processing capability including warehousing, retail, and estate management routines.

(*c*) *Mass market approaches.*

Kelloggs competes against all other breakfast cereals with Kelloggs Corn Flakes, and has been consistently one of the most successful food companies in the United States.

Many commentators consider that most UK companies spread their overseas activities too widely, and that a better use of segmentation techniques and concentration on the more viable segments would produce better results. These differences in approach are often called the 'shotgun' and 'rifle' methods, one achieving a broad scatter, the other being much more accurate and directed.

Avoiding the pitfalls of segmentation

4. Pitfalls in segmenting potential markets.

(*a*) *Accuracy of demand definition.* Crucial to the definition of market segments is the accuracy of the demand definition that is linked to it. This problem will be especially acute in industrial markets where demand is often influenced by:

(*i*) the degree of automation/technology in their production process;

(*ii*) the number of areas where the product can be used within the same organization;

(*iii*) the importance of price to the potential customer;

(*iv*) variations in the way the customers purchase;

(*b*) *The suitability of the segmentation criteria for the market.* Different companies will need to use varying methods to define market structures; what is appropriate for one company in one market may not be appropriate elsewhere. Thus a company active in selling fleet cars to large organizations will be guided by factors quite different from those applied by a company selling industrial detergents to the same organizations.

5. Features of successful segmentation policies. Segmentation is essentially a practical rather than a theoretical exercise.

Success or failure will depend on certain characteristics.

(*a*) *Is the identified segment* **measurable?** All market segments are to an extent hypothetical, but it is essential that the company's planning process is based on as much hard evidence as possible, and the size of each segment can be clearly defined; otherwise it will be difficult to allocate the correct amount of resources to exploit it.

American Express is able to accurately define the market size for its Gold and Platinum charge cards in Western Europe from government income statistics.

(*b*) *Is the identified segment* **accessible?** The market sector must be reachable with ease.

Sales of savings plans and life insurance are poorly developed in many parts of the world because the market sector though sizeable in many countries is very difficult to reach because of factors like poor communications and low levels of literacy.

(*c*) *Is the identified segment* **sustainable?** The market sector must continue to be viable over a period of years.

5. Differences and similarities

The growing investment of many companies in the health and diet market reflects their confidence in this as a continuing facet of society. Examples include Weight Watchers (Heinz) and Lean Cuisine (Findus).

(*d*) *Is the identified segment* **profitable?** It will be essential that the company is able to service the segment profitably.

The 'international car' concept developed by multinational car companies illustrates the issues of profitable segmentation. Though there are individual preferences in cars, a supplier can still effectively produce a product which meets as many of the buying criteria as possible at a competitive price. This balance of maintaining high production volumes (with consequent low prices) is continually having to be balanced against the inability of this policy to exactly match consumer requirements.

Segmenting markets at home and overseas

6. At home.

(*a*) *Rate of return on investment.* Most companies will view their home market as being their most important profit-earning region. Studies of small companies show that on average they generate 1.5 per cent of their profit overseas, and though for the larger company this figure will be significantly higher, it is the case that, for the majority of UK companies, home activity will be more important than overseas. In consequence they will often invest heavily in the home market to determine the needs of specific sectors of the market by identifying a whole range of segmentation variables within the community. Such factors might include the following:

(*i*) Economic factors, including the earning power of individuals, and types of house ownership.

(*ii*) Demographic issues such as family size, age and sex; stage of family development – number of bachelors; families with children, number of retired people.

(*iii*) Behavioural factors including life style or the importance of the family.

While such detailed analysis is crucial for a company operating in its home environment, from which it derives the bulk of its profits, development overseas will initially mean that the company considers broader market segments for planned activity, as narrow market definition will make it difficult for the company profitably to develop overseas for reasons discussed below.

(b) *Information.* In many markets the information which the company would need to define narrow market segments accurately is lacking (*see* 8:8) and though basic research can be carried out to fill the gaps, it will be extremely expensive for the level of likely return.

Because of these two factors the initial approach to market segmentation for a company developing overseas will be a broad assessment of the likely potential of each individual market. The company that is fully established overseas, with a more sizeable market share will be better able to more accurately define specific market segments and requirements.

7. Approaches to international market segmentation. There are several ways in which a company can approach segmentation. These are:

(a) economic;
(b) demographic;
(c) cultural;
(d) degree of central government involvement;
(e) life styles.

8. Economic.

(a) *GNP per capita.* The most common approach to international segmentation is to divide countries on a GNP (Gross National Product) per capita basis.

This approach divides the countries of the world on average per capita incomes.

Broad divisions within the total variation of world economies include the developed world (the EEC, EFTA, North America, Japan, and Australasia); newly industrializing countries or NICs (Hong Kong, Brazil, Taiwan, Singapore, South Korea); and the lesser developed world or LDCs including Africa, many countries in South America, Bangladesh and others.

Unilever uses the concept of per capita GNP to help define its

5. Differences and similarities

detergent development policy. A low per capita GNP means that the local company will need to concentrate on bar soap, a higher GNP on detergent powder, a still higher GNP on washing-machine powders and the highest GNP on fabric conditioners and other washing supplementaries.

Though the use of per capita GNP is useful for many companies operating in the mass market, the inequalities in income distribution may mean that substantial markets are missed by the averaging process that occurs.

India, with a population of 900 million consists of two separate markets, a segment which is in the cash economy of around 150 million individuals and the remainder who are subsistence farmers.

GNP figures can also be very misleading in countries such as India where the majority of transactions occur outside the cash economy.

(*b*) *The nature of family income.* Because of the inequalities in income distribution that exist in a number of countries another method of defining overseas potential has been developed using family incomes as a base. Five types of society based on income distribution have been defined.

   (*i*) Universal low incomes which are characteristic of subsistence economies with an income of less than $350 per annum.

   (*ii*) Majority of low incomes as seen in some centrally planned economies with average incomes below $880 per annum.

   (*iii*) Mostly low but some very high incomes with the average below $880 per annum.

   (*iv*) Low, medium, and high incomes characterized by countries with an emergent middle class with incomes greater than $1250 per annum.

   (*v*) Mostly medium incomes: countries achieving a high level of income redistribution by taxation as in Scandinavia, or managing to create high levels of governmental employment as in countries of the Middle East.

(*c*) *The development of the middle class.* Another approach is to consider the evolution of the middle class as central to the growth of consumer demand. This divides countries into:

   (*i*) primitive societies;
   (*ii*) revolutionary societies;

(*iii*) transitional countries;
(*iv*) affluent countries;
(*v*) classless societies.

The difficulties of applying this approach to the practical issues of segmentation are considerable since it relies heavily on the definition of what constitutes the various elements – such as the 'middle class'.

9. Demographic approaches to segmentation. For many companies, particularly in the industrial and service sector, the degree of urbanization and industrial development may be of crucial importance. Urbanization is important because it will determine how accessible a potential segment of the market is. Construction, financial services, education and health provision will all be related in part to the degree of industrialization and the concentration of population in urban areas in overseas markets.

International markets by such definitions can be divided into a number of categories.

(*a*) A subsistence agricultural economy with little urbanization.

(*b*) A pre-industrial society with slow urbanization and heavy reliance on overseas manufactured goods.

(*c*) Underdeveloped countries with low capital and high labour intensive manufacture such as footwear, building materials and canned goods for the home market where urbanization is growing rapidly.

(*d*) Industrialized countries where the large majority of the population are involved in manufacturing activities and living in or around urban centres.

(*e*) Post-industrial society where only a minority of the population are involved in manufacturing and the majority will be involved in the service sector.

10. Cultural approaches to international segmentation. The exact importance of culture to the company expanding overseas is very difficult to define.

The acceptability of McDonalds, Coca Cola and Levi jeans throughout the world suggests that cultural divisions often put forward as barriers to common approaches in world wide markets may perhaps have been overstated. However there are a number of

5. Differences and similarities   47

cultural influences which remain important as means of segmenting markets which must be taken into account by any company expanding overseas. These include:

(*a*) *Religion.* The main religious divisions throughout the world exhibit different customs which will affect the level of demand of various products.

Perfume consumption is much higher in the Arabian Gulf than in Western Europe because of dietary law and social custom resulting from Islam which require the washing and perfuming of hands before eating.
  Fondue sets would be in little demand in the Far East due to the dislike of the Chinese community for cheese products; a consequence of the emphasis on fresh produce in the cooking process.

(*b*) *Language and education.* Common language and educational systems produce a degree of common interests throughout the world.

Educational computer software produced for the United Kingdom market will be inappropriate for either France or the United States; in France because of the different language and in the United States because of the different educational system.

(*c*) *Family structure.* Societies will differ as to the nature of the family structure. The extended family with close connections between relatives remains important in many societies whereas in others this is now significantly less important.

One of the growth areas of home building in the 1980s in Western Europe has been the construction of bachelor apartments. This mirrors the decreasing importance of the family as the backbone of social organization.

11. Degree of central government involvement. The nature of central government involvement may also have an important influence on the level of demand. This ranges from the highly centralized systems of Eastern Europe and a number of developing countries, to mixed levels of state intervention in Western Europe and the broadly non-interventionist policies of the United States.

48　Marketing Overseas

12. Life styles. Developing a scheme to slot the countries of the world into a particular framework, whether it is by per capita income, size of household and the like, is a major undertaking. The company attempting to identify international markets should however be aware that there may be individual differences in consumption patterns that are not instantly definable in terms of some economic or demographic criteria.

The average Frenchman uses twice as many beauty products as does a woman.
The average Belgian drinks double the quantity of pure alcohol per year consumed by the average Swiss.
The average Australian spends far less on indoor games/toys than the average European even allowing for the differences in climate.
The number of books bought per capita in New Zealand is far higher than in the United Kingdom.

Progress test 5

1. Give a definition of segmentation. (**1,2**)
2. Why is segmentation important? (**3**)
3. Explain (a) niche segmentation; (b) selective segmentation; (c) mass market segmentation. (**3**)
4. What factors affect the accurate segmentation of a market? (**4**)
5. Give the key criteria for a successful segmentation exercise. (**5**)
6. Compare and contrast the factors relevant to segmentation in home markets with those overseas. (**6**)
7. List the approaches available to the company interested in segmenting a market overseas. (**7**)

6
International strategic development

Determining an international strategy

1. The elements of strategy. A company's strategic policies or plans must have certain characteristics.

(*a*) *They should be* **attainable.** Company goals can be met with the available resources.

(*b*) *They should be* **objective.** The plans take account of all the features of the environment in which the company operates.

(*c*) *They should be* **consistent.** The strategic goals chosen must not conflict with each other.

Central to the development of a consistent international strategy will be the understanding of the constraints that exist in the international environment as otherwise the plan will fail to meet the important criteria.

2. Key international strategic decisions. These can best be explained as finding the answer to questions in certain areas.

(*a*) *The international investment decision.* Should the firm expand or expand further overseas? Will the investment in the international sector be more effective in the short-term or long-term than comparable investments in the home market?

(*b*) *Selection of markets.* Which markets are most likely to meet the strategic objectives that the firm has set?

(*c*) *Marketing mix decision.* What issues of distribution, product, promotion and price need to be considered? What are their implications?

50 Marketing Overseas

(d) *Organizational decision.* Does the structure of the firm accurately reflect the requirements of the strategy? Does the organization have sufficient control and understanding of the issues involved?

The Midland Bank followed a strategy of investing in one of the growth areas in the United States by buying the Croker Bank of California. Failure to exercise sufficient control over the operation allowed the subsidiary to run up huge losses.

3. Setting specific strategic objectives. When the company has examined the strategic constraints (*see* **5**) existing in its overseas markets it will be in a position to take realistic decisions about specific issues in a number of areas.

(a) The desired return on capital employed, sometimes referred to as ROCE.
(b) The desired level of market share.
(c) The speed of payback that is required for further investment in the overseas market.

The targets adopted will affect:

(a) the level of investment that the firm will make;
(b) the level of risk that it is prepared to accept and the degree of flexibility that is desired;
(c) the speed at which market development should be pursued.

4. The timescale of the company goals. Different developments within the company's overall plan will take place over varying periods of time.

(a) There will be short-term goals; objectives set for the next year.
(b) Medium-term goals; objectives to be achieved within one to three years.
(c) Long-term goals; objectives more than three years ahead.

A company with substantial international activity will develop a matrix allowing it to structure the type of objectives it is trying to achieve, the timescale over which they will be applied, and the costs of entry (*see* Fig. 6.1).

6. International strategic development

Control issues

Costs of entry		Favourable	Moderate	Difficult
	High	Local subsidiary	Joint venture	Management contact
	Moderate	Joint venture	Industrial co-operation	Management contact/licensing
	Low	Local office	Distributor/ third party manufacture	Exporting

Figure 6.1 *Strategic analysis*

International strategic constraints

5. The main considerations. In order to create an effective strategy, a firm must have a clear understanding of issues that might affect the eventual outcome of the plan. These factors are known as constraints or barriers to entry, acting as a brake on the progress of the firm.

The problems that a company faces in defining an overseas strategy vary considerably from those in the home market.

Apricot, the successful business computer manufacturer, failed to appreciate the different constraints on operating in the USA compared with the UK and was eventually forced to withdraw with a loss of more than £10 million.

The degree of importance that is ascribed to each element will differ according to the level of investment that the firm is making and the speed of return which is envisaged, but the main factors that need to be considered include:

(*a*) political systems;
(*b*) investment aid;
(*c*) planning procedures;
(*d*) currency stability;
(*e*) legislation;

52 Marketing Overseas

(f) market size;
(g) competitive position;
(h) nature of buyers;
(i) nature of suppliers;
(j) nature of distribution;
(k) local business practice;
(l) local customs;
(m) market conservatism;
(n) personnel;
(o) logistics.

6. Political systems. Political systems can be vitally important in affecting and determining the success or otherwise of foreign involvement.

(a) *Stability*. The degree of stability within a political system will be crucial for large-scale investments. Expropriation of assets has occurred in many states – the Soviet government for example is currently negotiating to pay compensation for seizure of foreign assets in 1917.

(b) *Level of civil disorder*. Even in stable political systems the actions of a minority can cause considerable disruption to manufacturing industry. This is clearly shown in the difficulties that Northern Ireland continues to have in attracting overseas investment.

(c) *Government attitudes towards overseas investment*. Governments vary in their support of overseas investment. The nature of the political system will have important effects on the company's strategic planning.

> The high rate of growth of Singapore's economy up to the mid-1980s has been largely due to the success of official policies in attracting foreign investment including liberal attitudes towards the employment of expatriate staff and the level of control allowed to the foreign investing companies.

(d) *International acceptability of the political regime*. International political activity against both South Africa in 1985 and Rhodesia after the Unilateral Declaration of Independence, in 1965, damaged investment prospects in both countries.

6. International strategic development 53

7. Investment aid.

(*a*) *Grants*. For large scale investment such as new engine factories or assembly plants the amount of government assistance in grants and reductions in taxation either local or national can be a crucial factor in determining the site location of the new operation.

(*b*) *Tariff protection*. Some countries will provide tariff protection in return for local investment, which will substantially improve the local manufacturer's competitive position. Tariff barriers will be a major issue in the way in which a company can develop in an overseas market.

Tariff barriers after independence in 1947, along with restrictions on the level of control of overseas investment considerably reduced the level of overseas investment in the Indian economy.

8. Planning procedures.

The length of time that it takes to gain permission to build a new plant or factory will have important implications on the speed at which a company can become established in an overseas market. This is, in some countries, an extremely lengthy process whereas others have streamlined their procedures to aid foreign investment. A number of American companies interested in investing in Europe in the 1980s decided against the UK because of its cumbersome planning procedures.

Streamlined planning procedures including ease of acquiring manufacturing sites has made Hong Kong an ideal market for companies wishing to rapidly establish assembly operations in the Far East.

9. Currency stability.

Currency stability significantly affects:

(*a*) the profitability of the organization by adverse or favourable movements in relative currency strengths;

(*b*) the level of inflation which creates significant difficulties for forecasting and planning purposes;

(*c*) the degree of convertibility – how easy it will be to transfer money out of the country.

10. Legislation.

Local legislation will be a central limiting factor in the development of the firm.

54 Marketing Overseas

(a) *Ownership.* Each country will control the percentage shareholding that overseas companies can have in local enterprises. This will vary from nil (the case in some Middle Eastern countries), allowing minority stakes (Nigeria), to allowing totally owned local subsidiaries to be established. A minority stake in a company naturally will affect the freedom of the parent company to change direction as eventual control exists outside the organization.

(b) *Personnel.* Each country will control to a greater or lesser extent the nature of the personnel that an organization can employ, whether unionization is obligatory and so on. Italy has extensive union legislation that starts to take effect when more than 35 people are employed in a firm. Many firms solve the problem by keeping a small head office staff and then employing free-lance individuals in other areas such as the salesforce. Local legislation will also determine minimum levels of pay, redundancy terms, pension arrangements and the like.

(c) *Safety and other mandatory regulations.* Each country will have different regulations on what items should be included on the packaging, what safety regulations or emission standards need to be met in the factories and so on.

(d) *Price control.* Legislation may also include control over the prices that the company can charge in the market.

(e) *Patents and trade marks.* Legal protection will be more effective in some countries than others. The difficulties of enforcing trade mark protection in Taiwan have been well documented in many market sectors.

(f) *Control over monopolies.* Each country will have different mechanisms by which monopolies are identified and controlled; the point at which a business is identified as a monopoly will also vary.

In the United States the Justice Department maintains a strict watch over likely monopolies, forcing AT&T to split up its national telephone network. In the UK in contrast the official view is 'monopolies need not be against the public interest' and similar actions by the Monopolies and Mergers Commission are rare.

(g) *Contract law.* It will always be more difficult for a foreign firm to enforce contracts against national firms in overseas markets for a number of reasons. The overseas firm may be reluctant to cause adverse publicity, and the legal system may favour the nationally based firm. In some countries the legal system is so structured that contracts are practically impossible to enforce, and business operations rely much more heavily on trust than the force of law. Law based on British legal concepts can allow the company to specify terms and conditions whereas other legal systems may make this more difficult.

11. Size of market/market growth. The size of the market and its growth will naturally affect the strategy that the firm can follow. The nature of the business that the company does will very much determine what size of market will be sufficient for effective company operations. A company which needs to maintain service points or establish its own sales force will find that there are substantial fixed costs involved in overseas expansion. It will have to be sure that the profit achieved in the market will eventually be sufficient to cover these overheads. This is defined by many companies as 'critical mass' where sales value exceeds fixed costs (*see* Fig. 6.2).

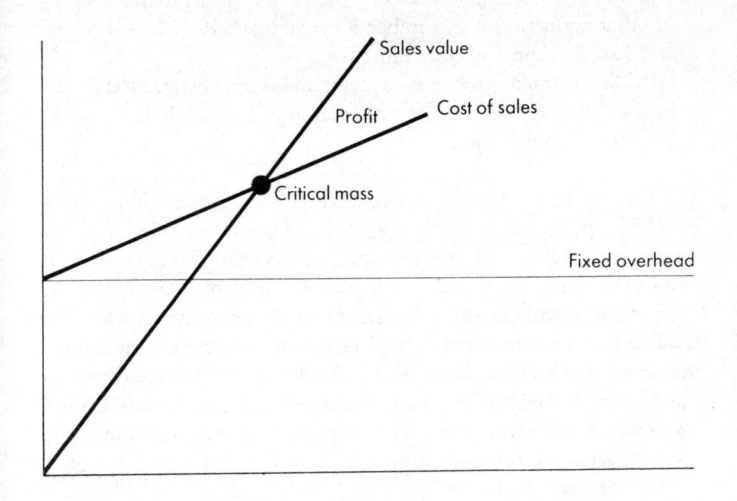

Figure 6.2 *Critical mass*

56 Marketing Overseas

12. Competitive position. The market share that the company has in each market will have a significant effect on the way in which it can develop.

In each market various market elements can be isolated:

(a) the market leader;
(b) the market follower(s);
(c) the market specialist(s);
(d) the commodity producer(s).

Each type of competitive position will require different approaches to the market. For example, the market leader will need to invest heavily in promotion and support services to maintain market leadership. The market follower may have to spend disproportionately greater amounts in research and development, or invest heavily in improving distribution in order to improve its market position. Each market will pose differing competitive problems which may serve as a brake on the achievement of strategic goals.

> Unilever still fails in the 1980s to achieve adequate returns from the United States detergent market, where, in contrast to the position in other countries, it is number 3 in the market – behind Procter and Gamble and Colgate Palmolive.
> IBM faces similar problems in trying to become better established in the Japanese market, the only country in which it does not far outsell the competition.

13. Nature of buyers. The structure of the market will in many instances pose fundamental problems for the development of international sales. The concentration of international business in a handful of firms, discussed in Chapter 3, is one of them.

In many countries the government or government services will tend to prefer to deal with a local rather than foreign company for major contracts. A Regional Health Authority was taken to court in the United Kingdom over the granting of a contract to ICL over foreign competitors. For the consumer goods company the concentration of retailing power in fewer and fewer companies creates identical problems.

In the United Kingdom for example, Sainsbury's, Tesco, and Dee each control around 13% of total grocery sales; in Belgium GB (23%)

6. International strategic development

Country	% grocery retail sales from top 5 retailers
Austria	70
Belgium	75
France	40
Germany	30
Italy	15
Switzerland	80
United Kingdom	60

Delhaize (12%) and Colruyt (11%) occupy similar positions.

Government buying organizations in many centralized economies and some developing countries provide the sole source of possible trade development, and have proved a major constraint in the development of trade with Eastern Europe.

A close relationship with a major buyer may provide an easy access point into a foreign market. Universal Toys of Hong Kong bought the ailing Lesney (Matchbox) group for whom they had been manufacturing.

14. Nature of suppliers. For a company manufacturing overseas, the nature of the suppliers may be important. Should all manufacturing firms in the market be required to buy raw materials and/or products from government trading organizations it may be difficult for the firm to establish a competitive position on either quality or price.

15. Distribution.

(a) *Availability.* Limited distribution facilities may restrict a firm's ability to expand overseas. For example, a frozen food manufacturer would be severely hampered by the shortage of frozen food cabinets in overseas markets and would have to invest in providing stores with them so that sales could develop.

(b) *Limitations on distribution.* Governmental or other controls may exist that define the nature of the outlets that are available.

The United Kingdom specifies the distribution channels for prescription drugs, and the prices at which they should be sold.

Alcohol is only available through government owned outlets in Sweden.

16. Local business practices. Much has been written about the differences in international business practice. Factors such as price fixing, and the nature of commissions to buyers, will vary from market to market and may either facilitate or hinder overseas development.

17. Local customs.

(*a*) *Religious.* Dietary laws are most commonly considered as major constraints to market development.

Jewish religious law forbids the combination of meat and dairy products making the sale of many frozen convenience food items impossible.

(*b*) *Gifting.* The items that are given as gifts will vary from country to country and have implications on product type and packaging.

A significant proportion of soap is given as gifts in the Japanese market which concentrates sales in two periods of the year.

(*c*) *Consumerism.* Local attitudes to products may exert influences in addition to those imposed by legislation.

Monosodium glutimate, a flavouring enhancer, though not legally restricted as a food additive has effectively been withdrawn in Western Europe due to pressure from consumer groups. By contrast, the flavouring is regarded as an important food additive in the Far East.

18. Market conservatism. Different markets will respond to new products at different speeds. For industrial goods, this poses a problem in all markets with the industrial buyer tending to be extremely conservative and only considering a re-purchase of the previous product. Consumer markets are often similarly affected.

Johnny Walker Black has long remained the premium Scotch in Middle Eastern markets even though strenuous attempts have

6. International strategic development

been made by other brands to become established in the market.

Such conservatism can extend to problems caused by the national origins of the overseas firm; strong market chauvinism may make the international firm carefully consider the nature of the product, brand name and communications package that it uses in overseas markets.

19. Personnel. A good overseas market strategy can collapse if the company does not have the right people available to carry it out. There are several aspects to this issue which must be considered.

(a) Local availability of employees.
(b) Skills of local employees.
(c) Costs and difficulty of training local employees.
(d) Costs of employing local staff versus expatriates.

Should the firm need to employ local personnel the skills available and the costs of employment will be factors that may act as constraints upon the planning process (*see* Chapter 23).

20. Organization structure. The way in which a firm is organized may itself create many barriers to overseas development; will the company be able to handle the increased distance and product complexity that development overseas may imply? (*see* Chapter 22).

21. Logistics.

(a) *Communications.* The ease with which the market can be controlled from overseas will often be important – the nature of air links and telephone systems may have important implications on the siting of overseas operations.

Bahrein in the Arabian Gulf remains the local centre for banking operations partly as a result of its good communications and ease of access.

(b) *Research data availability.*
(c) *Infrastructure.* Nature of internal transport systems. How good are communications within the country? Are water and power supplies adequate?

60 Marketing Overseas

Progress test 6

1. What characteristics should a company's strategic goals have? (**1**)
2. What are the key issues involved in international strategy planning? (**2**)
3. What is a barrier to entry and how many can you list? (**5-11**)

7
International marketing strategy and market investment

The level of investment

1. Options of market development. The level of investment that the company is prepared to make in the market will largely determine the way in which the international operation will be structured.

  (a) Low levels of investment in the overseas market:
      indirect export methods;
      licensing.
  (b) Medium levels of investment in overseas markets:
      direct export;
      third party manufacture;
      franchising;
      local sales subsidiary.
  (c) High levels of investment in overseas markets:
      joint ventures;
      local manufacturing subsidiary;
      the purchase of an overseas company.

Assessing the risk

2. Risk. The level of risk is closely associated with the level of investment. Firms without direct investment in the market in any form face the lowest risk of loss if the market becomes closed to the firm; the greatest risk is if the firm has a large, totally owned local manufacturing subsidiary, or has invested heavily in buying an already existing overseas operation.

62 Marketing Overseas

The Imperial Group bought the Howard Johnson hotel group in the United States for $630 million. Five years later after a steadily declining profit performance the Group sold the operation for around $300 million.

3. Assessing the level of risk. To offset the higher level of risk, firms investing overseas should seek higher levels of return than can be achieved in the home market.

Companies can relate the likely degree of return on investment to the probability that that return can be achieved by using one of the international comparison studies.

(*a*) BERI, Business Environment Risk Index, ranks the main markets of the world on a number of criteria including:

political stability;
attitude to foreign investment;
nationalization;
inflation;
balance of payments;
bureaucratic delays;
economic growth;
currency stability;
legal system;
infrastructure – communications/distribution;
local personnel skills;
availability of local finance.

Ratings are achieved out of 100; scores above 80 indicate an extremely favourable investment climate, below 40 a country which is unlikely to present a worthwhile investment risk.

(*b*) EMF. An index developed by the EMF foundation provides an international analysis of industrial competitiveness and can be used to determine where the overseas manufacturing company can best invest. Its survey is limited to 22 industrialized countries and 9 industrializing countries including Hong Kong, Taiwan and Singapore but it provides a comprehensive survey based on both independently collected data and expert opinion.

The criteria used include inflation, the level of private savings and the access to low cost finance. In 1986 the EMF ranked countries as follows:

Top: Switzerland, Japan, US.
Second rank: West Germany, Sweden, Norway, Denmark.
Middle rank: United Kingdom, France, Italy.

(c) Country environmental temperature gradient. This divides countries into three categories – 'hot', 'medium', and 'cool' on the following basis:

Item	Hot	Medium	Cool
Political stability	High	Medium	Low
Market opportunity	High	Medium	Low
Economic growth	High	Medium	Low
Cultural homogeneity	High	Medium	Low
Legal barriers	Low	Medium	High
Infrastructure problems	Low	Medium	High
Cultural barriers	Low	Medium	High

Both the business environmental risk index and the country environmental gradient suffer from a degree of subjectivity in the assessment of risk. The assessment of Iran for example under the Shah illustrates this issue; most commentators perceiving the political system as inherently stable, with the events of history showing a totally different perspective.

4. Other strategic models. The common strategic models used by companies to determine investment decisions in their home markets can also be applied to help in the definition of overseas activity.

(a) *Product life cycle or PLC*. The product life cycle holds that products and product categories will go through a period of introduction, growth, maturity and decline (*see* Fig. 7.1), reflected in sales in the market-place.

This movement in sales volume is accompanied by a slightly different pattern of profitability with an early high investment and maximum profitability during the maturity stage.

By using the PLC as a guide to profit and cash flow, an international organization can plan the nature of strategic investment.

Stage I: Export from home production base to main potential markets (introduction).

64 Marketing Overseas

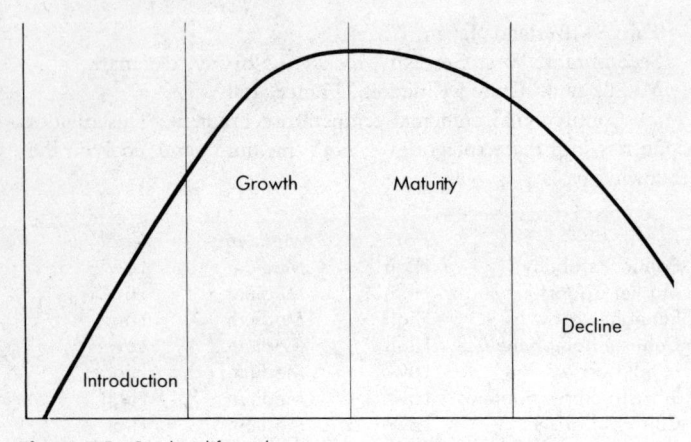

Figure 7.1 Product life cycle

Stage II: Manufacture in main overseas markets and export to minor markets (growth).

Stage III: Manufacture in minor markets (maturity).

Stage IV: Cease manufacture but licence technology to smaller companies wherever possible (decline) (*see* Fig. 7.2).

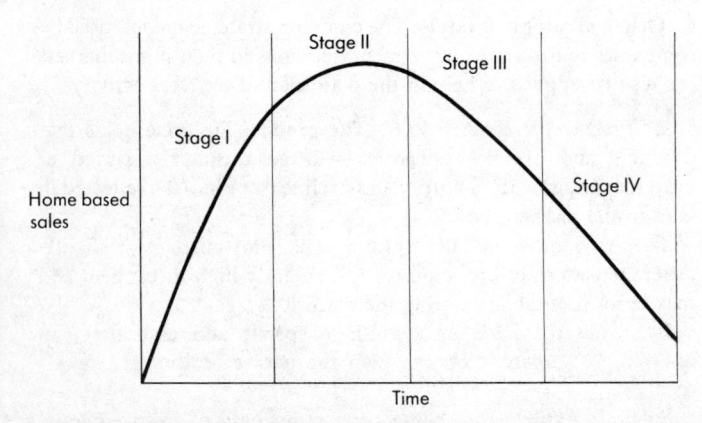

Figure 7.2 Strategic investment stages

This allows the international organization to maximize the profit contribution from its investment in the international environment. However the use of the PLC theory often produces the phenomenon of the self-fulfilling prophecy with management assuming that the product is declining, withdrawing support, thereby unwittingly precipitating a further decline. Not all products exhibit a classic PLC; fashion products have short cycles, and some products will show long term fluctuations (*see* Fig. 7.3).

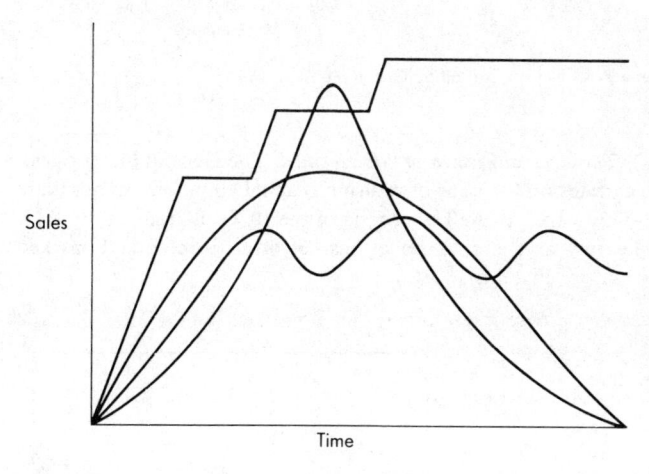

Figure 7.3 *Cycle variations*

(*b*) *BCG*. The Boston Consulting Group matrix (*see* Fig. 7.4) divides products on the basis of market share and market growth, into cows, dogs, question marks and stars. The application of this on an international basis provides the company with an overview of where it should be considering investing and what action should be taken with respect to the current products:

(*i*) Whether to invest.
(*ii*) Whether to maintain the current position.
(*iii*) Whether to run down activity or products.
(*iv*) Whether to withdraw from the market.

66 Marketing Overseas

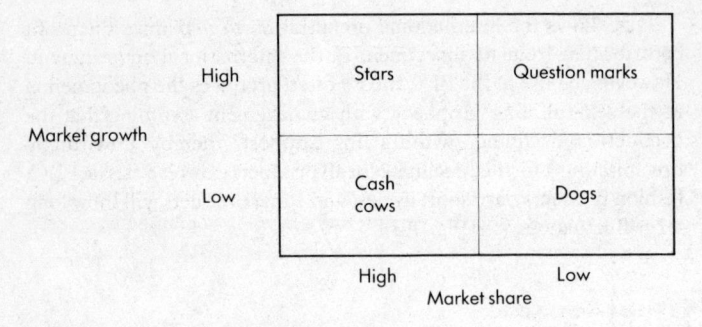

	High	Stars	Question marks
Market growth	Low	Cash cows	Dogs
		High	Low
		Market share	

Figure 7.4 Boston Consulting Group matrix

(c) *The General Electric or GEC method.* The General Electric grid concentrates on the issue of return on capital employed, rather than cash flow which is the key criteria of the BCG matrix.

The two axes are issues of market attractiveness and market position (*see* Fig. 7.5).

	High	1	2	4
Market position	Medium	3	5	7
	Low	6	8	9
		High	Medium	Low
			Market attractiveness	

Figure 7.5 General Electric grid

Within the 9 cells that exist, three different types of action are suggested.

(a) For cells 1–3, the company should invest to achieve continuing growth and development of activity.

(b) For cells 4–6, the company should consider maintaining the current level of activity.

(c) For cells 7–9, the company should consider withdrawing unless there are clearly defined strategic reasons for not doing so.

For the majority of companies involved in the international environment and concentrating on two or three key markets overseas, the use of strategic models will be a valuable aid to decision-making.

Other factors

5. Production issues. A key question that the exporting firm must resolve is whether production should be transferred overseas or whether the investment in overseas markets should be limited to the creation of a local sales subsidiary. Though the level of risk involved in overseas production is important, there are in addition a number of production-related factors that will often be just as important in determining the location of manufacture.

Factor	Local production	Centralized production
Product	Simple	Complex
R&D levels	Low	High
Unit price	Low	High
Quality control considerations	Low	High
Labour cost	Low	High
Labour skills	High	Low
Transport cost	High	Low
Transport availability	Low	High
Tariff barriers	High	Low
Customers	Local	Multinational
Capital availability	High	Low
Capital cost	Low	High
Political stability	High	Low
Economic stability	High	Low
Market potential	High	Low

68 Marketing Overseas

The issues are most clearly shown when the production policies of a highly technical company such as IBM or Boeing are compared with a low technology company such as the Bata shoe group. For Boeing the advantages of maintaining a centralized production unit are crucial; massive R&D (research and development) expenditure is required and the economies of scale are crucial for effective world production. In contrast Bata with low capital requirements, and low unit prices of its finished products, faces a different set of problems, all of which would suggest that a decentralized production process is advisable.

Progress test 7

1. What type of overseas operation is most appropriate for (*a*) low, (*b*) medium, (*c*) high levels of investment overseas? (**1**)
2. How does the level of risk affect the type of overseas investment operation chosen by the company? (**2**)
3. How can a company evaluate the likely level of risk in an overseas operation? (**3**)
4. Describe the strategic models used by companies as aids to investment decision-making. (**4**)
5. What factors must the company consider when deciding whether to manufacture abroad? (**5**)

8
Information systems for initial development overseas

The need for information

1. The importance of accurate market information. To plan for the future, a company must first find the opportunities that are available and must continually review its progress in taking advantage of these opportunities in the market. Good military intelligence allows the general to anticipate rather than merely react to what the opposition is doing – which is very similar to the problem faced by marketing departments in all companies with their role in the strategic process.

Information is crucial to both strategic and tactical planning. Obviously, different companies will need varying types of information but the company that has a better understanding of its market sector than its competitor will have a significant competitive advantage. With its enhanced knowledge of trends, such a company will be able to identify opportunities and challenges more accurately than its competitor, planning accordingly and benefitting from speedy reaction to changing conditions. Such advantages will only materialize if the company is able to interpret accurately, and use effectively, the information that is available.

Accurate marketing information will enable the company to:

(a) recognize developing trends more quickly than the competition;

(b) evaluate marketing action and planning more thoroughly;

(c) allow a large and diverse firm to integrate information for central planning purposes – essential for strategy development.

70 Marketing Overseas

2. Defining the information required. The discussion of trade, strategy and investment planning, segmentation and other topics, in earlier chapters, can be summarized in one word. Information. The company interested in marketing overseas must know about itself and its products, its competitors and their products, and about the environment in which they operate. Companies that appreciate the value of good information and how to use it will tend to be more successful than those with limited or non-existent information or dismissive attitudes to it.

The information of most immediate concern to the company can be summarized as a series of questions, and remembered as the mnemonic – the six 'Os' of marketing.

(*a*) Who are the potential consumers (Occupants)?
(*b*) What do they currently buy (Objects)?
(*c*) Why do they currently buy what they buy (Objectives)?
(*d*) Do consumers influence each other in the purchase decision, and if so, how (Organization)?
(*e*) When do they buy (Occasions)?
(*f*) Where do they buy (Operations)?

Information systems

3. Features of a good information system. Most organizations do not have sufficient data on which they can base realistic action strategies; some go to the other extreme in having too much. A good information system should be:

(*a*) simple;
(*b*) accurate and;
(*c*) useful.

A clear, company view about information needs is essential in order to achieve such ends. This will involve a company knowing the precise nature of its information needs, developing sources from which the information can be derived, and creating a system whereby this data can be organized into providing comparative analyses which can be used in helping to decide what action would be most appropriate for the company.

8. Information for initial development

4. Stages in development of an information system. The stages involved in the development of an information system can be standardized, whatever the action that the firm proposes.

(*a*) The information on a problem area should be defined as clearly, and specifically as possible. This will help in considering (*b*).

(*b*) The company must decide on the amount and type of information that will be required to solve the problem.

(*c*) A systematic method for collecting and analysing information will have to be established and maintained.

(*d*) The information collected will serve to delineate alternative possible action paths and establish criteria (action standards) by which their success or failure will be judged.

(*e*) The data should then be used with the action standards to determine the best possible course of action. This action will then affect the future information that the company receives. In other words a decision loop will be created (*see* Fig. 8.1).

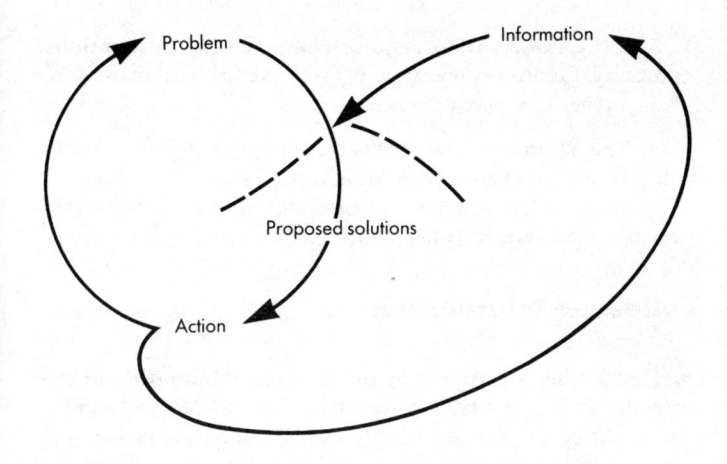

Figure 8.1 *Decision loop*

A structured approach attempts to remove the large element of subjectivity that tends to become established in information

72 Marketing Overseas

collection with managers often only accepting information that fits in with preconceived ideas.

However even when a structured information system is established, there is a danger that it becomes an end in itself. So that management remains alert about the role of the information system, certain key questions will have to be asked continually.

(*a*) What will management do with information if it is made available faster? Will management actually be able to use the available information effectively?

(*b*) What new types of decision will management be able to take if the information is made available?

(*c*) How flexible should the system be? How many different types of information requirement must it service?

(*d*) What range of inputs will be required to reach the acceptable level of risk?

(*e*) How much internal and external information is required to reach an effective decision?

5. Specific information requirements for the international company. Companies operating in overseas markets have two fairly distinct types of information need.

(*a*) The information that the company requires to define markets and products for overseas expansion (Chapter 8).

(*b*) Information required to control and plan once an overseas presence is established (Chapter 9).

Collecting information

6. Developing an approach to market definition. Collecting information will be a time-consuming and often expensive exercise. To minimize the amount of information collected, the company considering overseas expansion should have some form of screening process by which the majority of overseas markets are discarded at a fairly early stage without wasting too many resources.

A proposed selection process might have up to eight stages (*see* Fig. 8.2).

8. Information for initial development

```
Product analysis         (1)
        ↓
Customer analysis        (2)
        ↓
Screen available markets (3)
        ↓
Reject unfavourable markets (4)
        ↓
Concentrate on key markets  (5)
        ↓
Identify detailed opportunity (6)
        ↓
Plan actions             (7)
        ↓
Implement                (8)
```

Figure 8.2 *Eight-stage selection process*

(a) Defining current products and potential customers.
What criteria determine current purchase patterns?
High income levels?
An agricultural community?

(b) Using basic segmentation data (*see* Chapter 5) the company will be able to rapidly evaluate world markets and discard those that do not offer adequate potential.

(c) Select suitable markets.

(d) Carry out more detailed analysis on the selected markets to identify the order of acceptability by considering the possible barriers to entry (*see* Chapter 6) and weighing the issues according to their importance to the company on some form of grid system (*see* Table 8.1).

(e) Select specific market(s).

(f) Carry out specific research on the market (if appropriate).

74 Marketing Overseas

Table 8.1 Acceptability/importance of selected markets

	Importance	% chance of favourable outcome	Outcome
Political stability	3	60	1.8
Currency stability	8	70	5.6
Good distribution	6	40	2.4
Language problems	2	80	1.6
Technical skills availability	7	60	4.2

Using existing sources of information

7. Using information sources. In common with a structured approach to market definition, organizing the collection of information will help the company to reduce the cost and maximize the efficiency of the exercise.

A sifting process might involve five stages.

(*a*) Internal company information. This would include the experience of any members of staff in other companies, any contacts that have been made within Chambers of Commerce.

(*b*) Desk research in the home market. There will often be large amounts of data available:

   (*i*) from banks and other service organizations;
   (*ii*) from national and international governmental reports;
   (*iii*) from trade magazines and journals;
   (*iv*) from competitors' catalogues;
   (*v*) from trade associations;
   (*vi*) from trade directories;
   (*vii*) from specific literature on the market.

These information sources will often provide the small company with sufficient information from which to take the decision to develop indirect, low risk exports to a particular market or markets. Where the firm is considering a more intensive investment in the market, such as the appointment of agents, it will need to carry the research process further.

8. Information for initial development

(*c*) Desk research overseas.

(*d*) Purchasing audit data or previously commissioned market research data from research companies.

(*e*) Joining new omnibus surveys or commissioning specific market research.

8. External information sources for overseas trade.

(*a*) *Government or official publications.* There are an increasing number of data sources available to the company interested in overseas trade. Government and public agencies produce vast libraries of information which may be useful to the marketing team. For example Social Trends is a valuable indication of overall changes in consumer attitudes in the UK market, Customs and Excise maintains records of imports, the Department of Trade and Industry maintains information on industrial production. The OECD comments on West European economic development, the United Nations and subsidiary organizations publish data on such diverse facts as family planning and food production levels. The British Overseas Trade Board maintains detailed analyses of all major overseas markets. Similar information sources exist for many overseas countries. The BOTB will in fact prepare a short report on the potential of the company product in the proposed overseas market at minimal cost and this may suggest problems that the company did not initially foresee.

(*b*) *Trade/telephone directories.* These are available in major libraries for major overseas markets, and provide details of locations and numbers of firms in particular sectors.

(*c*) *Trade magazines.* These provide a valuable source of background information for the firm on overseas markets including issues such as duties, trading conditions and particular problems in the market.

(*d*) *Commercial databases.* In addition to official publications there are an increasing number of commercial databases which allow access to a wide range of specialist information. Indeed one of the distinguishing advantages of the large multinationals or conglomerates over their rivals, is the continuing development of intergroup data bases from which any of the operating subsidiary companies can derive consumer or market information which may

76 Marketing Overseas

have originally been commissioned by some other company within the group.

(e) *Banks, advertising agencies, freight forwarding companies.* These can all provide valuable additional information on specific areas of interest in overseas markets.

(f) *Sales audit data.* There are a number of firms which can provide information on competitive market shares in major markets. Examples of such firms include Nielsen (sales data on major consumer markets in Western Europe, and the Americas) and AGB. Other specialized firms provide data on areas such as the electronics market in which a firm like Mackintosh International operates.

(g) *Shared research activities – omnibus studies.* The same firms (*see* (f)) operate to provide research on common topics of interest to a range of companies on an intermittent basis.

(h) *Specific market research.*

9. Shortcomings in collected information. All information which is collected is likely to be inaccurate, some more than most. The saying 'Lies, damned lies and statistics' came from a fundamental understanding of the nature of all government statistics. Information may suffer from the following problems:

(a) It is extremely out of date.

(b) The way information is categorized may either be wrong or misleading.

(c) The way in which the information is collected will often change over time.

(d) The information may be recorded in a particular fashion for political reasons and not accurately reflect the underlying situation.

> There are no accurate population figures for Saudi Arabia as no census has been conducted. The situation in Nigeria is similar where censuses are politically sensitive.
> There have been 16 changes in the way the UK records unemployment figures between 1979 and 1985.

10. Using international statistics. International statistics will provide an indication of the likely position in each market, but will

8. Information for initial development

never be a totally accurate guide. Researchers need to review the material and clarify several issues.

(a) What exactly is included in the data – how does the organization define the category?

(b) Has the base line changed over the years – has the organization changed the way it collects the information?

(c) Does the data correspond roughly to other (independent) sources?

(d) When was the data collected and by whom; were there major upheavals at the time it was collected?

Should key decisions depend on these statistics it will be important to clearly state the level of uncertainty in the material as an assumption in the planning process.

11. Desk research overseas. Many countries will provide detailed information to the overseas businessman which can help in the definition of business opportunity. Though the cost of executive time overseas may be high, it will be substantially less than specific market research and – providing the sources of material are identified in advance via the commercial sections of overseas trade delegations and the journey effectively planned – the use of desk research overseas may be highly cost effective. In addition, it will provide the company with first-hand experience of some of the market conditions.

12. Acquiring audit data and other market research information. The major market research firms maintain an extensive range of material produced for other clients some of which, like sales audit data, is available for purchase. Other material like specific market surveys is not.

Conducting specific market research

13. Specific market research overseas. Where the firm is considering a major investment, specific market research will be required to minimize the level of risk. Overseas market research will pose additional problems over research in the national market for the following reasons:

78 Marketing Overseas

(*a*) *Language.* The exact meaning of words will be important for a survey to be accurate – the respondent has to be clear as to exactly what is being asked and the questionnaire has to be clear as to what it is demanding.

Translation always has its pitfalls. The English phrase, 'out of sight, out of mind', meaning if it's not visible you won't tend to think about it, has been translated as, 'invisible lunatic' (out of sight = invisible, out of mind = lunatic)!

(*b*) *Social.* In many cultures it will be unacceptable to interview women, there may be overall hostility to the interviewers as strangers or potential government agents.

(*c*) *Content.* Individuals, like governments, vary according to the nature of the information that they are prepared to divulge. Financial details are particularly difficult to acquire.

(*d*) *Availability.* It may be very difficult to gain access to individuals – it is impossible in many countries to question on a door-to-door basis, few individuals may have telephones, and there may be restrictions on interviewing in the street.

(*e*) *Bias.* All research suffers from a degree of bias – the respondents telling the questioner what they think he or she wants to hear. Such problems may be far more acute in certain markets.

14. Minimizing research problems in overseas market research. Whether the company carries out the research itself or chooses a market research agency, the following issues will be important:

(*a*) A high training level of interview staff.

(*b*) Minimizing misunderstandings by introducing visual display cards or samples.

(*c*) Check with the local authorities whenever there is a possibility of the survey causing local unrest.

(*d*) Carry out detailed pilot testing to ensure that problematic questions and research procedures are minimized.

15. Market research agency selection. For the majority of firms without a well-established local subsidiary employing a number of national citizens, market research overseas will inevitably mean the

8. Information for initial development

appointment of a specialist international market research organization. The options available are outlined in Table 8.2.

Table 8.2 Specialist international market research organizations

Type of research agency	Market knowledge	Control problems	Cost
Nationally based	Good	Substantial	Standard
UK based with overseas associates	Fair	Reduced	Standard
UK based – part of international group	Good	Minimal	Costly
UK based with overseas travelling staff	Poor	Reduced	Costly

In selecting an agency the company should check the following:

(*a*) That the agency chosen has recent expertise in the actual field or closely allied topic.

(*b*) That the results obtained will remain confidential.

(*c*) That the agency employs suitably qualified and trained individuals who will be able to cope with all potential local problems.

(*d*) That the agency can produce the required work on time and within budget.

16. Financial aid for overseas market research.

(*a*) *Initial market survey.* The BOTB provides via British representation overseas a market viability assessment for individual companies.

(*b*) *More detailed research.* For surveys that are likely to help substantially expand overseas trade, the BOTB will subsidise research at varying rates:

Individual firms: 33.3%
Groups of firms: 50%
Trade associations: 66.6%

Progress test 8

1. Why does a company need good information? (**1**)

80 Marketing Overseas

2. What are the six 'Os' of marketing? (**2**)

3. Explain the stages in the development of an information system. (**3**)

4. Describe the process whereby information could help a company chose its overseas markets. (**6**)

5. List the available sources of overseas market information. (**8**)

6. To what information shortcomings should the company be alert? (**9**)

7. What problems are associated with overseas market research, how can they be minimized? (**13, 14**)

9
Information systems for controlling international markets

Information needs in established markets

1. Introduction. When a company is established in an overseas market its information needs are rather different from those of the new entrants in the market (*see* Chapter 8). Such a company will want to:

(*a*) measure the effectiveness of its current activities in the market;
(*b*) define trends for future development.

2. Measuring current performance. The company established overseas will need a system to isolate and review key operating factors including the following.

(*a*) *Financial*
Balance sheets of overseas companies.
Cash flow statements.
Debtor analysis.
Orders outstanding.
(*b*) *Sales*
Sales volume by product group and location.
Profitability by product group and location.
Sales volume by customer type (important for many industrial companies).
(*c*) *Distribution*
Shipping costs.
Packaging costs.

Level of distribution achieved in the market compared with the competition.

(*d*) *Promotional expenditure*
Actual expenditure by type of material.
Commitments for future expenditure.

(*e*) *Pricing*
Current market pricing versus competition.

(*f*) *Market conditions*
Changes in duties.
Remittance procedures (particularly important for the multinational organization having to determine the nature of the transfer mechanism that should be adopted).

3. Additional information requirements. Most of the information the company will use will come from either internal sources or from contacts with outside sources, with relatively little contributed by specifically commissioned market research. This view of the information-gathering process is supported by research on established international companies which shows that though more information is gathered from outside the organization than inside (66 per cent against 34 per cent), the main source of external information comes from:

(*a*) service organizations – banks, advertising agencies;
(*b*) publications – trade journals, government reports;
(*c*) customers, competititors, suppliers.

This survey indicates that less than 1 per cent of the total information used by major companies is received in the form of commissioned market research. Market research commissioned in the United Kingdom totals around £160 million per year, much of it being continuous or sales audit information, and includes a substantial element of overseas research which is paid in the UK. This figure should be contrasted with an expenditure on advertising of £3000 million in the UK alone.

4. Costs of maintaining information. Each item of information considered necessary to improve company decision-making will incur a level of cost: the greater the amount of data, and the faster the speed of access to it, the higher the cost. Large sophisticated

9. Information for controlling markets 83

companies maintain continuous or on-line information systems for continuous monitoring purposes; in a smaller company off-line or intermittent information will be used.

As with specific market identification (*see* 8:**5**), internally available information will be the least expensive to collect, specifically and individually commissioned market research the most costly. It is possible to compare sources with the type of information that they will provide and a summary easily demonstrates the sources that are likely to be most useful.

(*a*) *Internal financial data* – sales, product costs.
(*b*) *Reports on external events* – competitors' activities, visits to major customers, changes in the market overseas.
(*c*) *External publications from government or trade publications* – statistics, changes in the environment, in living standards, in legislation.
(*d*) *Shared research information* – market shares, consumer purchasing habits.
(*e*) *Specifically commissioned market research* – specific reactions to products, advertising campaigns.

The level of risk involved in a particular decision is obviously an important factor in weighing the relative value of each information source and its cost to the company. In general terms the more important the decision, the lower the level of acceptable risk that the decision will be wrong, and the greater the need to ensure that all possible information has been collected to minimize the likelihood of the decision being based on incorrect or erroneous assumptions.

The steadily decreasing cost of data storage has meant that companies are more able to effectively analyse the internal information that they have at their disposal: a computer costing £750,000 ten years ago which filled two rooms can now be purchased for £30,000 and occupy the space of two filing cabinets. The inevitable tendency is for information systems to become steadily more complex with the reducing costs of data storage.

Identifying trends

5. Forecasting in the information system. Part of the firm's information gathering system will be directed at developing its

84 Marketing Overseas

capacity to forecast trends and movements, not only with respect to the level of sales, but political and social change as well. The forecasting process is all to do with the minimization of risk. One of the largest risks that an organization can face is the inability to foresee rapid change. This can either cause a dramatic increase or decline in demand. Either will cause the company greater problems than it can immediately deal with. Advance warning of these 'turning points' allows the firm to make resources available in other areas of the business – more production, more promotion, or whatever.

> Some firms dealing with Nigeria faced a dramatic decline in fortune when the oil revenues declined. One subsidiary of an international trading group reported earnings down from over £6 million to £230,000 the following year.

6. Forecasting and the environment. In a simple environment of one company supplying a long-established loyal customer with a component in short supply, demand is largely pre-determined and there is a minimal risk that the environment will change sufficiently to affect the supplier's production, for even if overall demand drops this will be offset by the shortage of supply. A company in this situation could plan with a high degree of confidence for the future.

At the other extreme a company with a volatile customer base, and a surplus of product available in the market, faces a very different set of demand problems. These will be made even more acute should the sector in which the firm operates face rapid political, economic, social or technological change, which will be very hard to quantify.

7. Demand problems. These largely imponderable problems can be remembered by the mnemonic PEST; as they are the problems that lie at the heart of many companies' forecasting problems.

(*a*) *Political*. What happens if political systems collapse or governmental policies change direction?

> The decision of the Common Market to introduce milk quotas had a dramatic and severe effect on many small farmers especially those in developing dairy areas such as Wales.

> Whether the major debtor nations, Brazil, Argentina and Mexico, would default on their massive debt repayments has

9. Information for controlling markets

overshadowed the planning process in many large banks. Here their ability to act is largely determined by the attitudes of Western governments to Third World debt.

(*b*) *Economic.* What are the likely changes in economic activity both at home and abroad over the next five years?

At what level oil prices will stabilize has been a factor of major importance to many companies. Its sudden collapse in 1986 for example was predicted by few.

(*c*) *Social.* What important social changes will take place over the next five years?

The number of people regularly playing bingo in the UK has dropped from 5.5 million in the 1970s to 3.5 million by the mid-1980s. Ladbroke, one of the major operators of bingo halls, has taken the view that this decline will continue; the Rank Organization, purchasers of their halls, take the opposite view.
Black African states have been campaigning against apartheid and calling for economic sanctions against South Africa since the early 1960s. It was not until 1985 that attitudes in the West to apartheid had changed sufficiently for governments to give serious consideration to sanctions.

(*d*) *Technological.* What effect will changing technology cause over the next five years?

The introduction of the tape cassette virtually eliminated the market for reel-to-reel tape recorders except for professional applications.

8. Reaction to changing trends. Some firms consider that the problems that these changing trends cause are too severe to combat effectively, and withdraw from any attempt to determine long-term demand.

The major record companies find it impossible to forecast demand for particular recording artists. Bands surface for six months, a year, and then mysteriously disappear from the public consciousness. They respond to these extreme fluctuations by keeping as many artists under contract as possible.

The record companies can adopt this approach because the investment involved is low; groups are paid on a royalty basis after their records sell. For other companies facing similar rates of change the solution is not so simple.

The Boeing Aircraft company currently faces the problem of assessing the future replacement of the 747. The investment that such a move will require will be immense; the pay back period well into the 21st century.

Companies like the Boeing Aircraft Corporation need to develop some system to minimize the risks that such investment decisions impose upon them. Any assessment of likely change will inevitably be subjective; in other words the research will be qualitative rather than quantitative, identifying trends rather than actual numbers.

9. Qualitative forecasting systems

(a) *Delphi.* The Delphi forecasting technique developed by the Rand Corporation attempts to use expert opinion to develop forecasts by an exchange of questionnaires. Members are kept unaware of who else is on the panel and there is no discussion – feedback is maintained by the group leader who analyses the questionnaires and asks individuals who deviate significantly from the group consensus to justify their answers. Companies such as the Lockheed Aircraft Corporation have found this a useful technique to attempt to minimize the problems of change in a rapidly changing technological environment.

(b) *Visionary statement.* A similar approach, albeit on a more simple level is to ask individuals within an organization for a 'visionary' statement, an attempt to forecast broad changes that may affect the organization.

10. Quantitative forecasting methods.
Even when the environment is rapidly changing the use of current information to forecast will increase the chance of the company identifying turning points within the planning horizon.

(a) *Historic projection.* The simplest approach is the straightforward historic projection, taking the current level of activity and

9. Information for controlling markets

projecting forward from that base. Such a forecast will be unlikely to identify major changes in the environment as it will be far too affected by short-term fluctuations.

(b) *Customer projection.* Where the bulk of the business is carried out with a limited number of customers direct contact with them over likely future demand will often provide one of the most accurate forecasting systems. This approach is very similar to the simple environment discussed in **6**.

(c) *Moving totals.* A method of removing fluctuations, such as those caused by high seasonal sales, is to combine the sales for the year or two years adding current months and removing sales which occur outside the time period. This system which is extremely easy to apply and fairly accurate as a short-term indication of likely trends is particularly suitable where the change in sales levels is fairly gradual.

(d) *Exponential smoothing.* Where there are rapid changes in the sales history, recent events will be far more important in explaining the near future than sales of one or two years ago. Introducing a smoothing constant which gives greater importance to more recent sales is one way of overcoming this problem.

The comparison between historic projection, moving averages and exponential smoothing is shown in Fig. 9.1.

(e) *Time series analysis.* More sophisticated analyses such as the Box-Jenkins method, attempt to take a number of elements of the company sales record and produce a model to explain the underlying trends. Both this system and the more complicated X-11 system produced by the US Weather Bureau require computer assistance and a degree of statistical expertise. Both systems do however reduce the element of risk in the forecast process by more accurately identifying possible turning points within a one year projection period.

(f) *Environmental factors.* The use of the PLC as a forecasting system has already been commented on (*see* 7:**4**). This, and the experience curve *see* 10:**6**, are used by some firms as additional forecasting tools.

(g) *Causal analysis.* The main shortcoming in all time series analyses is the fact that the information used to develop the forecast is internal. The company will not be able to rapidly relate violent change in the external environment to the effect on demand. To do

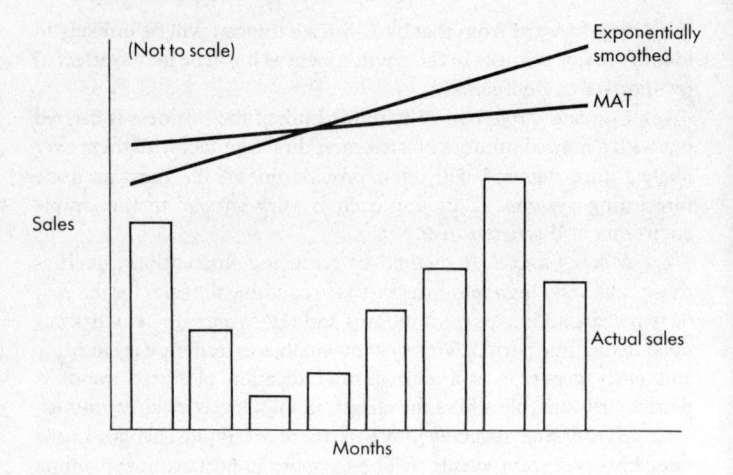

Figure 9.1 *Historic projection, moving averages and exponential smoothing*

this the firm will need to determine a factor in the external environment causally related to the demand for the company's products. Unilever's detergent policy – relating on a world wide basis the amount of detergent consumption to gross national product (GNP) per head – is one such relationship. Rising GNP appears to have an effect on the overall consumption of detergents.

Other relationships identified by companies include the level of consumption of consumer durables (on fast food consumption in the United States), the level of unemployment (on demand for holidays in the United Kingdom). Such causal systems allow the firm to predict demand patterns more accurately. The main problem in using them is the complexity of data analysis required, the removal of spurious inter-relationships, and critical assessment of what are in fact independent rather than dependent variables. For example there might be a relationship between the numbers of miles of motorway and overall ice-cream consumption; the real underlying factor would perhaps be increases in GNP. Secondly there would be a clear relation between the number of new cars and demand for number plates; one would be a dependent variable on the other.

At its simplest level regression analysis of a single factor against another will yield information about underlying demand trends.

9. Information for controlling markets

Often more than one factor will be important in influencing demand and therefore multiple regression techniques will be important for complex sales relationships. In many large companies this is built up into an econometric model which attempts to provide an explanation or a simulation of all the main external factors affecting sales.

> Bowater Scott and Beechams are two companies that have developed sophisticated models to explain the effects of environmental factors upon their leading brands. The logic underlying the model suggested to Bowater Scott that continuous advertising would be highly profitable for the Andrex brand; to Beechams that increasing price along with extra promotional expenditure would be the most profitable route for Dettol.

These econometric models at their most sophisticated simulate the external environment; they enable firms to test out hypotheses such as the effects of increasing distribution, lowering price, and raising promotional expenditure on the total market sales.

As forecasting systems become more complex, they tend to become divorced from the operational level and require the services of trained statisticians. The results of such forecasts tend to be treated with a degree of caution, as line managers often feel that the figures arrived at do not accurately reflect the market place.

11. The company and its forecasting requirements. As risk increases, the need for forecasting investment will grow. The following will exert a crucial influence:

(*a*) The level of investment.
(*b*) The speed of return on that investment.
(*c*) The uncertainty in the environment.

More investment means more risk, as do longer and longer pay back periods.

Progress test 9

1. What information does the established company need to measure its current performance? (**1,2**)
2. What useful information can a company gather from (*a*) internal, (*b*) external sources? (**3**)

3. Explain the connection between data collection and forecasting. (**5**)

4. Explain PEST. (**7**)

5. Describe two qualitative forecasting systems. (**9**)

6. How useful is (*a*) moving totals, (*b*) causal analysis as a forecasting technique. (**10**)

10
International product management

The product and the market

1. Introduction. The product itself is central to the marketing mix and the firm's positioning activity in the market place. This involves giving detailed consideration to certain aspects of the product.

(a) *Product features.* What is special or different about it? The question has to be asked whatever the product. The answer will involve describing both tangible and intangible elements of the product – the nature of which will vary with the product – from highly tangible products, such as cooking salt, bought mainly for their usefulness; to intangible products such as Porsche motor cars bought mainly for social status rather than basic transportation.

(b) *Presentation features.* How will the product be presented to maximize the special features? This involves not only the packaging which surrounds the product but extends also to such issues as after sales service, guarantees and the like (*see* Chapter 11).

Product options

2. The options available. Any company has a number of options regarding the future of its products whether it is selling at home or abroad.

(a) Abandonment of the product in one or more markets.
(b) Maintenance of the product without change in the marketing mix.

(c) Attempting to expand sales of current product in current markets.

(d) Attempting to expand sales of current product in new markets.

(e) Attempting to improve or modify the product or its packaging elements to improve sales volume or profitability.

(f) Introducing totally new products to meet consumer demands in overseas markets.

The interaction between product and market is clearly shown in what is normally called the Ansoff matrix (*see* Fig. 10.1).

		Market	
		Old	New
	Old	Market penetration	Market development
Product	New	Product development	Diversification

Figure 10.1 *The Ansoff matrix*

3. Product abandonment. Product abandonment will be important under a number of circumstances.

(a) If the product remains unprofitable.

(b) If sales of the product demand small production runs which interfere with the economies of scale possible on the company's main product lines.

(c) If the product needs to receive high levels of research and development investment to maintain what is a declining product in the long-term.

(d) If the product takes up a lot of time of the sales force and management which could be more profitably used elsewhere.

4. The implications of abandonment.
Management will however need to carefully consider the implications of the decision to abandon a product or market.

(a) Is the product in fact serving some competitive function by denying a competitor a strong and potentially profitable market position?

> The *Evening News* and *Evening Standard* both lost money in the evening paper market in London in the early 1970s. The withdrawal of the *Evening News* allowed the *Evening Standard* to improve its pricing in a monopoly market and move into profitability.

(b) Whether the reported loss is not in fact a feature of the costing system in operation within the firm. This may mean that the product is making a valuable contribution to overheads.

For example one can consider three products:

Product	Sales	Overhead cost	'Profit'
A	800	300	500
B	400	200	200
C	200	170	30
Total	1400	670	730

Removing product C because of low profitability would produce the following picture:

Product	Sales	Overhead cost	'Profit'
A	800	400	400
B	400	270	130
Total	1200	670	530

(c) What, if any, 'service' function does the product afford the company?

> Small packs of detergents may not be profitable in terms of sales volume but provide a vital part in initiating trial of powder detergents in overseas markets.

94 Marketing Overseas

The key issue for the international company is to identify service products and to budget for them within overall promotional expenditure.

(d) Can the product continue to generate money for the company via licensing or other royalty arrangements in overseas markets? Third party manufacture may also be a route worth exploring. These considerations will be especially important for the export marketing organization without overseas manufacture. Where it has a declining market at home for a profitable product overseas, the initial step should be to consider overseas manufacture rather than follow solely the dictates of the home manufacturing unit.

(e) Whether the product with a degree of investment can be effectively rejuvenated to produce new growth in profit and volume. The shortcomings of the Product Life Cycle have alrady been mentioned in this respect (*see* 7:4).

The issue of standardization

It is in the interests of the company operating overseas to maintain the maximum possible level of standardization for a number of reasons.

5. Economies of scale. The greater the amount produced the lower the cost per unit. Economies will also exist if the company does not have to produce specific advertizing material for the overseas market but can using extant film or promotional material without modification.

6. Learning curve. A firm can also lower cost per unit as cumulative production increases; in other words, the firm learns how to manufacture more efficiently becoming more skilful in speeding production, reducing component costs and the like.

7. Research and development costs. The longer the production run the greater the amortization of R&D expenditure.

8. Mimimizing stock costs. A small product range will minimize the cost of maintaining stock.

10. International product management

9. Maintaining international consistency. Certain international trends act as an incentive for companies to achieve a level of consistency with their goods or services across countries.

Legislation to protect consumers is now an almost universal feature of everyday life. In the area of mass marketed goods this means that the weight or volume of a product and its constituent ingredients must be displayed on packaging.

To facilitate trade between members, trading blocks like the EEC increasingly standardize their regulations on measures, health and safety. It therefore makes sense for European mass market companies to standardize products and packaging.

Within many markets, especially those providing goods or services in a well-defined sector, international trends again argue for standardization. The high level of mobility of management has encouraged the reduction of international variation in hotels ensuring that the Hilton in Bahrein offers the same level of service as the Hilton in Frankfurt.

10. International sourcing of components. Where the company manufactures internationally it will be in their interests to maintain component inter-changeability for three reasons:

(*a*) economies of scale;

(*b*) it allows the company to multi-source its components reducing risks inherent in single production sites, such as strikes or damage to plant;

(*c*) it allows the company to develop an international team of managers that have a common body of knowledge and experience of the company's products.

11. Constraints on standardization. Each product will, however, face varied demands and constraints in overseas markets which may operate against standardization.

(*a*) *Mandatory local requirements.* Despite the trends mentioned in **9** above areas of argument and conflict between countries remain, particularly in the area of health. These will generally affect the nature of the packaging, but may also include necessary action on additives, colourings and the like.

96 Marketing Overseas

Perfumes sold in the Middle East may not be ethanol-based, because of national laws against alcohol.

Scandinavian countries generally have more stringent controls on food additives than Britain.

The EEC has decided that British milk chocolate is not chocolate in the European context.

(b) *Taxation.* Tax bands may mean that the unmodified product is uncompetitive in price.

The move to King Size cigarettes in the United Kingdom is partly caused by taxation being calculated not on the tobacco weight but on a per packet basis – manufacturers can improve their positioning by increasing the length of each cigarette.

(c) *Climate.* Hot tropical conditions may make demands on the barrier qualities of the packaging (*see* Chapter 13), and on the stability of the formulation, sunlight may affect printing inks. Equipment will often have to be designed for the effects of additional cooling (or heating).

The Japanese car industry made major inroads in many tropical countries by providing small air conditioning units as low cost extras for many family saloons.

(d) *Tariff barriers.* For many countries import duties will be based on an ad valorem system – the landed cost of the product plus x per cent. Should these duties be high it may be in the interests of the company to export the product in kit form and assemble it locally thus reducing import duties and also improving the subsidiary's standing in the overseas market by adding a major percentage of local components.

(e) *Servicing arrangements.* Where servicing arrangements are inadequate the company would need to consider providing heavier duty material than would be normal in the home market.

(f) *Socio-economic and cultural factors.* Extreme variations in socio-economic and cultural factors may prevent the company from selling the same range of products in the overseas market.

(g) *Specific market requirements.* Where there are major market opportunities available for a modified product, the pressure for product standardization will naturally be minimized.

10. International product management

12. Using standard products in expanding in-market sales. The firm will have a number of options for expanding sales within a particular overseas markets.

(*a*) Changing distribution methods – expanding the sales force or using intermediaries to increase market spread.
(*b*) Increasing promotional expenditure.
(*c*) Changing price policy.
(*d*) Buying competitive firms.

13. Changing the product to meet market conditions – product development. The most common approach of the company involved in international trade will be to modify the product, in a number of ways, to make it more acceptable in overseas markets:

Product reformulation. This is often necessary to meet local conditions, in areas of performance, health, taste, size, durability, ease of maintenance, noise reduction and method of operation.

> Export Surf, sold in West Africa and other tropical countries, has a far higher level of active detergent than UK Surf to reflect the fact that the two areas have different wash problems – one a high temperature washing machine culture, the other a low temperature hand wash.
> International cigarette companies have introduced low tar variants in some countries in response to health campaigns.
> CPC reformulates Hellman's Mayonnaise to meet local tastes throughout the world, while retaining the same packaging.
> Where there are fewer supermarkets, the product range will need to concentrate on offering packs of smaller sizes.

14. Changing the product to meet market conditions – product extension. The company may find that the strength of the product position in some overseas markets allows them to introduce new variants to take advantage of the market conditions which do not exist in the home market or in other overseas markets.

(*a*) *Reduction in complexity:*

Raleigh introduced a range of more basic bicycles, without gears, for some markets to exploit sectors of the market that did not exist at home.

(b) New applications:

The range of Rexona soaps are sold overseas in many hot countries with a high use of showers. The introduction of a Rexona shower gel was designed to fill this market segment which was considerably larger than that in the UK or Western Europe.

15. Producing entirely new products for overseas markets – diversification. In order to become established in some overseas market, or to maximize market opportunities where it is already firmly established a firm may diversify away from its area of initial expertise into other market sectors. There are various options:

(a) Developing new products to sell to the same market sector.

Dalgety steadily expanded the products that it sold to the agricultural sector both in its home markets of Australasia and in the United Kingdom, moving from agricultural feedstuffs to distributing agricultural machinery and chemicals.

(b) Developing new products from the existing production expertise.

(c) Entering totally new markets with entirely different products.

16. Quality control considerations. Central to the success of products in an international environment is the maintenance of high levels of quality. There are a number of reasons for this.

(a) To ensure that service requirements are minimized.
(b) Intermediaries in the distribution chain are more likely to accept lower margins because of the reduced rate of product problems.
(c) The product gains in distinctiveness over the competition and enhances the reputation of the supplier for future purchases.
(d) Finally, good quality control will have the effect of reducing working capital as very few products will need repair or replacement.

The firm that institutes and maintains rigid quality control standards will therefore have significant advantages over other international or national firms.

10. International product management

The rapid acceptance of the Amstrad PCW 8256 in overseas markets was due in part to its low rate of product failure in contrast to another innovative home computer, the Sinclair QL.

17. New product development. In many respects, the problem of new product development is similar for all companies whether operating overseas, or at home. The exercise can be divided into distinct phases.

(*a*) Idea collection.
(*b*) Idea screening.
(*c*) Pilot production and concept testing.
(*d*) Test marketing.
(*e*) National or international launch.

The international company, however, has several advantages over the nationally based company, some of which have already been mentioned.

(*a*) A wider source of new product ideas because of its international exposure.
(*b*) A wider range of possibilities in pilot production and test marketing.

However many international companies with strong centralized controls find the development of new concepts difficult to achieve as subsidiaries are often either unwilling to invest in new product development or once a new product is developed they are unwilling to allow the transfer of expertise to other overseas units.

Multinationals or transnationals have attempted to overcome this problem in two ways. The first is called intrapreneurism whereby a new company is created within the organization to handle the entire new project, with total responsibility for its eventual profitability and performance.

General Motors have created a new company, the Saturn corporation, with the responsibility for the development of a new family car for the world market using all the latest technical developments in robotics, plastics and microprocessors.

IBM set up an independent unit to handle the development of the IBM Personal Computer.

100 Marketing Overseas

The second approach is to allow one subsidiary within the organization the lead on a particular product. This is called a world product mandate or WPM.

Progress test 10

1. What are the factors relevant to product positioning in the market? (**1**)
2. List the options available to a company in deciding on the future of a product. (**2**)
3. Explain why a company might choose to keep a seemingly unprofitable product on the market. (**3**)
4. What are the benefits of standardizing a product for overseas markets? (**5–10**)
5. What factors operate against standardization? (**11**)
6. What are the options for expanding product sales in an overseas market? (**12**)
7. Explain the differences between product development and product extension. (**13–14**)
8. Explain the rationale for product diversification; what are the options? (**15**)
9. Why is quality control important in export markets? (**16**)
10. Give the steps in the development of a new product. Illustrate how multinationals cope with the stresses encountered in this area. (**17**)

11
Further aspects of international product policy

Factors affected by nature of product

1. Introduction. In Chapter 10 we were concerned with the strategic options of product policy overseas which were available to the company. There are, in addition, other factors which are affected by the nature of the product and which were mentioned initially in 10:**1**. The most important are:

(*a*) packaging and branding issues;
(*b*) trade mark protection;
(*c*) the service support the company needs to provide should the product be technical or complex.

Packaging

2. Packaging factors. The factors that the firm will need to consider are similar to those of the home market. These are:

(*a*) consumer related factors;
(*b*) brand related factors;
(*c*) production related factors;
(*d*) distribution.

3. Standardization of packaging. Standardization of packaging will provide the same benefits that accrue from the standardization of product mentioned in 10:**5-9**.

Proctor and Gamble produce Head and Shoulders shampoo at

their plant near Newcastle for all major European markets. They have managed to standardize packaging in what might be considered a 'cosmetic' product which would benefit from specific packaging to meet individual market conditions.

4. Packaging and the consumer.

(a) *Mandatory information.* The amount of information that the company must provide under the law varies from country to country. In most markets, firms are obliged to provide a minimum of information about the product itself but the rules in some markets may also extend to the way in which this information is presented with specifications about the size of type deemed necessary to protect the consumer, and the language in which the consumer information should be provided on the packaging.

(b) *Additional usage information.* The level of literacy and education will vary from country to country and the use of simple graphics may be essential to the acceptability of a product in certain markets.

(c) *Safety.* Different markets will have different legislation concerning the provision of child-proof caps for medicine bottles, for example – drugs may have to be packed in different quantities to comply with local laws.

Advice on labelling overseas can normally be obtained from the relevant trade department. The BOTB, for example, maintains a register of the main factors in overseas packaging.

5. Brand related factors in packaging.

(a) *Name.* International naming of products poses all sorts of problems. Names that are appropriate in one market may be totally wrong in another.

Japan named a Toyota car Cedric and a truck the Little Bugger; Rolls Royce realized that they could not name a car Mist as this means dung in German.

(b) *Logo.* A logo may have an important role to play in the developing of branding, but again will have implications in the international market. In some markets cats will be regarded as especially lucky and snakes as unlucky. Stars and moons may have religious implications that would be best avoided.

(*c*) *Numbers.* 7 is lucky in Chinese communities whereas 13 is neutral; 13 is unlucky throughout Western Europe.

(*d*) *Colour.* Cultural associations of colour remain strong throughout the world. White is the colour of mourning throughout the Far East; green which has connotations of freshness in the United Kingdom market is regarded as a 'masculine' colour in Holland. In India, saffron is a colour associated with priests and red with brides.

(*e*) *Design.* Historical links and culture also influence the preferred design of products and packaging. Much of West Africa will prefer French styled products because of the strong historical ties with France.

6. Production related factors in packaging.

(*a*) *Strength.* The strength of the packaging may have to be altered to meet the demands of overseas markets – for example, the effects of high humidity, and rough handling, may necessitate a re-design in the nature of the container.

The increasing use of container transport methods in Western Europe is leading to a steady decrease in the strength of the outer cartons; for markets in other parts of the world additional strength outer cartons may be essential.

(*b*) *Extended storage requirements.* Transporting a product to Australia from Western Europe, and storing it in a distributor's warehouse before eventual re-sale may add four to five months to the required shelf life of a particular product. This might be important for products with restricted shelf life and could mean that the best option available is to manufacture the product locally.

7. Distribution related factors in packaging.

(*a*) *Visibility on the shelf.* Different retail systems will have varying approaches to the product on the shelf and packaging may need to take account of this fact if the retailer is a major customer.

(*b*) *Retailer information.* It may be necessary to provide specific information on the outer carton to tell the local retailer how to store the product, though the increasing use of international symbols is largely overcoming this problem.

(c) *Pack acceptability.* The pack will have to meet certain size, shape and material criteria.

> Supermarkets in Western Europe increasingly require that liquids be provided in PET plastic bottles or cardboard containers rather than glass.
> Some airlines are similarly demanding that alcoholic miniatures be provided in PET rather than glass – the saving in fuel for a Boeing 747 is estimated at £12,000 per annum!

8. Effects of overseas manufacture on packaging design.

(a) *Component availability.* Local manufacture will normally require some form of modification as the availability of components (cardboard, inks, plastic elements) is not universal.

(b) *Pack design.* The type of pack design will be determined by the type of machinery used and the distribution system. The situation in the overseas market may therefore be different from that at home.

Branding

9. The branding decision overseas. Branding has already been identified as one of the key elements of a successful overseas marketing development. Certain key issues will need to be resolved.

(a) What level of investment will be needed over time to make the branding exercise effective?

(b) Can the brand name be protected in the international environment?

(c) What is the likely level of return to the company?

(d) How should the branding be defined? Should it be company wide or umbrella – for example, the range of DIY and gardening machinery all identified under the Black and Decker company name; or on a product-by-product basis – Signal toothpaste, Harmony hair spray, Sunsilk shampoo, Sure deodorant are all products of the Elida Gibbs company but all advertised separately?

(e) Should the company consider the development of an

11. International product policy

international brand or should the product be branded on a country-by-country basis?

10. Advantages of the international brand name. There are a number of circumstances where international brand names will be very appropriate.

(*a*) Where there is a high degree of purchase by the international travelling community as in the case of films and spirits.

(*b*) Where there is substantial benefit to be gained in the development of common advertising campaigns.

(*c*) Where there is a strong possibility of media spillover.

(*d*) Where, as in the industrial goods sector, international trade magazines can be used to promote a branded reliability and guaranteed performance.

11. Legal protection for international companies – terminology. A trade mark is a 'brand or part of a brand that is given legal protection because it is capable of exclusive appropriation'. A brand is a 'name, term, sign, symbol or design which is intended to identify the goods or services of one particular supplier and to distinguish it from others'.

12. The importance of protection. Trade mark protection is crucial for many companies but especially those with a reputation as pioneers of high quality, innovative products. These include companies involved in fashion – Levi jeans, Gucci leather, Chanel perfume; companies with best-sellers whether they are producing films, songs or books; electronics innovators – computers, hi-fi; and car components, for example Ferrodo brake pads.

Infringement can occur in a number of ways.

(*a*) *Counterfeiting* – attempting to duplicate the product exactly.

(*b*) *Duplicating* – copying technology, but not attempting to pass off as identical copies. This is increasingly common in the microcomputer market.

(*c*) *Similarity* – copying the main elements of name, pack colours and logo to come close to the original.

A Greek manufacturer produced 'Lucky' liquid for the Middle

106 Marketing Overseas

East market similar in shape and colour to the market leader 'Lux'. Other infringements include Coalgate for Colgate toothpaste, Del Mundo for Del Monte juices.

(*d*) *Use in other market sectors* – manufacturers using a well-known brand name in other product sectors.

(*e*) *Trade mark piracy* – a company or individual registering a trade mark of an overseas company in a particular market in order to sell the rights to the trade mark to the operating company should it want to enter that market using its own trade mark.

The company developing overseas can obtain protection for a number of the product components. Each action involves cost and the company will need to evaluate the risks and benefits associated with each.

(*a*) Present and future potential of the added value of registration in the proposed markets over the period of the protection.
(*b*) Total cost of both registration and protection.

13. Methods of protection. The elements of protection include the following.

(*a*) *Trade marks.* These can either be the manufacturers' name or the logo that the company uses to identify its products. Protection is available via the Madrid arrangement (mainly limited to the main industrialized countries) which allows registration in one country to be acceptable in all others and the Paris Union which requires registration of trade marks in all participating overseas countries.

Registration may be extremely expensive, for small potential gains. The company will need to consider carefully the benefits of world-wide registration, and most firms tend to register only in key markets.

What exactly can be registered as a trade mark varies according to the nature of the legal system; some will allow packaging styles and use of colours, others only the name and style of lettering. Trade marks will also be limited to specific categories – Colt is used as a firearm, air conditioning, a lager beer, and a car by different companies.

(*b*) *Brand names.* Most countries maintain some form of brand registration system, of which broadly two types can be identified.

(*i*) *Prior use.* This exists where the company is able to show that for the preceding six months the product has been on sale somewhere in the world.

(*ii*) *Local registration.* The company will need to register locally the brand name to ensure that it receives protection.

The registration of brand names is relatively inexpensive.

(*c*) *Patents.* There are currently three patent agreements; the European Patent Convention, one for the European Community and the Patent Co-operation Treaty which covers all major trading countries. Patent protection in one of the signatories automatically gives protection in other countries. Maintaining patents is however a costly process on a world-wide basis and companies need to carefully consider the rate of potential return. It may cost up to $40,000 to maintain a patent in the EEC.

(*d*) *Copyright.* The Berne Convention is recognized in the majority of countries and serves to protect published material (including entertainment and computer software) against illegal reproduction.

14. Action against counterfeiting. Even where a clear case of product infringement exists, the costs and difficulties of taking legal action may often be immense. Small manufacturers of counterfeit goods will often move and re-establish themselves under a new company structure requiring a further round of legal action.

The most effective response to counterfeiting is either to invest to make the copying more expensive – by changing the inks on the packaging, introducing special tapes into the weave of cloth and so on – or to take action on the distribution channels in major overseas markets.

Trading Standards officers in the United Kingdom have become increasingly important in policing the sale of videos, records, cosmetics and clothes, both confiscating counterfeit items and bringing legal actions against the importers.

Service warranties

15. Guarantees or service warranties in international development. For the industrial product the availability of service facilities will be one of the key issues in buying an expensive piece of technical equipment.

Caterpillar, the major construction equipment manufacturer of the United States, offers a 24-hour service for any Caterpillar machinery anywhere in the world. Such a guarantee is a major inducement to construction companies even if Caterpillar equipment is more expensive than the competition.

The nature of the warranty offered will depend on certain facets of the product and the market.

(a) The competitive advantage it may offer.

(b) The quality of the product – will warranty returns be extremely expensive?

(c) The nature of the international servicing arrangements (*see* **18**).

16. The advantages of standardizing international guarantees.

(a) Where the product is international, differences in warranties on a national basis may be impossible to define. The example of Caterpillar above is one such – a construction company such as Bechtel with world-wide interests will want the same level of service in the Middle East that it receives in Munich.

(b) Where there are major safety factors associated with the product.

(c) Where the product has a single production source, the definition of warranties for a range of overseas markets may be difficult to administer.

17. Disadvantages of international guarantee standardization.

(a) Variation in conditions overseas may make common guarantees impossible.

A European bus company reviewing the conditions under which their vehicles were likely to be used in a North African city decided that their normal warranty of one year would have to be reduced to one month.

(b) Different production points will produce variations in quality control and in the particular problems that the product is likely to encounter.

(c) Competitive value: as guarantees are a valuable competitive weapon, international standardization will often limit the use of this tactic on a market-by-market basis.

18. Defining international servicing arrangements. The company selling technical products overseas will face three options.

(a) Maintaining the product from its home base, using employees of the parent company.
(b) Setting up an overseas servicing operation using directly employed engineers.
(c) Being represented in the market by a distributor which can provide service back-up.

The criteria that will determine the most appropriate method are the following:

(a) *Strategic issues.* The firm may decide that for strategic reasons a high level of service is essential.
(b) *Cost.* The comparative costs of providing the service by the three methods will need to be considered.
(c) *Complexity.* The type of servicing required is the key issue in determining the way in which the company deals with the servicing issue. Complex tasks especially those involving safety issues will mean that the firm must directly employ service engineers overseas, as it will be difficult to achieve the necessary high level of training with overseas distributors.

All major airlines maintain engineers at their major stop-over airports to ensure that servicing to the necessary level of safety can be achieved.

(d) *Market profitability.* The more potentially profitable the market, the greater the incentive to provide a high level of local service support.
(e) *Speed of communication.* Where the market can be rapidly reached from the home territory it may be cost-competitive to service the market from the home base.

Marketing Overseas

Progress test 11

1. What aspects of packaging for overseas markets must the company consider? (**2-8**)
2. What are the packaging problems associated with international branding? (**5**)
3. List the key issues associated with international branding. (**9**)
4. Give the advantages of an international brand name. (**10**)
5. Define (*a*) a trade mark, (*b*) a brand. (**11**)
6. What forms can trade mark infringements take? (**12**)
7. What influences international standardization of company guarantees or warranties? (**15-17**)
8. What considerations affect the servicing decisions taken by a company selling a technical product overseas? (**18**)

12
Distribution channels: design and management

Distribution channels

1. Definition. A distribution channel is the means by which goods are transferred from the supplier to the end user.

Channels are either direct - the supplier has immediate contact with the end user; or indirect - with intermediaries between the supplier and the end user (*see* 14:**9**). Figure 12.1 illustrates the various distribution channels that exist in four overseas markets.

2. International distribution channels. Two issues confront the company operating in the overseas environment:

(*a*) Defining distribution channels between countries.
(*b*) Defining distribution channels within markets.

In choosing between the alternatives that are available, the company will have to achieve a working balance between the characteristics of each market and its own operating needs to succeed in that market. The balance has to be realistic: a method of distribution that works in one market may be out of the question in another.

Distillers delivers container lorries of Johnny Walker whisky direct from Scotland to major retail customers in Belgium. In contrast it ships whisky to an agent in Japan for distribution through the wholesale network. This is not simply a question of distance from the market but a reflection of the crucial controlling role of large Japanese buying houses in the country's system of distribution.

112 Marketing Overseas

Bahrein
(Consumer goods)

```
              Manufacturer
                   |
                 Agent
                   |
              Wholesaler ———— Own retail outlet
                   |
               Retailer
```

Japan
(Consumer goods)

```
              Manufacturer
                   |
              Wholesaler
                   |
              Wholesaler
                   |
              Wholesaler
                   |
               Retailer
```

Western Europe
(Many industrial +
consumer products)

```
              Manufacturer
                   |
            Retailer/end user
```

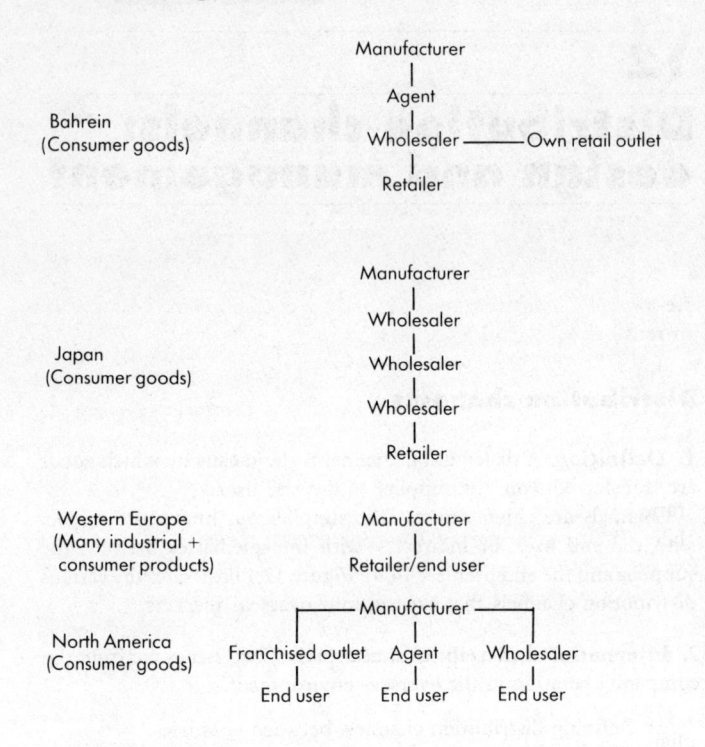

North America
(Consumer goods)

```
    ——————————— Manufacturer ———————————
    |                 |                |
Franchised outlet   Agent          Wholesaler
    |                 |                |
 End user          End user         End user
```

Figure 12.1 *Distribution channels in four overseas markets*

3. Importance of distribution channels.

(*a*) *Cost.* Controlling distribution costs can be an important, but often ignored, issue in improving profitability.

The percentage of cost that is attributable to distribution depends very much on the product. An industry average, however, suggests that around 19 per cent of manufacturers' selling price is attributable to distribution costs including transport, warehousing, inventory cost, order processing and administration.

12. Distribution channels

Item	% cost
Transport	6
Warehousing	6
Inventory cost	3
Order processing	2
Administration	2

Re-appraisal of distribution channels can therefore be very important in reducing costs and improving profit.

Direct distribution to a large number of companies overseas would mean high transport and administration costs. Employing one intermediary enables substantial savings to be made.

Transport, it can be seen, is a major cost. The nature of the transport system employed will also affect other distribution costs as there will be a continual pay-off between the cost of the transport system and the cost of maintaining stock (*see* 13:5).

(*b*) *Competition*. There are major competitive advantages open to the company through efficient distribution – by providing a higher level of service than the competition or reducing the length of time that customers have to wait for spare parts, for example.

(*c*) *Pricing*. The inclusion of intermediaries in the distribution chain will affect the pricing policy of the firm. Wholesale discounts will need to be included in the pricing structure.

(*d*) *Profitability*. Intermediaries in the distribution chain will lower the per unit profit when compared with direct distribution methods. This can obviously be offset by lower per unit distribution costs and greater volume, so that the net effect of the use of intermediaries will be an overall increase in the level of profit.

(*e*) *Long-term implications*. The choice of distribution channels will often have long-term implications particularly in some overseas markets.

Commercial law in the Arabian Gulf prevents overseas suppliers changing local distributors unless they agree to the change. This means that distribution agreements once entered into are extremely difficult to change.

(f) *Control.* The distribution channel chosen will also affect the amount of control that the supplier can exert in the market, particularly in areas of promotion, pricing and sales activity.

The amount of control that a particular distribution channel organization permits also extends to the amount of market information that the firm will receive. Where intermediaries are employed it is unlikely that the supplier will have a clear concept of what is happening in the market.

One of the perennial problems in the management of overseas distributors is to maintain the flow of the monthly stock and sales reports. Other information such as price structures and competitive pricing are rarely if ever provided; only by visiting the market is the supplier company likely to receive such basic data.

(g) *Flexibility.* The type of distribution channel chosen will have important implications for the ability of the manufacturer to deal with fluctuations in demand.

(h) *Conflict.* Within each distribution system, there will be conflict between companies fighting to achieve maximum profitability in the market: wholesalers against wholesalers (an example of horizontal channel conflict); suppliers against end users (vertical channel conflict); and wholesalers against retailers (inter-channel conflict).

Parallel exporting is an example of channel conflict: the exporting by wholesalers to overseas countries bypassing the traditional distribution channels of the manufacturer, substantially improving the profitability for the wholesaler (see Fig. 12.2).

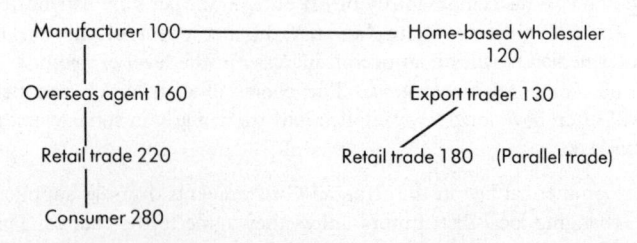

```
Manufacturer 100 ───────────────── Home-based wholesaler
      │                                       120
Overseas agent 160                     Export trader 130
      │                                      ╱
Retail trade 220                   Retail trade 180   (Parallel trade)
      │
Consumer 280
```

Figure 12.2 *Parallel exporting*

Some overseas distribution firms especially in specialist areas such as toys maintain retail outlets. Competing retail outlets will often be unwilling to stock the products distributed by these firms.

The distribution channel selected will obviously affect the type and level of conflict that will occur within the market.

(*i*) *Coverage.* The extent of the market coverage desirable to the supplier will in turn affect, and determine, its distribution decisions. The more intermediaries that are involved the greater the degree of market coverage.

(*j*) *Skills.* Where servicing is important, this will affect the choice of distribution channel as it is often essential for the supplier company to be able to provide these services through the distributor. Intermediaries will need to be trained and it may be difficult, where they handle a range of additional products, to ensure that the standards achieved are equal to those of the supplier company.

Using intermediaries

4. Advantages of using intermediaries. Intermediaries in the distribution chain will provide some or all of the following services:

(*a*) Provide a wider coverage than would be possible by direct deliveries.

(*b*) Adapt a product in such a way that it becomes acceptable to the local market.

(*c*) Provide credit to the overseas end user.

(*d*) Reduce the paperwork that the overseas supplier needs to be involved in; one customer instead of dozens.

(*e*) Carry out local sales promotion and advertizing.

(*f*) Be legally responsible for the product sales in the local market.

(*g*) Carry out testing and development work for the supplier.

(*h*) Increase the local customer base.

(*i*) Set local prices and discounts.

(*j*) Provide a local level of buffer stock which copes with fluctuations both in supply to the market (shipping delays, customs problems) and within the market.

(*k*) Reduce distribution costs by allowing the supplier to ship in bulk.

(*l*) Perhaps reduce the amount of credit that the supplier would have to offer in the market thus improving cash flow.

5. Disadvantages of using intermediaries.

(*a*) *Pricing.* As the intermediary has its own profitability criteria, it may choose to price product at uncompetitive levels, either reducing potential market share or encouraging parallel trading.

(*b*) *Concentration.* Intermediaries will tend to concentrate on their most immediately profitable products and not give their attention to developing new products.

(*c*) *Conservatism.* Intermediaries may resist the introduction of new types of product/service as they are not acceptable to the way that they carry out their business.

(*d*) *Distribution.* Intermediaries may be specialists in one specific type of distribution, and when the market changes or the strategy of the supplier alters they may be unwilling or unable to change the pattern of trade.

A distributor of spirits in Italy had an extensive range of major brands until the late 1970s when the growth of supermarkets meant that distribution emphasis had to be shifted away from the specialist shop sector. The distributor was unable to respond effectively and the suppliers were forced to change distribution methods to meet changing market conditions.

(*e*) *Product range conflict.* Intermediaries by their very nature maintain an extensive range of similar products of manufacturers competing in the same market. Over a ten-year period, product range A of manufacturer A will often become identical to product range B supplied by manufacturer B, as the competitors encroach on each other's sector of the market. This will cause considerable conflict if both companies use the same intermediary in the overseas market.

(*f*) *Promotional timing and content.* Intermediaries, because of their extensive product range, will often have promotional plans that conflict with their suppliers.

Strategic implications

6. Risk/return considerations. The first issue in the development

12. Distribution channels

of distribution channels will be the strategic issue of the level of investment, its risk and likely return (*see* Chapter 13). Where the market potential is high, the overseas supplier will need to evaluate the rate of likely return comparing local distribution with establishing a local sales subsidiary or production plant. The greater the level of investment the greater the level of control that the firm will have over the market.

There are a number of alternatives to using a local distributor:

(*a*) Buying an already established local distributor.
(*b*) Developing an entirely new distributor operation by recruitment.
(*c*) Developing a new distribution system within the market.

Unilever pioneered a new method of selling in Africa using vans to sell detergent products direct to the customer as well as showing promotional films.

7. Continuity. The length of commitment that the firm will need to make in the market will be the second important issue that it needs to consider. Will the market ever be sufficiently large for direct investment? How rapidly can distribution arrangements be altered?

A small market like Qatar in the Middle East, with 300,000 inhabitants is unlikely to ever be of interest for direct investment for many firms, and it would be acceptable to enter into long-term distribution arrangements with a local intermediary. The Indian market poses a different set of problems. Though the market has been difficult to enter for a variety of reasons, the long-term potential is such that flexibility of local distribution arrangements would probably be advisable.

The firm will also have to consider carefully the amount of time that changing distribution methods can involve – removing one distributor and replacing it with another will often take over a year, even if the agency agreement is carefully designed (*see* Chapter 15).

Seagrams, the owners of Sandeman port, took the policy decision to concentrate sales of major brands in the French market via an owned sales subsidiary. The changeover from the previous distributor meant that the product lost distribution and sales which had to be recouped by substantial promotional investment.

8. Product issues. There are a number of product attributes that make the use of intermediaries more necessary, and some that encourage direct distribution.

Factor	Intermediary	Direct
Unit price	Low	High
Purchase frequency	High	Low
Number of customers	High	Low
Location of customers	Widely spread	Concentrated
Servicing arrangements	Simple	Complex
Level of price negotiation	Low	High

Thus a manufacturer of gas turbines will deal direct; a firm selling sweets will need to employ an intermediary.

9. Legal issues. Legal constraints in the market will influence the choice of distribution channel and how it operates. Some countries do not allow foreign firms to own any assets in the home market, others a limited amount (*see* Chapter 6).

Maintaining a competitive distribution channel

10. Maximizing channel effectiveness. Once established the channel must be controlled and monitored by the overseas supplier. There are a number of important issues concerned here.

(*a*) *Monitoring channel effectiveness.* Does the channel continue to meet the supplier's strategic objectives and the market conditions? What changes should be introduced to achieve the maximum match between the channel and the supplier's goals on
 (*i*) price;
 (*ii*) promotion;
 (*iii*) market coverage?
(*b*) *Motivating members of the distribution channel.* This is an

extremely important part of the overseas sales task (*see* Chapter 15) and includes a number of issues.

(*i*) Training distribution staff.

(*ii*) Providing local promotional support.

(*iii*) Running competitions or providing awards for effective performance.

(*iv*) Visiting the market to understand local conditions.

(*v*) Providing the channel with information on new products, achievements, promotional material.

11. Reviewing other channel possibilities. The supplier should always review the possibilities of using alternative channels to achieve a greater level of market sales in conjunction with the local distributor.

> A British toy company was able substantially to increase sales in the Spanish market by directly approaching the major store group Corte Ingles. This did not conflict with local distribution as the store group maintained local market prices.

12. Changing channels. Should the channel currently in use be failing to meet the company's requirements alternatives will need to be considered. The following issues will however be important:

(*a*) The costs of termination. This will not only include the compensation that may be payable to the current channel member(s) but also the interval between leaving one channel and starting distribution via another.

(*b*) Whether the proposed change in distribution is too short-term a solution and if additional investment in the market could not produce a viable long-term answer to the distribution issues in the market.

Progress test 12

1. What is a distribution channel? (**1**)
2. Explain the difference between direct and indirect methods of distribution. (**1**)
3. Itemize the cost factors involved in distribution. (**3**)

120 Marketing Overseas

4. Summarize the key issues needing consideration in choosing a distribution channel. (**3**)

5. What are (*a*) the advantages, (*b*) the disadvantages of using intermediaries? (**4-5**)

6. What are the strategic issues involved in choosing a distribution channel? (**6**)

7. How can a company ensure that distributors overseas function effectively? (**7-9**)

13
Factors in physical distribution

Physical distribution implications

1. Introduction. The distribution of the company's products involves not only the intermediaries the firm uses to reach the end consumer (the channel concept discussed in Chapter 12) but also the physical movement of the product from A to B. This is known as physical distribution. For many service companies physical distribution will not be a significant cost factor in the price of the 'product' that is being sold (*see* Chapter 24).

Physical distribution will have a number of important implications for the firm operating in an overseas market.

(*a*) Cost – the 'total distribution cost' concept.
(*b*) External packaging for export goods.
(*c*) The type of transportation used for goods between countries and within countries.
(*d*) The effects on warehouse organization of overseas activity.
(*e*) The effects on stock control.

Total distribution cost

2. The concept. With a wide variety of distribution systems and destinations available, the exporter will need to continually review the situation regarding possible savings on transport, warehousing, stock holding and administration costs (*see* 12.3) that constitute the total distribution costs that are involved in the distribution process.

122 Marketing Overseas

A company operating in the North-West of France might for example have an important customer in Munich in Germany. Currently the company ships, via road, direct at the cost of £0.14 per mile. Investigation of the available competitive methods indicates that by using rail transport via Brussels, transport costs will drop to £0.10 per mile or a combination of road and rail via Paris would mean a cost of £0.09 per mile. The company could also make savings by reducing its stockholding and simplifying its order-processing procedure.

The distribution costing system therefore involves a number of inter-acting factors the optimization of which can make a considerable impact on the overall profitability of the company.

3. Factors affecting total distribution cost. Factors will include:

(a) The size and – very important – the value, of the individual consignments.

(b) The chosen location for shipment and delivery.

(c) Frequency of shipment.

(d) Physical characteristics of product – perishability and resistance to crushing, for example.

(e) Speed of required delivery and stock levels in the overseas market.

Export packing

4. Important considerations. As distribution channels and methods overseas will often differ from those employed at home, the company will have to consider the way in which the product is packaged and protected for its journey to its final destination. The following factors will be important:

(a) Resistance to climatic conditions.

(b) Resistance to handling in overseas markets. (Problems in this area will be reduced by the use of containerization, *see* 11:**6**(*a*) and **6**(*a*).)

(c) The use of internationally agreed symbols to designate handling conditions.

(d) That the packaging meets the requirements of the distribution channel.

13. Factors in physical distribution

Many specialist spirits outlets in Belgium prefer to order product in boxes of six rather than dozens. Altering the outer cartons to meet this market condition improved sales acceptability.

The large hypermarkets in Europe may mean that product is stacked thirty feet above the floor. Clear external identification of the product is an important part of acceptability within the warehouse and will help overall product performance.

(e) Ensuring that the outer carton is easily opened to minimize damage to the product inside.

Transport

5. Important considerations. The interaction of a number of factors will determine the final physical distribution decision.

(a) *Cost.*

(b) *Service considerations.* Firms may consider that the faster delivery system meets their strategic requirements even though it may be more expensive.

(c) *Speed.* The total speed of the delivery method will have to be carefully monitored to ensure that the advantages are maintained.

The port of Lagos became extremely congested in the 1960s with over 300 ships waiting to discharge cargo. It then became far quicker to deliver overland via the Sahara by truck, and many companies starting using this route. Similar problems at ports of Southern African countries in the late 1970s and 1980s meant that goods for these countries were increasingly shipped through the more efficient ports of South Africa and then transported inland by road.

(d) *Convenience.* Door-to-door delivery by lorry in Europe gives the organization far more flexibility than arranging delivery by ship, ship to shore and then onward delivery.

(e) *Stock cost.* There will be a pay-off between the speed of delivery and the amount of stock that the company needs to maintain in the pipeline (*see* Fig. 13.1). Thus for a company with expensive products, the cost of maintaining stock in the delivery chain may be offset by an increase in the speed of delivery.

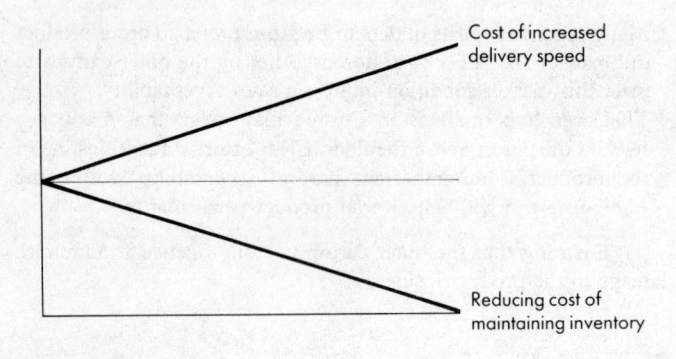

Figure 13.1 *Stock cost: speed of delivery and stock availability*

(f) *Security.* The nature of the product will determine its security requirements – high added-value products demanding the greatest level of security, bulk goods such as coal and oil the lowest.

(g) *Extra packaging requirements.* The physical distribution system used will determine the need for extra packaging, if any. Non-container shipment, for example, demands that the company provide extra-strong outer cartons.

(h) *Transport infrastructure.* Each country will pose slightly different problems arising from the efficiency of the transport system – some countries will have well-developed rail networks, others may have better roads, still others may have neither; it is possible to use river transport in some European countries.

(i) *Risk/political considerations.* Some transportation routes will be more open to delay than others – border conflicts, or industrial disputes for example.

6. Transport trends.

(a) *Containerization.* Since 1965 there has been a steady increase in the share of world trade shipped via container. The container provides certain advantages.

(i) *Security.* Goods can be effectively secured against pilferage/loss far more effectively than loose stowage. This reduces the cost of insurance over loose cargo.

(*ii*) *Packaging savings.* Because of the strong exterior box, the company can make significant savings on packaging material.

(*iii*) *Speed.* Container systems offer far more rapid cargo handling and customs clearances.

There is, however, one main disadvantage.

The sizes of containers 20, 30, and 40ft containing maximum loads of 20, 30 and 40 tons means that the company will find it difficult to send small quantities of products to overseas markets. Much of the work of international freight forwarders now consists of providing the means of consolidating less than full container loads for overseas markets. Some companies see this potential disadvantage as an advantage by persuading overseas buyers to purchase in larger quantities than they might otherwise do, to gain the benefits of full container loads.

(*b*) *'Multi modal' transport systems* (also termed combined transport or CT). As a result of the standardization of containers, there is a trend towards integration of sea, road and rail transport, containers being switched between systems to achieve the best compromise of the company's transport requirements and cost.

(*c*) *Centralized packing and despatch.* As a result of the growth of containerization ports are becoming less and less important and there is increasing development of inland clearing depots where the documentation for containers is handled for both inward and outward despatch.

7. Sea transport.

(*a*) *Shipping lines.* Shipping lines are organized in trade association 'conferences' for certain areas of the world. Conference traffic follows the same pattern as the International Air Travel Association (IATA) in charging the same rate for freight to the same destination. Certain other lines 'non-conference' offer savings in freight but do not provide as frequent a service to the chosen destination.

(*b*) *Cost.* Sea transport offers the lowest cost option per mile for heavy goods occupying a fairly small space (or cube).

(*c*) *Speed.* This will vary according to the nature of the route chosen and the number of ports a ship will be calling at. In general transport by ship will be the slowest option available due to port clearance delays, for example.

(*d*) *Flexibility.* Sea transport is a fairly inflexible means of physical distribution; companies have to plan in advance for shipment booking space on forthcoming boats and arranging for delivery from factory to port.

8. River transport. In certain countries river transport may offer the most logical transport method available.

The Rhine in Germany is still heavily used as a method of transporting heavy industrial materials within Germany and the Low Countries.

Recently there has been the development of the LASH (lighter aboard ship) concept. This employs 400 ton lighters that can use river transport and then be hauled upon larger container ships completing their journey by river at the other end of the sea voyage.

9. Road transport.

(*a*) *Growth.* In the United Kingdom and most of Western Europe road transport has grown, year by year, in importance as a means of physical distribution and comprises around 80 per cent of total transport useage. The development of roll-on roll-off (RORO) sea transport has further expanded the use of road transport over fairly short sea passages – the English Channel, Baltic, and Mediterranean.

(*b*) *Advantages.* Road transport offers maximum flexibility, it is faster than sea transport, and has a fair degree of security. Firms are also able to sub-contract a large part of their transport to small independent operators and need not tie up capital in large distribution systems.

(*c*) *Disadvantages.* The EEC and other countries impose limitations on the size of lorries, the length of time that drivers can operate (8 hours in the EEC), and the nature of the goods that can be carried, particularly noxious chemicals.

10. Rail transport.

(*a*) *Growth.* Rail transport has declined in the majority of industrialized nations as a major factor in physical distribution. However, in countries with large land masses, it offers several advantages.

(b) *Cost.* Rail transport is substantially less expensive than road transport over long distances.

An invention of the mid-1980s is to 'piggy back' containers on railways, with two containers on one flat car. This has the result of reducing freight costs by a further 40 per cent and makes rail transport even more cost effective.

(c) *Speed.* Because of possible 24-hour rail services, shipment by rail within markets may often be faster than road alternatives.

Evergreen Shipping Services of Taiwan uses rail transport between the West coast of the United States and Chicago with journey times of around 60 hours.

(d) *Security.* As rail consignments can, with suitable track arrangements, be delivered door-to-door, security of transport can be good. Rail transport offers a cost effective distribution method for products of relatively high weight and low added value.

Taunton Cider, relatively close to a main line track, replaced road with rail transport and is estimated to save around £250,000 a year.

(e) *Flexibility.* There have been a number of advances in the integration of rail services with other means of transport. The rail ferry system used in some parts of Europe is designed to combine the advantages of rail and sea for the transport of particularly bulky or heavy products, which could only with difficulty be moved by road.

11. Air transport. Air transport offers a number of substantial advantages over other transport systems.

(a) *Speed.*
(b) *Security.*
(c) *Possible reductions in inventory levels.*

However it suffers from certain disadvantages.

(a) *High cost.* However, as air freight is calculated on weight and not normally on cubic dimensions there is a point at which air freight becomes cost competitive with sea freight which costs on dimensions rather than weight.

(b) *Containers.* The need to provide non-standard containers for air freight. Air freight cannot be easily integrated into standard container distribution systems because of the physical constraints within aircraft holds.

12. Evaluating freight systems. Assessing the risks and benefits involved in chosing a freight system involve finding answers to a series of questions.

(*a*) What are the packaging implications of the different freight systems? Could the company reduce packaging costs by moving to air freight and what would be the level of the potential saving?

(*b*) How will the insurance charges be affected by the freight system?

(*c*) How are freight charges calculated (on dimensions or weight) and how does this affect the freight system chosen?

(*d*) How will the freight system affect the level of working capital – if stocks are reduced by faster distribution will this provide an overall net improvement in profitability?

(*e*) Will changes in the freight system allow the company to expand the selling season in an overseas market?

(*f*) Are out-of-stock problems a major difficulty in overseas markets and how will changes in the freight regime affect this service issue?

(*g*) Will changes in the freight system allow the company to handle its production plant more effectively, for example by permitting longer production runs of single items thus improving economies of scale?

Other factors

13. Warehousing. Warehousing makes up a major element of the total distribution cost. Companies in the international environment need to consider how changes in warehouse organization can help in the development of efficient export business development.

(*a*) *Warehouse organization.* The structuring of the warehouse into specific export areas can substantially improve packing and dispatch efficiencies.

(*b*) *Packing systems.* By prepacking product onto pallets and by using computer packing programmes the company can improve both

13. Factors in physical distribution 129

the speed of container 'stuffing' and the amount that each container holds, thus improving freight costs per unit.

(c) *Order processing.* The use of appropriate technology can help to improve the speed of completion of the order and match this with the documentation that is required (*see* Chapter 21).

(d) *Freight.* Changes in the freight system can have an effect on warehouse organization overseas by reducing both the stock held and the total numbers of distribution depots required.

14. Freeports. A freeport is a geographical entity which is outside the fiscal framework of the host country. Many companies use freeports of which there are now 300 world-wide as distribution and assembly centres (*see* Chapter 15). Freeports have a number of advantages.

(a) Allowing the company to maintain stocks overseas or assemble goods from components brought in from overseas without paying duty or sales tax.

(b) Allowing the company to ship goods rapidly because of the lack of customs formalities in the freeport area.

(c) Providing improved security over normal dockyard areas.

Successful freeports such as Galveston in the United States have provided a substantial increase in trade for the area, with an estimated 20,000 locally employed.

15. Stock control. Overseas development will increase the stock control problem facing the firm. Orders will tend to fluctuate and mean that the firm involved in overseas trade will have to maintain a higher level of buffer stock than one trading within one market (*see* Fig. 13.2).

These problems can be minimized:

(a) If the company is able to agree an annual plan with the overseas outlets it supplies.

(b) If the company develops a forecasting system (*see* Chapter 9) which can cope with the entire range of overseas markets.

(c) If the company continually reviews the product range that it manufactures for markets at home and overseas (*see* Chapter 10).

130 Marketing Overseas

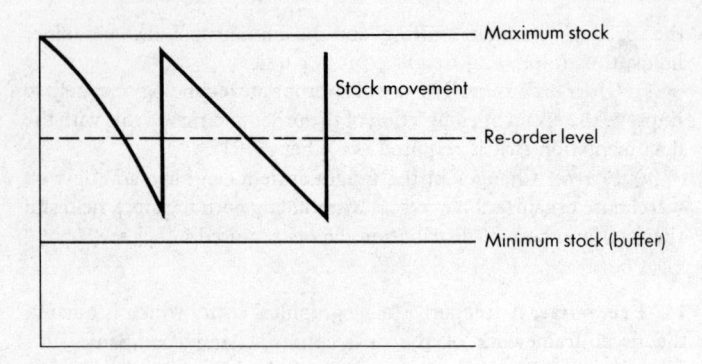

Figure 13.2 Stock control: buffer stock

Progress test 13

1. Give the factors which are important to physical distribution in an overseas market. (**1**)
2. What are the criteria involved in a distribution costing system? (**2**)
3. How would a firm decide on the most appropriate transport method for its goods? (**5-12**)
4. Why has the quantity of goods transported in containers increased? (**6**)
5. Describe the various transport options available to the company giving the advantages and disadvantages of each. (**6-11**)
6. How can efficient warehousing improve export performance? (**13**)
7. What is a freeport? How do they contribute to efficient distribution? (**14**)

14
Indirect exporting opportunities

Indirect export

1. Definition. Indirect export involves the use of intermediaries including agencies which handle the purchase and distribution of products from within the home market to overseas outlets. Indirect export involves the transfer of ownership of the company's products to another organization for overseas despatch normally within the home market of the supplier.

Export agencies

2. Types of export agencies.

(*a*) Export wholesalers, who act on their own account, buying from the home market and selling overseas.

(*b*) Overseas buying representatives for foreign firms, buying on behalf of an overseas principal.

(*c*) Specialist export agencies, acting on behalf of firms in developing overseas markets. These companies often import as well for home-based companies; the import/export agency.

(*d*) International trading companies, which may act to buy a product in the home market and distribute it overseas. Most commonly, the international trading companies will act as agents overseas (*see* Chapter 15).

(*e*) Co-operative export groups which provide a method by which small firms can combine to develop overseas markets.

132 Marketing Overseas

It must be remembered that export agencies may often be acting in a variety of roles in one market, acting as a buying representative for one firm and as a wholesaler for another, and so divisions between categories of activity will rarely be as neat as the student would wish (*see* Fig. 14.1).

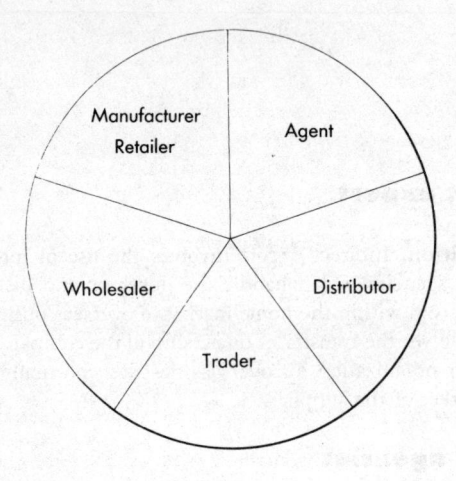

Figure 14.1 *Activity by category of an international trading company*

3. Importance of export agencies. It is estimated that there are around 800 established companies involved in export agency activity in the UK, though the percentage of trade for which they account has tended to decline as the importance of African and Latin American markets decreases as a percentage of international trade. By the mid-1980s they were thought to account for 12 per cent of UK trade.

4. Advantages of dealing through export agencies.

(*a*) The export agency takes all the risk of financing the transaction, buying the product in the home market in local currency.

(*b*) The agency handles all documentation procedures.

(c) The agency will have specific expertise in dealing with the market with well-established local contacts and trade links. This will be particularly true of companies dealing with COMECON and other countries with centralized buying systems.

(d) Export agencies may have specific expertise in financing local sales through, for example, barter arrangements.

5. Disadvantages of dealing through export agencies.

(a) The agent will determine which market or market sector is most attractive, at what price the product should be sold, and how it should be promoted. In other words the supplier has no control over the market; indeed the use of export agencies often may encourage parallel trading (*see* 12:3 (*h*)).

> Distillers supplied an export agency with whisky ostensibly for a COMECON market via Rotterdam. The product turned up in one of their most profitable Middle Eastern markets.
>
> A toy manufacturer secured what appeared to be a major order for the Yugoslav market which was priced significantly below normal sale price. The large quantity of product re-appeared in the home market via a major retailer over the Christmas period.

(b) The supplier has no guarantee that demand will continue from the market; the export agent as the single source of demand in the market may drop the line if a competing product appears more attractive.

(c) The supplier is dependent on the export agency rather than the market itself for the price that it can obtain, and this will mean that profit on sales to export agencies will tend to be lower than those via other distribution methods.

(d) Export agencies tend to be more interested in short-term rather than long-term returns, and will not be prepared to invest either time or money in product development.

(e) Export agencies will often handle large numbers of competing lines and the supplier has no means of controlling this competitive activity.

(f) Export agencies are generally unable to cope with technical products requiring a sophisticated salesforce or provide the warranty backup necessary for equipment.

Other intermediaries

6. Export wholesalers. Export wholesalers buy products on their own behalf, ship overseas and sell on the open market via established outlets. They tend not to maintain a separate salesforce to build sales but act as a traditional wholesaler. They may offer a means of developing a particular market area, but distribution is likely to be limited. The company achieves its profit by the mark-up on the goods that it sells in the overseas market.

Gibraltar is an example of an overseas market that is mainly supplied by wholesalers operating from the United Kingdom.

7. Confirming houses. The confirming house acts on behalf of an overseas buyer, such as a store group or government agency. It purchases the goods in the country of origin, arranges shipment and insurance, provides credit for the overseas buyer and receives commission on the total value of the order. Confirming houses will often allow the supplier firm to enter markets where there are particular payment problems. The importance of the confirming house has significantly declined in the 1980s as they have been particularly badly hit by the restricted availability of foreign exchange in Africa.

8. Buying offices of overseas retail outlets. As retail concentration continues, the buying offices set up by overseas retail outlets are becoming of increasing importance to the small firm wishing to become established in overseas markets.

All major Japanese retail outlets maintain buying offices in Europe; Macy's the well-known American store group has buying offices in Paris, Dublin, Florence, Tel Aviv, Copenhagen, Frankfurt, Madrid, Bogota, Lima, Buenos Aires, Sao Paulo, Osaka, Seoul, Manila, Bangkok, Singapore, Hong Kong, Bombay.

The buying office is essentially a service organization for the home-based retail company. However, on many items they can act in competition with other buying offices of the retail group if it is trying to find a source of international production. As the retail groups grow in size and importance in all major markets (6:**13** gives examples of

14. Indirect exporting opportunities 135

the size of retail operations in Western Europe) the percentage of outlet own brands that they sell is tending to increase on a world-wide basis. These pressures may lead to the exporter being unable to establish his own brand but nevertheless achieving profitable export activity by manufacturing own brand for these buying offices.

> Many textile firms in Taiwan and Hong Kong have achieved profitable export activities by providing own-label garments for major store groups in Western Europe and the United States without ever establishing their own branded product.

9. The specialist export agency. The specialist export agency acts to purchase products in the home market and then develop sales in specific overseas market(s). The involvement of the export agency will vary from a straightforward one, acting as a trading company, providing stock for a range of outlets in overseas markets, to groups that actively plan and promote their suppliers' products in overseas markets.

There are a number of advantages of using a specialist export agency:

(a) They provide the manufacturer with a ready made export department.

(b) They increase the level of control that the manufacturer has by building up distribution and therefore demand in an overseas market.

(c) The long-term development of a product in the marketplace is of equal interest to both the specialist export agency and the manufacturer.

> The Caribbean poses special problems to many exporting firms. The islands are extremely widespread – the distance from Trinidad to the Bahamas is over 2500 kilometres – and individually small in population. The use of specialist export firms which deal with this area will have many attractions.

However there are a number of disadvantages:

(a) The specialist export house will often only be prepared to accept either a global brief or a regional agreement – that the manufacturer agrees to allow the export agency to develop sales within a given area. The nature of the agreement may be too restrictive.

136 Marketing Overseas

(*b*) The specialist export agency will often tie the supplier in to one type of distribution system for long periods of time, which may interfere with the supplier's long-term plans for the market.

(*c*) Specialist export agencies though offering a wide ranging service may only be especially skilled in one market area.

10. International trading companies. The international trading companies are particularly important for the development of Japanese and Korean trade (*see* 4:**2**(*d*)) where they act very much in the role of co-ordinating trade activities showing some of the activities of a co-operative export venture (*see below*). European international trading companies can provide important means of establishing an overseas presence. Generally international trading companies will act as agents for principals in overseas markets, but may pay for the product in the country of origin, as they ship in combined loads to overseas markets.

Involving international trading companies in the distribution overseas will have a number of advantages:

(*a*) They will act as a traditional agent in an overseas market with a long-term interest in product development.

(*b*) They will often be able to supply the technical back-up which is lacking in most export agencies.

(*c*) They will pay in the country of origin and handle all shipping and documentation.

The main disadvantage is that as widely spread trading companies they are unlikely to give the individual products the attention a supplier may wish; they will also be carrying a large range of competing products.

UAC, the Unilever subsidiary has interests in both Africa and the Middle East. It owns retail outlets (Kingsway stores in West Africa) and business equipment manufacturing plants and acts as a distributor for a very wide range of European products.

Hagemeyer, one of the oldest established European trading companies has subsidiaries throughout Europe and South America and handles a wide range of industrial and consumer goods.

11. Co-operative exporting.

(*a*) *Complementary arrangements*. In these a major exporter will

14. Indirect exporting opportunities

carry other lines overseas, a process often known as 'piggy backing', either

(i) achieving profit on a commission basis; or
(ii) buying and re-selling the products.

The advantages for the minority partner in the arrangement are that they receive vastly expanded distribution and market presence at little or no investment, even though the price at which their goods are sold may be below national levels. The majority partner is able to provide additional product lines which may enhance the acceptability of the product; add-ons for sports cars are an example of such activity. The disadvantage of such a system is that the small exporting company is heavily dependent on the major and will often have to meet specific pricing and packaging criteria (for example packaging under the major company's logo) which may limit potential overseas expansion.

(b) *Co-operative exporting*. In some areas such as toys, individual manufacturers may combine to form co-operative ventures. The co-operative acts as a trading entity to further the interests of the members by promoting their goods, paying for the product in the home market and then trading overseas. The development of co-operative ventures have been limited as the interests of the members and their product ranges are continually changing.

Brittoys is an example of a British toy consortium established in the United States. The advantages for the members has been the ability of the co-operative in concentrating on the development of their own products of which there are sufficient to form a comprehensive range and sufficient volume to cover the overheads of a sales operation which would not otherwise have been possible.

(c) *Export consortia*. Where large industrial tenders are involved for the provision of large sites, a consortium will arrange the purchase of the necessary equipment for the entire project.

A series of large hospital projects in the Arabian Gulf enabled a manufacturer of pumps for industrial cleaning equipment to become rapidly established in the market. Initial orders enabled them to learn about the market and then to expand into other areas.

Consortia generally exist as companies in their own right, with separate profitability criteria and management staff.

138 Marketing Overseas

The advantage of consortia exporting is that it allows the company to gain a foothold overseas without establishing a long-term commitment. However the provision of after-sales service will need to be carefully reviewed by the firm entering into such an arrangement.

The importance of indirect export

12. The role of indirect export as a distribution channel. Indirect export methods serve as an important distribution channel in a number of instances.

(*a*) For the company lacking the resources to establish a long-term overseas operation they can provide an extra source of revenue and enable the company to gain some international exposure.

(*b*) For the established company they provide a means by which marginal markets can be serviced – those markets which are unable to provide sufficient volume because of economic or political considerations.

Companies will need to continually review their use of indirect methods of export for two reasons:

(*a*) The potential conflict that may occur between different indirect distribution methods over which the supplier can exert little control and markets where other distribution systems are involved.

(*b*) The way that indirect distribution methods may limit growth potential in overseas markets where a higher level of investment would yield greater rewards.

Progress test 14

1. List the various types of export agency. (**2**)
2. Explain the benefits and risks associated with selling through an export agency overseas. (**4–5**)
3. What do confirming houses do? (**7**)
4. Why has the importance of overseas buying offices increased? (**8**)
5. What are the advantages and disadvantages of using international trading companies? (**10**)

15
Direct exporting opportunities

Direct exports

1. The nature of direct export. A direct export channel consists of one in which there is a contractual relationship between the supplier and an end user in a defined overseas market.

2. Direct export as a method of distribution. There are a number of alternative methods of direct export that are available to the company.

(*a*) The use of agents (*see* **4** *below*) and distributors (*see* **9** *below*) established within the overseas market.
(*b*) Direct sale of the product from supplier to end user.
(*c*) Supply via mail order.

The key difference between indirect and direct exporting arrangements is one of control established through a contractual agreement. Such an agreement between the supplier and the overseas agent allows it to increase the level of control that it is able to achieve in the market. This is because the agreement will give the supplier control over price, place and promotion which it cannot achieve via indirect methods. With indirect methods the company relinquishes control over the product once it is sold to the overseas buyer. As part of the increased control secured through a direct export agreement, the company must expect to raise the level of commitment in the market, accepting that a longer-term involvement and a greater amount of investment will be required. Direct export does not require the establishment of a legal presence within the overseas

140 Marketing Overseas

country and avoids the complications of local taxation and labour laws (*see* Chapter 16).

3. The role of agents and distributors. Most companies operating overseas use agents and distributors in some or all of their overseas territories. Over 60 per cent of American companies use distributors for some or all of their export activity, and for European firms the figure rises to over 70 per cent.

Agents

4. A definition. An agent, in the case of direct export, can be defined as an individual or organization that acts on behalf of a principal to bring the principal into contact with third parties to which the principal's products can be sold. Agents normally never own the goods which they are selling; they act as intermediaries between the supplier and end user.

5. Types of agent.

(*a*) *Commission agent*. The commission agent achieves profit by approaching potential customers on behalf of the principal and passing the resulting orders, on each of which he receives an agreed level of payment, back to the supplier. The agent is unlikely to hold any stock, and will not have any responsibility for the credit-worthiness of the local firms. Commission agents are particularly suitable in areas where there is no service element (e.g. consumer goods) and where there are particular problems in gaining entry to the market and orders are limited and spasmodic.

(*b*) *Agent providing spares and servicing facilities*. While not holding stock of the finished product, there may be advantages in certain markets from an agency agreement where the agent not only achieves commission on sales but is also able to provide service in the local market on an agreed cost basis and charge local customers. These agents are particularly suitable for industrial products in certain markets as they provide the local servicing back-up many firms will require.

(*c*) *Stocking agent*. This arrangement is especially suitable for freeport distribution arrangements (*see* Chapter 13). The agent acts as a wholesaler for the overseas principal, maintaining buffer stock in a central warehouse for which the principal is charged an agreed rental sum.

6. Advantages of using agents.

(*a*) The supplier company has access to an individual or company which is established in a clearly defined overseas market. This enables it to build up knowledge of the market and market conditions enabling it to plan more effectively.

(*b*) An agent can only deal with a specific market and therefore the company has greater control over the distribution channel, as the number of competitive products the agent handles can be limited by contractual agreements.

(*c*) The supplier does not have to invest heavily in the market as all sales costs are paid for on a marginal basis when the sale is achieved.

7. Disadvantages of using agents.

(*a*) The market conditions may change and the nature of the agency arrangement might be such as to preclude rapid alteration in distribution methods.

(*b*) Agents are rarely prepared to cover the credit risk involved in dealing with the overseas customer (though the agency agreement can be structured so that they accept a *del credere* position, *see* Chapter 21).

(*c*) Should the market grow in size, high levels of commission on orders will mean that the market is not as profitable to the supplier as it might be if alternative methods of distribution were used.

(*d*) Individual customers in the market may require different packaging, labelling and credit arrangement all of which add to the administrative load of the supplier.

(*e*) Commission agents may order in small quantities which lead to uneconomic shipping arrangements – though this can be solved by alterations in the pricing structure (*see* Chapter 20).

(*f*) Commission agents, though to an extent limited by the agency agreement, will still tend to handle a wide range of competing products and therefore be unlikely to give the product the necessary level of attention.

142 Marketing Overseas

8. Defining the need for agents. Agents must be considered as part of the entire distribution channel for overseas markets. They will be particularly suitable where:

(*a*) The market potential is limited due to either shortage of foreign exchange and/or economic size.

(*b*) Where orders are likely to be small or spasmodic.

(*c*) In markets where the company cannot see any long-term potential.

The level of market investment made by the supplier company is likely to be limited where agents are used. However, the existence of a single contact within the market with the responsibility of developing the sales of the company's products enables the supplier to provide promotional material and carry out market visits to expand the overall level of demand.

Distributors

9. Distribution or full service arrangements. Distributors are customers in an overseas market who have been given the (normally sole) right to purchase and sell-on the goods of a supplier organization. They differ from the agent in the fact that they contract to maintain stocks of the product in the market, and receive income from the difference between the price for which they buy the product and the price for which they sell it in the market place.

10. Advantages of distributors.

(*a*) Distributors take all the credit risks in the market.

(*b*) Because they depend for their livelihood on the sale of stock in the market and often have high overheads with large salesforces (a national distributor in France for example would spend around 8 per cent of turnover on the salesforce alone), high sales volumes are important.

(*c*) As they hold stocks, the fluctuations on supply and demand on the supplier's organization will be much reduced especially if the product is seasonal.

(*d*) They will often have the facilities to carry out special packaging and handle servicing arrangements in the market.

15. Direct exporting opportunities 143

(e) The supplier will be able to ship in bulk to the distributor using the most cost-effective freight rates and methods.

(f) The distributor will often be quite sophisticated at planning in-market activities, local sales promotions, exhibitions, which reduce the work-load of the supplier in this area.

(g) The distributor is more likely to be able to provide the level of information about the market that the supplier needs to accurately plan and develop the product in the overseas market.

11. Disadvantages of distributors. The disadvantages of distributors are all those mentioned in 12:5, which can be summarized as a problem of control. Many of these issues can be minimized by well-designed agency agreements, but there are specific areas of conflict that are likely to arise.

(a) *Pricing levels.* Suppliers and distributors will often be extremely suspicious of each other's profit margins.

(b) *Stock holdings.* Suppliers will tend to consider that distributors should carry more stock.

(c) *Coverage.* Suppliers may either want the coverage increased or re-directed (e.g. from specialists to general outlets or vice versa).

(d) *Promotional expenditure.* Both the level and share of promotional expenditure will continue to be a problem.

(e) *Competitive products.* The definition of what constitutes a competitive product is difficult to define and distributors will always be changing their product range.

(f) *Termination.* As distributors often invest more heavily in the market than agents the problems of terminating the arrangement are generally more acute – a company changing distribution methods will often have to pay substantial compensation to a long-established distributor.

(g) *Priorities.* Suppliers and distributors will often have very different priorities both in respect of the products that should be concentrated upon and the timescale over which activity should occur.

12. Defining the need for representation by distributors. The appointment of distributors in common with that of agents must be viewed as part of the strategic development of the firm. They will be particularly appropriate for certain markets.

(a) Substantial markets with regional or technical problems that the supplier company is unable to deal with.

(b) Markets far removed geographically from the home market.

Distributors will tend to be achieving a higher level of sales than agents. As a result the supplier company will need to provide a higher level of support in terms of product modification, promotional expenditure and market visits.

Choosing an agent or distributor

13. Defining the type of distributor/agent required. The supplier company will need to carefully consider the following issues:

(a) The nature of the market coverage required. Does the supplier consider that the product is mass market or is it sold purely to a narrow specialist sector?

(b) The level of distribution that the supplier is envisaging. What level of coverage is acceptable – 60, 80 or 100 per cent?

(c) The exact geographical area that is involved.

(d) The level of professionalism that is required in the selling task. For many products particularly those in the industrial sector this will be a crucial issue that will need to be resolved.

(e) The level of stockholding and/or service commitment that will be required.

(f) What complementary or competitive lines held by the distributor will be acceptable to the supplier?

(g) Corporate philosophy: should the distributor be marketing orientated, or only interested in sales volume achievement?

French and German firms consider whether or not the potential distributor has a marketing orientation as a key factor in selection. UK firms overseas do not tend to use this as a criteria.

This approach allows the supplier to create an agency selection profile (or ASP) against which potential agents can be reviewed. No agent is ever perfect but sufficient strengths in one area may offset weaknesses in others. Companies can produce an ASP which defines essential qualities as well as those that are desirable (*see* Table 15.1).

Table 15.1 Agency selection profile

Criteria	Importance	% chance of agent meeting criteria	Outcome
Market coverage			
Contact with key accounts			
Political acceptability			
Marketing expertise			
Salesforce expertise			
Pricing position			
Physical distribution control			
Competitive products			
Financial stability			

14. Finding potential agents and distributors. There will be a number of sources of information about potential agents and distributors.

(*a*) National trade organizations such as the BOTB provide details of potential agents/distributors overseas via the Economic Intelligence Service.

(*b*) Banks.

(*c*) National and overseas trade associations may provide lists of potential agents/distributors or publish magazines which provide a means of advertising in the local market for representation.

(*d*) Chambers of Commerce will vary in importance from industry to industry and market to market. The British Chamber of Commerce in Mexico for example provides a detailed back-up service for firms interested in developing overseas. The London Chamber of Commerce provides details of potential agents for subscribing members. Local chambers of commerce may also allow firms interested in export to meet firms currently established in overseas markets which can provide introductions to possible overseas agents and distributors.

(*e*) The International Union of Commercial Agents and Brokers maintain lists of agents/distributors in overseas markets which are available for purchase.

(f) *Local advertisement.*
Should all these avenues fail, the firm should consider advertising in local newspapers overseas.

15. Evaluation and selection of agents or distributors. The process of evaluating and selecting agents or distributors will require care. A systematic approach is advisable to ensure that the minimum of errors occur. A systematic approach would consist of the following:

(a) *Initial market survey.* A review of all possible agents/distributors from the available sources of information.

(b) *Additional sourcing.* Should the initial search be unsuccessful the company will need to consider additional activity such as local advertising.

(c) *Initial evaluation of agents.* Carrying out credit checks via the overseas trade representatives or banks; collection of brochures and financial data such as company accounts if possible.

Far too many companies developing overseas sales fail to take adequate precautions against bad debts, relying on commercial insurance cover to make up any shortfall. Credit checks are both simple and inexpensive to carry out and minimize potential disasters.

(d) *Initial contact.*
(e) *Market visit and discussion.*
(f) *Completion of agency agreements.*

Contact with agents and distributors

16. Initial contact. In many countries such as the United States and West Germany a professional approach to a potential agent is essential. Documentation should include not only full details of the product range, production facilities, and experience of personnel, it should serve as a selling document. It should:

(a) stress the unique selling points of the product;
(b) outline the progress that the product has made in the home

15. Direct exporting opportunities 147

market and where it has been most acceptable, sector by sector, and the reasons for its success;

(c) compare the competitive products;

(d) describe the back-up that the firm has provided for the overseas market;

(e) outline the firm's current and future marketing plans – the way it is developing, the way in which it supports its products, the nature of the training the salesforce receive.

It may be thought appropriate at this stage to ask the potential agent or distributor to provide detailed information on its activities via a questionnaire which covers the issues that the company considers essential for a local agent or distributor. This allows the supplier to identify issues that it will need to discuss further and investigate in the market before appointing an agent or distributor.

17. Market visit. It is essential that a firm visits the overseas market for the following reasons:

(a) To understand the local conditions.

(b) To evaluate the potential performance of a distributor by visiting customers, spending time with salesforce, looking over the warehouse. To help in structuring the collection of this information it may be valuable to use some form of checklist (*see below*) which can be modified for individual circumstances.

> *Checklist*
> Salesforce numbers
> Outlet coverage: major
>   minor
>   specialist
> % Advertising expenditure
> Exhibition attendance
> Number of marketing personnel
> Sales growth over five years
> Change in product list over five years
> Salesforce turnover
> Current operating margins
> Geographical coverage

(c) To find out whether the management personalities involved

148 Marketing Overseas

will work well with those in the company. In order to check this it is essential that the senior management of both supplier and distributor come to a clear understanding of how the arrangement will work.

(*d*) To complete the agency or distributor agreement.

18. Financial aid with overseas visits. Government trade organizations such as the BOTB sponsor visits by groups of firms to overseas markets; local Chambers of Commerce may also provide subsidized group visits.

The disadvantage of such group visits is that the itinerary may not suit the particular company, visiting countries in which it has no interest and spending too little or too long a period in the relevant countries. The advantage of such visits is in the support services such as pre-arranged appointments and the provision of translators.

Agency and distributor agreements

19. The importance of clarity. An agency or distributor agreement is a commercial contract and involves a long-term binding agreement between supplier and local representative. The nature of contract law will vary from country to country and therefore there is no hard and fast approach to the drawing up of agency documents. However as a general rule the more specific the document is the better it is for both parties as there will be no room for misinterpretation.

> The phrase ... it is the responsibility of the distributor to maintain a reasonable level of stock to meet demand ... can mean three months stock cover in the Middle East, and only 15 days in the United States and Japan. Different commercial practice in overseas markets will inevitably mean disagreement unless the issues are clearly identified.

20. Key issues. An agency or distributor agreement will therefore need to be clear on a number of key issues.

(*a*) *Parties*. Identification of the companies involved in the contract.

(*b*) *Territory*. The nature of the territory on which the agreement is based.

15. Direct exporting opportunities

(c) *Exclusivity*. This will define certain things:

(i) How the principal and agent handle orders placed direct with the supplier from other companies in the market – there may be some established customers that the supplier company wishes to continue supplying on a direct basis.

(ii) How the principal and agent handle orders for the territory arising outside the market – orders from an international head office requiring delivery in the local market.

(d) *Competitive lines*. The rights of the agent to handle competing lines and what constitutes a competitive line.

(e) *Products*. The exact products that are party to the agreement. It is in the interests of the supplier to state clearly that new products, and new activities, are not covered by some blanket agreement.

(f) *Duties of the distributor*. In particular:

(i) Servicing and guarantee arrangements.

(ii) The provision of sales information.

(iii) Whether the distributor provides part of the promotional budget and if so how it is calculated.

(iv) What clearance procedure the local distributor must follow for local publicity material.

(v) What stockholding the distributor needs to maintain.

(vi) The degree of freedom in setting price levels in the market and if there are stipulations on the maximum level of gross margin that the distributor can add to the product.

(vii) The degree of freedom in disposing of stock at below list price – obsolescent stocks for example.

(g) *Duties of the principal*.

(i) Supply of replacement product for faults in previous shipments.

(ii) Provision of spare packaging material and labels to deal with goods damaged in transit.

(iii) Translation costs of brochure material.

(iv) Speed of dealing with orders.

(v) The amount of notice to be given for price rises.

(h) *Duration*. The length of time that the arragement will remain in being in the first instance and then the length of time the contract will be renewed on an on-going basis provided that both companies are in agreement.

150 Marketing Overseas

(*i*) *Commission*. Where commission is payable:

(*i*) When it is payable, quarterly, half yearly.

(*ii*) The rate of payment payable on different categories of goods; the basis on which it is payable; CIF, FOB (*see* Chapter 21).

(*iii*) The rate of payment on orders received from organizations that cancel orders or become bankrupt.

(*j*) *Termination/problems with the agreement*. This will need to include:

(*i*) Amount of notice that either side will need to give for termination of the contract.

(*ii*) The rights of either party to dispose of remaining stock.

(*iii*) Effects of change of ownership of the agreement either on the supplier or on the distributor.

(*iv*) What body should be involved in arbitration should the agreement break down.

The International Chamber of Commerce in Paris has been an important arbitration body for agreements in the EEC. It is estimated that around 150 distribution agreements are involved in arbitration proceedings via the ICC every year.

(*v*) The laws under which the agreement is administered. This has important implications. Contracts within countries operating a system of common law can limit actions and liability to issues stated within the contract. In other countries operating a civilian system (such as France) there will be overriding statutory provisions outside what is specified in the contract.

Examples of typical contracts can be obtained from government trade organizations or supporting bodies such as the Institute of Export.

Motivating agents and distributors

21. The advantages of motivation. Once they are appointed the supplier will have to ensure that the agents and distributors are properly motivated. Distance creates a form of isolation which often suggests that the supplier is not particularly interested in the activities of the overseas agent or distributor. Proper motivation will benefit the supplier in a number of ways.

15. Direct exporting opportunities

(a) Distributors and agents are far more likely to provide the supplier with information concerning possible improvements in the marketing policy in the overseas market.

(b) Because good performance is recognized and encouraged distributors will be far more enthusiastic about developing sales of the company's products.

(c) A well motivated agent or distributor is unlikely to consider alternative or competing products.

Too many exporters consider that the distributor will be solely interested in the profit motive. Active supplier/distributor contact has proved to be crucial in developing new products or activities in overseas markets.

22. Important factors. Certain factors are particularly important:

(a) The continuing provision of information concerning pricing, changes in specification and packaging which will affect the performance of the product in overseas markets. Many firms are notorious for the limited amount of information with which they provide overseas companies; the overseas distributor in consequence feels isolated and ignored with the consequent deterioration in performance.

(b) Agreement and adaptation of promotional material: many distributors will have active promotional programmes within overseas markets which may not exactly fit the preconceptions of the suppliers' promotional plan. Compromise will ensure that the distributors consider that they are receiving adequate support.

(c) Market visits are essential for a number of reasons. They increase the knowledge of the market, particularly the problems that the distributor or agent is facing. They also allow the supplier to influence and train the salesforce in particular product areas. Finally they are important to convince major customers of the commitment that the supplier has to the market, often a crucial factor in sales development.

(d) Competitions and awards: there may be instances where competitions between agents and distributors serve a useful function, but more normally competitions within the national salesforce or awards can be very effective in improving the relationship between supplier and distributor.

Asbach, the German brandy firm, gives individuals who have worked for an overseas distributor for more than ten years an award at a dinner which is attended by an Asbach director.

(e) Planning: the development of joint plans between supplier and distributor for the common development of the market is very important. A common commitment ensures that the distributor feels that there is a partnership between supplier and his own organization.

(f) The provision of technical support: it is vital that the supplier ensures that the distributor receives technical support, even where the problem would appear to be simple and straightforward.

Direct sales

23. Direct sales. There will be a number of instances where direct sale to the end user is a possibility. These will include:

(a) Where the product or service is highly priced and highly technical – examples would include turbines for power stations, jet aircraft, ships.

(b) Where there is a major buying centre that can be easily handled on a direct basis. The existence of buying offices for large retail stores has already been mentioned (*see* 14:**8**) but there are many possibilities of approaching stores direct in overseas markets.

Germany in common with many European countries has a number of major store groups.

Store group	No of associated stores
Albrecht	1800
Deutscher Supermarkt	276
Karl Gaissmaier	130
Hussel Holding	522
Kaisers Kaffee-Geschaeft	611
Allkauf	102
CO-OP	1627

Some small companies in fact find it more worthwhile to maintain travelling sales representatives in overseas markets rather than rely on

15. Direct exporting opportunities 153

agency or distributor support. This approach will be particularly viable if the geographic distances involved are small and the potential returns considerable. Thus the costs of a similar approach in the United States would be considerable whereas in Western Europe with high population densities it is a practical possibility.

The Amstrad group managed to gain impressive distribution for their personal computers in the United States via an agreement with Sears Roebuck, the leading retail chain.

In other countries with centralized government buying offices the direct approach will be the only possibility.

24. Defining the role of direct sales in the distribution channel. Direct sales will be most effective where:

(a) the product occupies a fairly narrow and well defined niche;
(b) the buyers are well defined and geographically concentrated;
(c) the product requires little servicing and/or the market is close to the manufacturing source;
(d) the product is of high added value.

Direct mail

25. Direct mail as a distribution opportunity. Direct mail houses provide a major source of sales opportunities in a number of consumer fields such as fashion and household goods.

26. The advantages of direct mail outlets.

(a) They often buy products in large volumes.
(b) They provide the overseas supplier with a means of becoming established as a reputable force in an overseas market at minimal expense.

27. Disadvantages of mail order.

(a) The mail order house will often require exclusive rights to the product in the market.
(b) They will often be unwilling to take a product without minor modifications.

154 Marketing Overseas

(c) They will often demand very low prices.

(d) They will be generally unable to plan very precisely on the exact nature of demand which may lead to considerable fluctuations in the level of orders.

(e) Because of the time lag between the completion of the brochure and its replacement by a new one, mail order houses will often require that suppliers maintain their prices for a substantial period – often over eighteen months.

Progress test 15

1. Define (a) direct exporting (**1**); (b) a direct exporting agent (**4**); (c) a stocking agent (**5**); (d) a distributor. (**9**)

2. Explain the difference between direct and indirect methods of export. (**2**)

3. What type of agent would suit a company exporting (a) consumer goods, (b) industrial goods? (**5**)

4. When might a company consider appointing an export agent? (**6–8**)

5. What are the advantages and disadvantages of appointing a distributor for an export market? (**10–11**)

6. Agent or distributor? What factors would influence a company confronted with making such a decision? (**13**)

7. What steps should a company take in selecting an agent or distributor? (**14–18**)

8. Why is motivation of overseas agents or distributors important and how can it be achieved? (**21–22**)

9. What is the potential for direct sales? (**23–27**)

16
Overseas investment

Establishing subsidiary activities

1. The nature of overseas investment. In addition to indirect or direct export methods involving the physical movement of goods across national boundaries, there are a number of other ways the firm expanding overseas can become established. They involve the establishment of subsidiary activities in overseas markets in a number of ways by an investment of either capital or management. There are a number of options:

   (a) Industrial co-operation arrangements.
   (b) Licensing.
   (c) Franchising.
   (d) Management contracts.
   (e) Joint venture manufacture.
   (f) Contract manufacture.
   (g) Local sales offices.
   (h) Local assembly operations.
   (i) Acquiring an overseas company.
   (j) Establishing a majority owned manufacturing site.

2. Implications of overseas investment.

   (a) *Company legislation.* In all the instances of overseas investment mentioned in **1** above, the company is establishing a legal presence of some kind in the overseas market and becomes liable to tax on earnings overseas. It also becomes liable to an increased level of local control over its operations.

156 Marketing Overseas

(b) *Pricing.* Local regulations concerning the level of pricing will come into effect (*see* Chapter 20). The local controls on pricing may have important implications for the way in which the overseas operation is structured and how the organization prices and transfers payment between the various subsidiaries (*see* Chapter 21).

(c) *Personnel.* The company will become liable to a range of controls existing on the employment of personnel; levels of pay, working conditions, visa regulations if foreign staff are employed, fringe benefits expected (health insurance, works canteen), unionization.

(d) *Control.* Once the firm starts to maintain assets overseas the problems of controlling the business will become accentuated. Firms will have to ensure that they are still getting accurate information concerning their overseas investment so that opportunities can be maximized and problems minimized.

Industrial co-operation ventures

3. Definition. Industrial co-operation ventures are long-term agreements between manufacturers to share industrial expertise.

With the steady growth in research and development costs there has been a steady increase in the amount of industrial co-operation ventures, though the nature of them will vary.

(a) Sharing technology.
(b) Sharing manufacture of a particular item.
(c) Combining to manufacture a joint product range, one item manufactured in its entirety by one company, and sold in the market of another.

Zastava and Polmot, vehicle manufacturers in Yugoslavia and Poland exchange vehicle components with one factory specializing in a range of specific items.

4. Advantages. There are a number of advantages for the companies involved:

(a) Sharing the very high costs involved in the development of technical products.
(b) Sharing market information on other countries and com-

16. Overseas investment

petitors which would otherwise not be available to the individual partner companies.

(c) The ability to develop sales of components or other unrelated technology to the other partner in the venture.

(d) Low capital involvement in the overseas market – firms only provide their expertise and some form of management presence.

A considerable amount of East–West trade is now taking the form of industrial co-operation ventures.

5. Disadvantages. Disadvantages however are similar to those of licensing, discussed in **8** below.

Licensing

6. Definition. Licensing involves the agreement between two parties whereby one gains access to some commercial expertise of the other in return for a payment.

(a) *Nature of the agreement.* The agreement may cover certain items:
  (i) A patent covering a product or process.
  (ii) A trade mark or brand name.
  (iii) Technical expertise in particular manufacturing areas.

One of the most successful licensing operations worldwide has been Coca Cola. The company provides licensees in each country with the famous 'secret' Coca Cola essence, the companies bottle under licence to Coca Cola.

(b) *Content of the agreement.* The agreement will be very similar in nature to that established for an agency (*see* 15: **19–20**). It will include the following:
  (i) Parties to the agreement.
  (ii) Rights of the licensee to transfer the agreement.
  (iii) Duties of the licenser – for example, how far access to technology will be allowed, how much subsequent information will be provided, the level of capital investment required by the licenser, what publicity material/artwork or packaging should be made available, and whether the licenser or licensee is responsible for any action over trade mark infringement in the market of manufacture.

(*iv*) The territorial boundaries of the licence. This is particularly important in some countries such as India where extra-territoriality (sale outside the confines of the market) is a fairly frequent event.

(*v*) Duration of the agreement.

(*vi*) Degree of exclusivity.

(*vii*) Performance criteria of the licence. This will include minimum quantities produced, quality control methods, training of staff, confidentiality of process and other information, the right of the licenser to inspect both factory and sales records on an agreed basis.

(*viii*) Payment terms. This will include the way in which the royalty will be calculated, the dates on which it will be paid, the currency in which it will be made available, extra payment schedules for spare parts, additional management assistance outside the terms of the contract.

(*ix*) The effects of changing business environment. This will include the effects of devaluation, changes in ownership of the firm, liability for taxes.

(*x*) Legislation. How the agreement will be terminated, under what law the agreement will be administered, how arbitration will be arranged, the responsibilities for making sure that the agreement meets all local legal requirements.

7. Advantages of licensing.

(*a*) *Return.* Licensing allows a fairly high rate of return for minimal investment.

(*b*) *Additional income.* Income from licensing arrangements can if properly organized be increased in a number of ways:

(*i*) By technical, managerial and engineering assistance fees.

(*ii*) By sale of components to the licensee.

(*iii*) Through feedback of information and other technology and reciprocally reduced licence fees on other technology.

(*c*) *Market access.* As the payment levels are often low, licensing is of particular use where:

(*i*) there are high tariff barriers or export quotas;

(*ii*) the product is extremely bulky to produce and has low added value;

(*iii*) there is extremely strong and well-established competition.

(*d*) *Risk*. Risk of nationalization or loss of capital invested is minimized.

(*e*) *Access to distribution chains*. The licensee provides access to the market via an often well organized distribution system.

(*f*) Licensing. Licensing provides an opportunity to produce revenue from processes or technology which the firm no longer uses in its key markets.

8. The disadvantages of licensing. Licensing, however, has a number of disadvantages.

(*a*) It may create competitors within overseas markets. By the time that the term of the licence has expired the local manufacturer may have acquired sufficient expertise from the licenser and will be able to enter the market as an independent competitor.

(*b*) Returns will tend to be low – of the order of 3 to 5 per cent of sales with often a requirement to provide extensive management or technical expertise.

(*c*) The licensee may not be able to service the market adequately which will allow local competition to become firmly established. Thus strengthened, the competition may then become a potential threat in the licenser's other overseas markets.

(*d*) Changes in economic structure may alter countries to which the licensee also has access, thus threatening the licenser's other markets.

The creation of the EEC with the stated principle of free movement of goods between countries created substantial difficulties for some overseas firms from countries outside the Community that had licensed manufacturers in some of the member states. Some of the licensees used the Treaty of Rome to expand their sales into other member states.

(*e*) Changes in national laws may make the agreement hard to implement.

9. Defining where the potential of licensing exists in the distribution channel. Licensees will be most appropriate in certain circumstances:

160 Marketing Overseas

(a) Where there are high market barriers to entry.

(b) Where the technology supplied will not pose a threat to the current core businesses of the company.

(c) Where the product obtains its market edge from promotional activity – the brand is the most distinctive element of the product.

Licensing has proved particularly popular as a spin-off to the entertainment business and where there are well-established brand names in one particular business area. The Star Wars films led to a whole range of licensed toys, the stars of 'Dynasty' promote a range of lingerie, and the Harrods name is used to promote a brand of cigarette.

10. Choosing a suitable licensee. The procedure that needs to be followed resembles that of the agent or distributor (*see* 15:**13**).

Franchising overseas

11. Defining franchising. A franchise is the right to a particular business within a given area. It normally consists of a complete business system developed by a company (the franchiser) which then sells a local franchise in return for promotional and managerial assistance.

(a) *The importance of franchising.* It is estimated that one in three of new businesses in the United States is a franchised operation and that 10 million people in the developed world are now employed in this sector of the economy.

(b) *The scope of franchising.* Franchising is broadly a feature of the service economy, including restaurants, transport, household services, retailing.

Well-known firms that are involved in franchising include:

Benetton – retailing.
TNT – transport.
Dyno Rod – drain clearance.
McDonalds – fast food.
Kentucky Fried Chicken – fast food.
Budget – car rental.

16. Overseas investment

12. The advantages of franchising.

(a) The firm can achieve rapid market growth with a new, successful, product concept without major investment.

(b) Franchising allows the firm to maintain maximum control over the product concept.

(c) Franchising can be extremely profitable, often with high royalties on sales (10 per cent or more) and the requirement of the franchisee to buy the product from the franchiser.

13. Disadvantages of franchising.

(a) Firms can perhaps achieve a higher level of profit by running the operations themselves.

> McDonalds in the UK is a totally owned operation – there are no franchised outlets because of the high profit potential in the market, by contrast with the position in other European countries where McDonalds is franchised.

(b) It will often be difficult to maintain the motivation of the franchisees over a number of years particularly where they are required to maintain a high level of royalty payments.

(c) Franchising will often require a high level of initial investment both to find potential franchisees and also to build up awareness of the franchise operations.

(d) It may be difficult to maintain the quality of the franchised operations which will lead to an overall deterioration in the profitability and long-term potential of the franchised operation. Franchises will need continual and systematic supervision to ensure that quality is maintained.

14. Defining the potential of franchising in the distribution channel. Franchising will be most suitable:

(a) in countries with a high level of socio-economic development;

(b) in service industries;

(c) for concepts that require little training and can follow clearly laid down procedure.

Management contracts

15. Defining management contracts. A management contract is an agreement between one company and another to organize some or all of their activities.

The scope of management contracts: management contracts will be most common where the management task requires a high degree of expertise which may not be present in the overseas market, for example construction projects. International hotel groups also provide large numbers of examples of management contracts.

16. The advantages of management contracts.

(*a*) They allow a minimal investment and often a good rate of return.

(*b*) Management contracts involve a very low level of risk.

(*c*) They develop the firm's understanding of different market conditions, a necessary part of international development (*see* Chapter 23).

(*d*) They often allow the firm to offer a wider level of service.

17. Disadvantages of the management contract.

(*a*) Because of the normal high levels of investment in the project, the major shareholders will have considerable influence as to the way the project will proceed which may make management difficult.

(*b*) Management contracts are often of a short-term nature.

(*c*) It will often be difficult to staff the operation effectively.

18. Defining the potential for management contracts in the distribution channel. Management contracts for the majority of companies will be most effective if:

(*a*) they are considered as operations to produce marginal income using existing personnel resources; and

(*b*) they are considered as a means of achieving greater international exposure or providing a more comprehensive service which will be of advantage to the core operation.

Joint venture operations

19. Defining joint ventures. A joint venture is a project in which two (or occasionally more) parties invest in a venture. It normally consists of the creation of a new company in which the parties have shares, though neither party has effective control over the decision-making process – otherwise the operation is more correctly designated as an overseas investment (*see* **22** *below*).

Scott Industries, an American firm, formed a joint venture with Bowater, a British firm, to form a new company Bowater Scott to develop sales of paper products in the United Kingdom, with a 50/50 shared ownership between the two initiating companies. In contrast Levers Nigeria is now termed an associate company within Unilever as the Unilever shareholding has now been reduced to 40 per cent.

20. The importance of joint ventures. Joint ventures are particularly well developed in some countries where majority shareholdings of foreign firms in local businesses are either forbidden by law or made difficult by the local business structures.

Turkey for example used to forbid foreign firms holding more than 40 per cent of equity in local companies; Japan until the early 1970s restricted foreign ownership of local companies to 50 per cent of equity.

21. The advantages of joint ventures.

(*a*) They may be essential to overcome legislative problems in the overseas market.

(*b*) They provide substantial control over the manufacture and distribution process which is not available via other methods.

(*c*) They allow a company with limited financial and managerial resources to become firmly established in an overseas market.

(*d*) For the established company they lower the overall level of risk inherent in investment overseas.

(*e*) They may reduce local hostility to the presence of a foreign company operating in the market.

(*f*) Access to raw materials: a joint venture in one field may be

164 Marketing Overseas

politically necessary to achieve access to raw materials owned by the partner as another part of the business operation.

22. Disadvantages of joint ventures.

(a) Joint ventures often suffer from the fact that they are not exactly joint – one company is likely to hold more than 50 per cent of the equity. This means that the minority partner in the arrangement will often be under pressure to accept the majority partner's decisions. This will be especially true when one partner has provided the majority of management which is often the case. Management will naturally tend to favour their parent company against the interests of the partner in the venture.

> It is estimated that 30 per cent of joint ventures are substantially modified within the first five years of commencement due to factors other than market changes.

(b) Because the financial interest of both parties is effectively limited the joint venture will tend to be starved of resources.

> Scott Industries of the United States has had a successful track record of joint venture operations in overseas markets. It limits its shareholding in each case to 50 per cent of the total equity.

(c) The overseas joint venture partner is often required to make a substantial investment in an overseas production plant which may be reduced in value if the partners cease to be motivated to produce effective results.

> A European toy firm invested in a Singapore production base with major local shareholding. The interests of the local partners were diametrically opposed to the overseas firm with the result that the eventual sale of the production plant meant a £100,000 loss for the overseas firm.

23. Defining the potential for joint ventures in the distribution system.
There are a number of situations where joint venture approaches will be most appropriate:

(a) Where there are strong barriers, either legal or structural, to full ownership of local manufacture.

(b) Where rapid exploitation of a product or service in a local market is necessary to prevent the growth of overseas competition.

(c) Where local companies can provide additional resources that will advance the business in other areas, for example, low-cost labour and access to raw materials.

(d) Where the level of risk is unacceptably high.

24. Minimizing conflict in joint ventures. Companies entering into joint ventures should consider various issues:

(a) Maintaining the maximum amount of control over technology and brand names, including if possible supplying key components for the manufacturing process in the overseas market.

(b) Defining accurately the territorial boundaries within which the joint venture can operate including the nature of export markets.

(c) Maximizing equity control wherever possible, or trying to ensure that other parties such as banks and overseas investment houses achieve a shareholding.

(d) Appointing key managers such as financial and marketing staff to the organization.

(e) Clarifying the methods of arbitration, payment of dividends.

(f) Agreeing the prices at which components should be transferred and the cost of management contracts if they exist.

Xerox formed a joint venture with the Rank Organization which was given the rights, outside the USA, to the distribution of photocopiers. This agreement meant that the Rank Organization has continued to profit from investment made by Xerox at a cost estimated at over $200 million dollars by the early 1970s.

(g) Adopting rigorous quality control procedures and insisting that the joint venture is frequently visited by senior personnel.

Establishing a local sales or marketing office

25. Definition. A local sales or marketing branch office is a subsidiary of the international firm based in an overseas market. It may perform one (or more) of several functions:

(a) Manage a local salesforce to sell the company's product.

166 Marketing Overseas

(b) Supervise a number of local sales agents or distributors.

(c) Act as a holding company for the interests of the international company to minimize tax.

(d) Provide marketing support to a local distributor or joint venture operation.

(e) Co-ordinate local third party manufacture (*see* **30—32**).

26. Advantages of a local sales office.

(a) It provides a method of closely supervising the interests of an international company in an overseas market.

(b) Local sales operation greatly expands the control that the company can exert on the local market.

(c) As sales increase the per unit cost will tend to decrease, rather than remain static as in the case of distributors. Once the critical volume is reached the local sales subsidiary will improve the profitability of the total sales.

(d) It will substantially increase the amount of information that the parent company receives from the market.

27. Disadvantages of a local sales office.

(a) *Cost.* The running costs of a local office will be extremely high especially if expatriate staff are employed.

A European company would need to consider the investment of a minimum of £100,000 to establish an expatriate sales manager in Japan. Accommodation would cost at least £20,000, salary and expenses would run at £40,000 and even a small office would cost in the region of £40,000 to establish with secretarial assistance.

(b) *Legislation.* The firm will be required to meet all local taxation and labour laws relating to the national market.

(c) *Authority.* The overseas firm will have to delegate authority to the local branch to enter into commitments on behalf of the parent company. This will decrease the amount of control that the parent company has over the overseas operation.

28. Financial aid to establish an overseas sales office. The
BOTB makes available a scheme called the Market Entry Guarantee

Scheme to suitable applicants whereby up to 50 per cent of the cost of establishing a local office will be guaranteed should the venture prove unsuccessful.

29. The role of local sales offices in the distribution channel.

(a) A local sales office will be vital to the growing company when a certain level of volume is achieved in the overseas market. The costs of continuing to use independent distributors across a wide range of products or high volumes will tend to make the products uncompetitive compared with totally owned manufacturing and distribution arrangements of other companies.

(b) They will exist most easily where legislative and local market systems are fairly straightforward.

(c) They will be appropriate where there is the requirement for either a high level of technical selling or service requirements.

Contract manufacture overseas

30. Definition.
Contract manufacture involves the use of the manufacturing facilities of local firms overseas to produce batches of the product to the international company's specifications.

31. Advantages of contract manufacture.

(a) *Tariff barriers.* Contract manufacture enables the overseas firm to overcome tariff barriers and produce the product for the local market.

(b) *Adapting the product for local market conditions.* Contract manufacture enables the overseas firm to meet local requirements.

(c) *Reducing transport costs.* For bulky goods the cost of transport may be a particularly important factor in markets distant from the parent company.

(d) *Fluctuating demand.* Contract manufacture will enable the company to produce product against fluctuating demand, a substantial advantage in a seasonal market.

(e) *Investment.* The level of investment that the firm needs to maintain in productive capacity will be minimized though it will need increased working capital to maintain stocks locally in the market.

(*f*) *Minimizing local legal constraints.* By using contract manufacture the overseas firm does not become involved in employee legislation which remains the responsibility of the contractor.

32. Disadvantages of contract manufacture.

(*a*) *Quality control.* It will often be very difficult to maintain sufficiently high levels of quality control using contract manufacture.

(*b*) *Competition.* In common with licensing arrangements, contract manufacture provides local manufacture with experience which can be used to compete with the overseas firm once the contract ceases.

(*c*) *Complexity.* Contract manufacture is unlikely to be able to deal with complex or highly technical manufacturing.

(*d*) *Profitability.* Because the contract manufacturers will price the product to contain a measure of profit for themselves the contract product will tend to reduce the profitability of the overall product.

Local assembly operations

33. Advantages. Local assembly operations will be most appropriate where the company faces tariff barriers which weight the cost of finished goods more highly than components, and the cost of local labour is lower than the additional cost of assembly.

> Commodore Computers assembled home computers for the European market at Corby in the United Kingdom. The advantages of bringing in the complete circuit boards and assembling the product produces considerable savings over the import of complete units from the United States.
>
> Many drug companies use local assembly operations because of the low bulk of the active ingredients in relation to the finished product and because the required technology for tablet production is relatively simple.

Local assembly operations will also help to improve the company's acceptability in the local market while retaining the maximum permitted percentage of imported components.

Much of the importance of freeports (*see* 13:**14**) is in the role of providing centres for local assembly operations, where low cost labour in overseas markets can be utilized for assembly and then re-shipment without the product incurring the high levels of local duty.

34. Role of local assembly operations in the overseas distribution channels. Local assembly operations will be most suitable where the company requires slight modifications to a standard product; where the tariff barriers are such that components attract far lower rates of duty than completed product; and where the product can be assembled using simple technology.

Buying overseas companies

35. Overseas acquisitions. The foreign firm can become established overseas by buying a local firm in an overseas market. Acquisition of overseas companies is currently considered as the most cost-effective method of overseas expansion where the market is mature – examples include chocolate, soft drinks and building materials.

Cadbury Schweppes has expanded into the United States by buying a large interest in the Dr Pepper soft drinks company.
Hanson Trust has acquired large numbers of companies in mature industries in the United States. The purchase of the Smith Corona Corporation in 1986 was an example of this acquisition strategy with its interests in the production of industrial raw materials, and food manufacture and distribution.

36. Advantages of overseas acquisition.

(*a*) Rapid establishment of financial viability in an overseas market.
(*b*) Enables the firm to acquire distribution and marketing expertise quickly.

37. Disadvantages of overseas acquisition.

(*a*) The company will be unable to gain access to development grants and tax free holidays that are often available to the company that produces new jobs for the economy.
(*b*) Foreign companies are notoriously difficult to integrate into an

established operation for a number of reasons:

(*i*) Suspicion of foreign management.

(*ii*) Differing standards of action within the acquired company.

(*iii*) Differing approaches to the market.

(*iv*) The collection of information in a way that cannot be integrated with the parent company.

(*vi*) The inclusion, along with the core activity for which the company was initially purchased, of many additional fringe activities may involve senior management in a large amount of unproductive activity.

38. Minimizing the problems of overseas acquisitions.

(*a*) Thorough research into markets and activities before acquiring the firm will be essential.

> If the Imperial Group had more carefully researched the Howard Johnson hotel group they would have been aware of many of the problems that would haunt them after their acquisition of the group.

(*b*) Disinvestment of all non-essential activities. This will ensure that the new company only contains those areas about which the overseas management has knowledge and understanding.

(*c*) Replace key management and standardize information and reporting systems. It is essential that the corporate stategy for which the company has been bought is fulfilled and this will mean that the philosophy and control structure of the subsidiary mirror that of the parent company.

Creating a fully owned overseas manufacturing plant

39. Introduction. This will be the highest level of overseas investment that a company can make – it will often involve a major long-term investment in an overseas market.

40. Advantages of creating a fully owned overseas plant.

(*a*) It will allow the firm maximum control over the local product.

16. Overseas investment

(b) It will reduce transport costs and minimize tariff problems.

(c) It may provide the firm with favourable grants and tax-free periods.

(d) The presence of a local manufacturing plant will have political advantages in persuading the local community that the foreign firm is a 'good citizen'.

41. Disadvantages of creating fully owned overseas plants.

(a) There will be a lengthy period of investment and training before the project starts to generate revenue.

(b) The firm will have to carefully consider the effects of changing head office policy on local employment.

(c) The firm will have to meet all local laws concerning taxation, unionization, minority rights and the like.

(d) The firm will be under considerable pressure to steadily increase the percentage of components that are sourced locally.

(e) The firm will have large amounts of capital tied up in an overseas market which it will be unable to move quickly if political or social change occurs rapidly.

Disinvestment strategies followed by many overseas companies in the South African market in the 1980s meant that many investments had to be sold for well below their 'book' value.

Major overseas investments will pose the highest level of risk to the international company which will need to review the need for considerable investment in research into the market and market conditions before the decision is taken to carry out full-scale investment in local manufacture.

Progress test 16

1. List the overseas investment options available to a company. (**1**)
2. Explain the following:
(a) An industrial co-operation agreement. (**3**)
(b) Licensing. (**6**)
(c) Franchising. (**11**)
(d) Management contracts. (**15**)
(e) A joint venture. (**19**)

172 Marketing Overseas

(f) A local sales office. (**25**)
(g) Contract manufacture. (**30**)
(h) Local assembly manufacture. (**33**)

Briefly summarize the advantages and disadvantages of each.

17
International communications

The nature of communication

1. Definition. Communication is defined as the way in which the company informs its potential customers about the nature of the product or service. It includes the following:

(a) The activity of the salesforce.
(b) Sales promotional ventures such as exhibitions, competitions, special offers.
(c) Public relations.
(d) Paid media promotion or advertising including press, television and radio.

2. The importance of a communication or promotion policy. Different companies will place different emphasis on the various functions of promotional material.

(a) *Gaining new customers.*

Many companies in the consumer goods field provide sample products attached to others for trial, coupons in magazines or delivered door-to-door and advertisements that encourage trial.

(b) *Developing market acceptability.*
(c) *Expanding trade distribution.*

Promotional incentives for wholesalers to handle a particular product, or to develop a franchise network will be vital to many companies' promotional strategy.

174 Marketing Overseas

(d) *Maintaining existing customers – repeat purchase.*

Continually reminding current customers of the benefits of the product, persuading previous users to switch back to the product will be essential to hold the product in the marketplace.

(e) *Supporting the salesforce.*
(f) *Minimizing competitor's effectiveness.*

Heavy promotional expenditure during test markets by competitors is not unusual. A company must also react to competitive advances in the market by calling attention to special features of its products.

This chapter deals with the implications for media investment overseas, which includes all types of advertising. The balance between advertising (often termed above-the-line expenditure) and other types of expenditure (below-the-line) varies from country to country. In Western Europe with the increasing dominance of the retail chains and the steady growth of promotional expenditure in the industrial sector, below-the-line expenditure is generally equal to that of media expenditure. In other countries media expenditure often takes a higher proportion of the total promotional budget.

Communicating with an international market

3. International variations in the nature of media investment. Different markets will show variations both in the total amount of expenditure and also in the way this expenditure is allocated between media.

Country	per capita media exp $	% TV	% print
Germany	92	12	75
France	50	18	55
UK	85	30	60

The variations are partly due to differences in per capita income between countries – the United States predictably has the highest per capita expenditure on advertising; partly by the media available for

17. International communications

advertising (*see* below) and partly by the nature of the market.

Most cars in Japan are sold by door-to-door salesmen, in contrast to the showroom approach adopted in European and North American markets.

4. The range of media available. The international company is faced with an often bewildering diversity of promotional channels available in overseas markets. The more sophisticated, the greater the diversity of promotional channels. Each overseas market will offer a variety of opportunities which may not be immediately apparent when the company reviews the likely channels in the market. The importance of different channels may also change fairly rapidly.

Increasing affluence in the Indian sub-continent is quickly increasing the popularity of television and decreasing that of the cinema. It is reported that there are over 30 million television sets in India, a figure growing at 15 per cent per annum. Radio, which has been an extremely important information medium in a continent with high levels of illiteracy, is also declining in popularity.

The channels open to the international company include the following:

(*a*) Television.
(*b*) Consumer magazines.
(*c*) Trade magazines.
(*d*) National press.
(*e*) Local press (including the increasingly important free newspapers in many European and North American markets).
(*f*) Commercial radio.
(*g*) Cinema.
(*h*) Posters.

Print material which is developed as part of below-the-line or sales promotion activities includes the following:

(*i*) Leaflets.
(*j*) Brochures.
(*k*) Direct mail shots.

(*l*) Exhibitions.
(*m*) Point-of-sale material – shelf strips, display racks.
(*n*) On-pack (added to the packaging).
(*o*) Menu cards, table mats.
(*p*) Trade material such as keyrings, calendars, notepads.

Strategic factors affecting promotion

5. Promotion and the strategy of the firm.

(*a*) *Promotion and return on investment.* High levels of expenditure on promotion will need to be often regarded as one of the necessary investments to be made in order to become established in a foreign market, exactly in the same light as investment in plant and machinery. As an investment the firm will need to control the effectiveness of the advertising expenditure via the management information system.

(*b*) *Speed of promotional effects.* The reaction of market and product to promotion will vary. Research has shown that the maximum effectiveness of consumer advertising is fairly rapidly achieved. Industrial and service sectors require longer periods for maximum effect.

In the United States it appears that consumers reach maximum response to advertisements for products like toothpaste if they have seen them two or three times within a short period. Industrial buyers require four times this amount of advertising before maximum effectiveness is achieved.

A further complication to these findings is that individuals forget advertising fairly rapidly; around 30 per cent of the content of an advertising message is forgotten for established brands within a month, and often 100 per cent for new brands in the market.

(*c*) *Promotion and price.* Promotion will interact with the pricing level adopted by the firm to determine the speed of return on investment within the market (*see* Chapter 20).

(*d*) *Long- and short-term effects of promotion.* Research suggests that sales promotion expenditure is short-term in its action, whereas investment in media promotion leads to a long-term change in market share (Fig. 17.1).

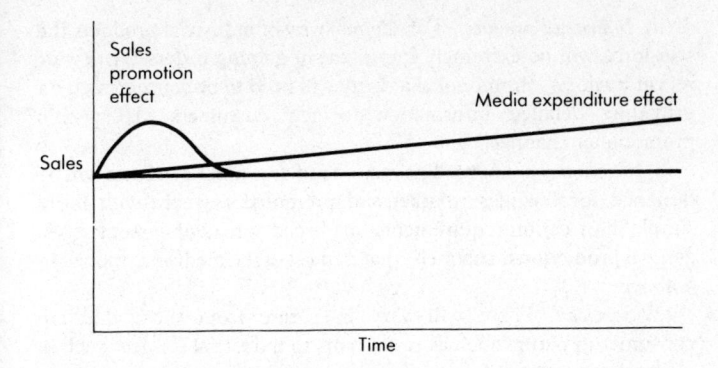

Figure 17.1 *Effects of short- and long-term promotion*

6. Promotion and the product. Different products will demand different promotional approaches both in the home market and overseas (Fig. 17.2).

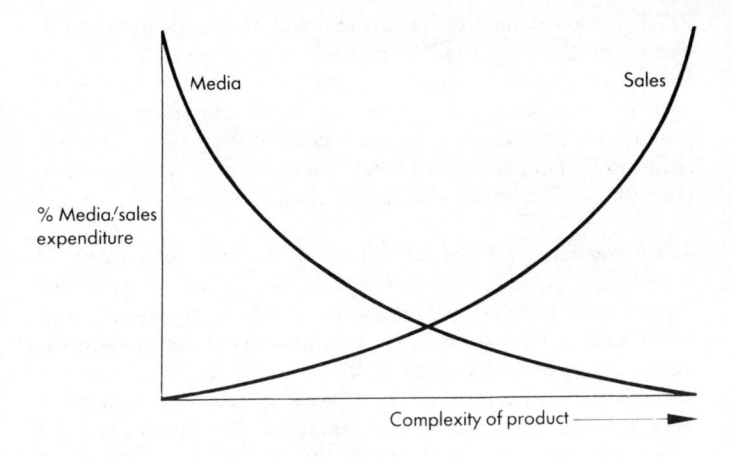

Figure 17.2 *Promotional approaches*

178 Marketing Overseas

(a) *Industrial products.* For the majority of industrial products the salesforce will be extremely important in gaining orders for new or repeat business. Promotional activity will need to be concentrated on providing detailed information to new customers via specific promotional channels.

(b) *Consumer products.* The majority of consumer products will be designed for the mass market and promoted as such, with fairly simple information requirements to a broad spread of customers via general promotional channels, that is, most of the media mentioned in 4 above.

(c) *Services.* These will vary in nature from those that are consumer in nature such as restaurants to industrial services such as office cleaning.

The way in which the product or service is promoted will have an important influence on the way in which it is perceived. A premium product will have to be promoted via a premium promotional campaign.

Gucci, the Italian leather firm, chooses only the most prestigious magazines in which to advertise, particularly those with an international circulation such as *Vogue*.

The nature of the product may also require specific promotional techniques. For many products colour is an essential part of the brand identity and premium price, for example the striking red and white pack for Marlborough cigarettes. In others movement must be portrayed to fully demonstrate the benefits of the product, in others sound will be important. All these factors will have an influence on the nature of the promotion channel chosen.

7. Promotion and the distribution channel. The choice of distribution channel overseas will influence the way in which the promotional material is developed. If the company is using intermediaries such as dealers in one country and not in others the advertising material will need to reflect these differences. Similarly the power that each member of the distribution channel manages to wield will affect the overall balance of expenditure. Thus major retail chains have succeeded in increasing the percentage expenditure on sales promotion of mass manufacturers.

17. International communications

8. Promotion and product change. There will be a series of options available to the firm transferring expertise from the home market overseas.

(*a*) Uniform product and uniform communication strategy: Coca Cola is the classic example of a standardized product with a standard advertising message. It should however be noted that the advertising medium has to be changed in some countries because of local conditions so even with a 'global' product there often has to be some form of adaptation. So although Coca Cola has to an amazing extent succeed in designing cross-national television advertising slogans these may still not be considered appropriate for all its markets at any one time.

(*b*) Uniform product but varied communication strategies: cars though similar in construction often need to be promoted differently within each market as consumers are interested in different benefits.

(*c*) Modified product but uniform communication strategy: many detergents fall into this category – Lux and Lifebuoy soap for example are formulated to meet different market conditions, but are providing similar benefits in all countries.

(*d*) Modified product and varied communication strategies: examples of these include many items of food and clothing. For example, Heinz baked beans have both a different formulation and communication strategy in the United States compared with the United Kingdom.

(*e*) New products for overseas markets that will require entirely new communication strategies.

9. Promotion policy and stage of market development. Mention has been made of the product life cycle concept which suggests that a product passes through introduction, growth, maturity and decline phases (*see* Chapter 7). The same product will often be at different stages in its market development in various overseas markets.

(*a*) *Introductory stage.* The nature of the communication strategy must be to encourage trial of the new product by explaining the benefits.

(*b*) *Growth stage.* The promotion policy will need to be directed

180 Marketing Overseas

towards improving the awareness of the brand or individual product itself as the benefits of the product will by this stage be better understood.

(c) *Maturity stage.* The promotion policy will be primarily aimed at maintaining position within the market place by improving the product's competitive position. Sales promotion expenditure will claim an increasing proportion of overall expenditure.

Standardization

10. The advantages of standardization. The advantages of standardization in advertising are less extensive than in the product area. Nevertheless, there are some:

(a) Reduce production costs of material – a television commercial, for example, may now cost well over £50,000 to produce which is a substantial sum for individual small markets.

(b) The amount of time that management will have to invest in the creation of the campaign will be minimized.

(c) Develop an international brand image which may have the effect of increasing the product's acceptability.

(d) Allow the group to develop advertising through international media channels such as satellite television systems that will become increasingly important in the 1990s.

The current audience for the European satellite television system SKY is small at around 3.0 million. Falling costs of satellite dishes and improvement in the programming may dramatically change this figure and a European audience of 100 million by the end of the century for major events and new films is a strong possibility.

11. The extent of standardization. In common with global products it is clear that the standardization of advertising campaigns will only extend to a common central theme.

Unilever Export Ltd produced what was called an NSD – non-soapy detergent – kit. This consisted of a series of film sequences which could be combined to produce a variety of tailored detergent commercials for particular markets. The central 'washing sequence' could be surrounded by specific sequences for particular markets.

Standardization will be most appropriate under certain circumstances:

(*a*) Where all media are available.

(*b*) There are no government restrictions on the nature of the advertising campaign.

(*c*) The product has no strong cultural connotations, for example it is an industrial product or one that is bought on fairly objective criteria.

(*d*) Where local advertising agency expertise is limited.

(*e*) Where there are strong possibilities of media cross-over from one country to another.

In parts of Belgium it is possible to receive English, Dutch, French, and German television broadcasts. Standardization of advertising ensures that the consumer receives a single advertising message and there are possible economies in the advertising expenditure. The expansion of satellite television in Europe will undoubtedly encourage the trend.

12. Factors discouraging standardization.

(*a*) *Media availability.* Countries will vary considerably as to the availability of media. In many there is no commercial television (for example Saudi Arabia), or commercial radio. In others the press is only regional in coverage (United States), posters may be controlled. The extent of media opportunities that are truly international are limited but include the following:

(*i*) Satellite television systems.

(*ii*) Continental radio stations such as Radio Luxembourg.

(*iii*) International trade and consumer magazines with worldwide circulations.

(*iv*) International newspapers and magazines – *The International Herald Tribune, Financial Times, The Economist, Time,* are examples.

(*b*) *Variations in coverage.* There will be wide scale differences in the international environment in the way in which media reach the individual consumer.

The numbers of commercials shown on Dutch television in a week is rigidly controlled and even the most avid watcher is unlikely to see more than 150. In comparison it has been estimated that the average American could see over 1000.

(c) *General controls on media usage.* There are a variety of general controls that operate within markets to different extents to control what is or is not allowable. Among these are the following:

(*i*) Controls against inaccurate or misleading advertisements – claims must be substantiated.

(*ii*) Minority rights protection.

(*iii*) Controls against the use of superlatives in advertising – this will include the exact definition of words that are acceptable; for example the word 'natural' may run into restrictions in some markets.

(*iv*) Controls on the amount of advertising – limiting advertising time on radio and television.

(*v*) Controls on the timing of advertising – for example limiting the amount of advertising of alcohol around the Christmas period.

(d) *Specific legislative controls on advertising.* In addition to the general controls that are placed on advertising there are many variations internationally in the type of advertisement allowed – either on the nature of the media which may be used to advertise products like contraceptives, or on the commercial style of presentation that is permissible. These include:

Category	Country
Use of non-nationals in advertising	Malaysia
Alcohol advertising	Many EEC, Muslim world
Violent toys	Scandinavia
Cigarette advertising	UK (TV)
Comparative advertising	Germany
Semi-clothed female form	Muslim world
Advertising to children	Canada
Foreign language content	France
Contraceptives	Many
Pharmaceuticals	Most

(e) *Language.* Though a single visual approach to demonstrating a particular product or concept may be possible it will often be very difficult to standardize the explanation or slogan that accompanies it.

17. International communications

Qantas, the Australian airline used a successful advertising concept for the UK market – 'Don't be a wallaby'. Such a play on words (the similarity to the English term 'wally' meaning someone stupid) would not be transferable outside the country.

Because of the differences in the understanding of words and often the difficulties of translation, the transfer of identical advertising copy from one language to another is a potential minefield.

(*f*) *Literacy.* The level of literacy in the market will affect whether the written word or symbols will be important in the market.

Promotion in West Africa in the 1960s relied heavily on the use of brand symbols 'Elephant' – a detergent, 'Star' – a beer, being two well-advertised brands.

(*g*) *Print quality.* The ability of the international company to translate advertising material locally will be affected by the sophistication of the printing industry if there are restrictions on the import of printed material as there are in many countries.

A German company developed a four-colour plastic point of sale unit for a consumer product which was highly successful in Europe and around which much of their promotional activity was based. The campaign could not be run in many overseas markets because the printing technology required to print onto three dimensional plastic was generally not available and the promotional material could not be imported as it was classified as print, the import of which was banned.

(*h*) *Taxation.* Certain media may attract high levels of sales tax in overseas markets which may mean that the budget allocations will need to be reassessed.

(*i*) *Trade expectations.* The standard of trade literature in Japan and the United States is of a generally higher quality than that used in Western Europe and firms trading in these important markets will have to meet local standards of presentation.

13. Minimizing the problems of adaptation. The problems of transferring promotional material across countries can be minimized in a variety of ways.

(a) Employing a professional agency which is able to advise on the issues involved.

(b) Making the language in the material used as simple as possible so that translation is less complex and less open to misinterpretation.

(c) If the campaign is designed for world distribution, maximize the amount of information that is provided visually and minimize the written copy.

(d) The company should remember that regional variations may still occur even when the same language is being used and should therefore employ translators who are nationals of the particular country or region where the campaign is planned.

(e) Once the translation is completed the material should be checked and translated into the original language in the market for which the campaign is designed. This process is termed back-translation and is an essential control for the international company.

Agencies

14. The role of the advertising agency. The advertising agency will provide a range of facilities to the international firm for the development of campaigns in overseas markets. The support that they can provide includes the following:

(a) The design of advertising campaigns.

(b) The creation of advertising copy – the message that will be used in the advertising campaign.

(c) The preparation of the necessary photographic work.

(d) The printing and production of the advertising material.

(e) The translation of home market material into the overseas language.

(f) The booking of media space in overseas markets and the despatch of advertising material to the appropriate contacts.

(g) The organization of market research in overseas markets to test advertising and product concepts and their acceptability.

A company is able to choose between a full service agency (one which will provide all the above listed activities) or specialist companies offering one or more of the required services – media buying, translation services, print specialists and the like.

15. The advantages of the full service agency. With the complexities of the international advertising environment most companies with limited resources will tend to find that a full service agency will offer the best option, significantly reducing management involvement in what is often a time-consuming activity.

16. Defining the options available in agency selection. There are a number of options available:

(a) Using the current domestic agency which will be able to operate via associates in overseas markets.

(b) Using an international agency with branch offices on a world-wide basis.

(c) Using national advertising agencies in each of the markets in which the firm operates.

17. The criteria for agency selection.

(a) *Degree of campaign standardization.* Where the product and promotional concepts vary on a market-by-market basis, it will often be more sensible to employ local agencies who will tend to be more fully aware of local needs.

(b) *Complexity of coverage.* As the number of markets and products being promoted increases, the management control will become steadily more difficult unless the expenditure is centralized and progress in individual markets can be reviewed within a single forum.

(c) *Budget size.* As the level of investment increases, the control that the company wishes to exert will increase. This will be most easily managed if the organization of promotional expenditure is maintained centrally.

(d) *Distributor relationships.* In certain markets the distributors will take an active role in promoting the products and joint local campaigns will be a major motivational factor. The effect of removing the control of promotional expenditure from the local market will need to be carefully considered.

(e) *The relative importance of media expenditure compared with sales promotion.* Advertising agencies do not normally specialize in sales promotion activities. Where this makes up the major proportion of the expenditure, local organizations that are fully aware of all the

186 Marketing Overseas

current legal conditions that are attached to sales promotion will be a more effective choice than an overseas advertising agency.

18. Evaluating agencies. The requirements of individual companies will differ but the following factors in agency selection will be important:

(*a*) *Degree of expertise in specific markets and products.* Does the agency understand the markets under consideration and the particular factors that are important in the product? What similar work has it done in the past?

(*b*) *Level of contact with the overseas market(s).* Will the agency use associates or is there a branch office locally? What are the relationships like between head office and the local level?

(*c*) *Competing products.* Does the agency handle competing products in either home or overseas markets? Does this raise security issues?

(*d*) *Translation expertise.* Has the agency demonstrated their ability to take concepts from the home market and effectively use them overseas?

(*e*) *Personnel.* What personnel in the advertising agency will be working with the client and what is their experience of the overseas market conditions?

(*f*) *Cost.* How will the involvement of the advertising agency be costed? Will it take agency commission (receiving a fixed commission on the value of the advertising space it books overseas) or will it require a fixed fee? How will this be calculated?

19. Possibilities of co-operative advertising. Certain trade groups provide a format within which common promotional expenditure can be channelled to the benefit of individual members.

The International Wool Secretariat promotes wool products from member countries on a world-wide basis.

Progress test 17

1. Define and explain the components of the term promotion. (**1**)

17. International communications

2. Explain the relevance of promotional activity to the company. (**2**)

3. List the media available for promotional activity. (**4**)

4. What factors must a company take into consideration in developing an overseas promotions strategy? (**5–8**)

5. Explain the link between the product and the promotional strategy used. (**6, 8–13**)

6. How can a company benefit from a standardized advertising campaign? What are its limits? (**10–12**)

7. What services will an advertising agency provide and how should a firm go about selecting one for its overseas promotions? (**14–18**)

18
Sales promotion and public relations

Defining sales promotion

1. Definition of sales promotion. Sales promotion covers those activities that attempt to directly stimulate customer interest other than media advertising and personal selling. The scope of sales promotion can be divided into three main areas:

(*a*) In-store promotions (demonstrations, competitions, on-pack offers).
(*b*) Direct mail.
(*c*) Exhibitions.

In-store promotions

2. Importance of in-store promotions.

(*a*) *Growth of retailer power.* With the steady increase in the power of retailing chains in many overseas markets, in-store promotions have become more and more important for the company involved in the marketing of consumer goods overseas. It is estimated in the West German market for example that in-store promotional expenditure now exceeds media expenditure.

(*b*) *As a short-term tactical promotional tool.* Sales promotion has essentially a short-term effect (*see* 17:**5**(*d*)); competitive pressures may mean that the international firm will have to make use of it in the market to offset other companies' actions.

18. Sales promotion and PR

3. Implementing in-store promotional activity.

(*a*) *Legal restrictions.* Markets vary as to the permitted extent of sales promotional activity. Scandinavians restrict any use of sales promotions that require proof of purchase.

(*b*) *Size of sample unit.* The definition of what constitutes a sample will often vary from country to country and whether the size of product normally used by the company for sampling purposes meets the necessary local conditions will need closely checking.

(*c*) *Control.* As it is difficult to offer prizes across national frontiers, the company carrying out in-store promotional activity will have to arrange for local control of the project, involving the distributor or advertising agency. Retailer co-operation will often be difficult to achieve in some overseas markets and the length of the planning process, to ensure that the promotion is a success, will have to be carefully considered.

(*d*) *Stock implications.* The printing of special packs will add to the stock control problems of the supplier company as it will mean special production runs, and stocking costs. It will be simpler for the company to arrange the addition of material, such as collars for banded packs, in the market overseas.

4. Major pitfalls in sales promotion.
Unfair or poorly organized sales promotions can have a major deleterious effect on the brand in the market.

Heinz ran a promotion to provide sports goods for schools in return for a number of labels off Heinz products. The very large number of labels required for each individual item resulted in a storm of protest from parents and teachers who accused the company of meanness and abusing the appeal of its foods to the young. Heinz had to make a number of additional presentations to the educational sector.

5. Co-operative in-store activities.
Major store groups in many countries of the world carry out 'theme' promotions on a particular country's goods on an intermittent basis.

'British' weeks are a feature of department stores in both New York and Tokyo.

190 Marketing Overseas

There are several advantages for the contributing company:

(a) It can draw attention to a product already on sale within the store.

(b) It can provide an opportunity to demonstrate the product to potential agents, distributors or local partners.

However there are limitations:

(a) It is often an expensive way of becoming established overseas.

(b) The range of goods that can be developed in this way is fairly limited and tends to be restricted to premium or up-market products.

6. Financial assistance with in-store activity. The BOTB supports major store groups in running promotions for British goods and similar schemes exist in other overseas markets. The Festival of India was run in major European capitals in the 1980s to promote knowledge of the country and its products.

Couponing and direct mail

7. Couponing and direct mail in overseas markets. The potential for direct mail and couponing as a means of developing sales in overseas markets is generally little explored by exporting companies, particularly those in the industrial field, which tend to rely on exhibitions most heavily as a source of contact with potential buyers.

8. The potential of direct mail. Direct mail is most manageable where there are specialized agencies available to produce lists of potential customers and where the postal authorities allow the despatch of samples through the mail.

The Swedish Post Office provides lists of potential contacts broken down by size and business category for companies interested in direct mail opportunities.

Direct mail and couponing activity will be least effective where individuals cannot be identified easily – as in the Middle East where post boxes are common and directories of addresses rare – and where the postal authorities are unwilling to distribute material of this nature.

9. The advantages of direct mail. Direct mail can benefit the company developing overseas in several ways:

(a) It can be very cost effective.
(b) Companies can easily evaluate the way in which each particular type of direct mail is working.
(c) It can reach all major decision-makers for a particular product.

10. The disadvantages of direct mail. There are a number of disadvantages associated with direct mail:

(a) The company must maintain a contact point in the overseas market to handle all enquiries.
(b) Mailing lists will rapidly become outdated.
(c) Building a mailing list on the firm's own account will often be time consuming and expensive.
(d) The market may be hostile to the direct mail concept.

The international exhibition

11. Important considerations. Exhibitions are major avenues of overseas product development, particularly for companies with complex industrial products. When evaluating the possible use of exhibitions the company will need to consider various issues.

(a) The purpose of exhibiting and its connection with the company's overall strategy.
(b) For what products and markets the use of exhibitions will be particularly relevant.
(c) The nature of the available exhibitions.
(d) How to evaluate alternative exhibitions.
(e) Preparing for the exhibition.
(f) Evaluating effectiveness.

12. The purpose of exhibitions. As the cost of most exhibitions will be extremely high the company will need to be clear as to the exact role of exhibitions within the promotional strategy, only by this means can evaluation be properly carried out (see **17**). Exhibitions can serve several purposes:

(a) Obtaining orders direct on the stand.

192 Marketing Overseas

(b) Obtaining enquiries to be followed up later.
(c) Helping with the search for potential agents or distributors.
(d) Evaluating the acceptability of products in specific overseas markets.

13. The international role of exhibitions. Though exhibitions are a major promotional tool in Western Europe, in many overseas markets they may be especially important.

(a) They may be the only method of contacting government buying agencies, for example in Eastern Europe.
(b) In markets with limited specialist media they will be a popular venue for potential buyers.
(c) They often allow the exporting firm to introduce samples and working models free of charge into an otherwise heavily protected market.

14. The types of exhibition available. Publications carry details of major overseas exhibitions up to two years in advance. The options open to the international company include the following:

(a) Specialized exhibitions relating to the specific interests of the company.
(b) General trade fairs.
(c) Permanent exhibition sites. Taiwan maintains a large permanent exhibition site, the CETDC, with over 1200 booths displaying a wide range of industrial products.

Many companies also use the exhibition concept by hiring small industrial premises or hotel space to carry out promotional activity for their products in isolation.

15. Criteria for exhibition selection. The main criteria will be the way in which the exhibition meets the objectives (*see* **12**) set by the company for involvement in exhibition activity versus the cost of the investment. This can be checked by obtaining from the exhibitors analyses of the following factors:

(a) The nature and the numbers of individuals attending previous exhibitions.

18. Sales promotion and PR

(b) The proposed investment in promotional expenditure for the proposed exhibition compared with the previous years.

(c) It will also be worth checking whether other companies (particularly competitors) continue to use the exhibition on a year-to-year basis. Satisfaction of previous customers is likely to be the best reference possible.

(d) The nature of the organizing body – whether it has detailed experience in running previous exhibitions in that and other markets.

16. Preparing for exhibitions. As an exhibition often involves a major expenditure on the part of the company, systematic planning and attention to detail are key elements in effective use of exhibitions as a means of promotion. Listed below are some of the key elements that will need to be considered and the order in which they occur.

(a) Define exhibition opportunities in the light of market requirements.

(b) Define other activities that might be possible with the exhibition (fringe meetings for example). Liaise with local agent if there is one.

(c) List products that would be exhibited.

(d) Check product implications – packaging, labelling, operating conditions – suitable for the local market and whether local servicing arrangements can be made for faulty product during the exhibition or whether servicing personnel will need to be included in staffing requirements.

(e) Clearly allocate responsibilities within the company – what the marketing department is required to do; what the shipping department should complete.

(f) Define space requirements and other back-up facilities – water, power (and whether the product will go through doors and in the elevators), availability of local personnel to carry out exhibition construction.

(g) Check import duties and any other legal aspects (patent, trade mark protection), whether there are exemptions for the purposes of a trade fair, for example, that may present problems.

(h) Analyse proposed layout checking that it conforms to any specifications of the exhibition organizers, and chose appropriate area. Prepare budget for total expenditure. Book space with organizers.

(i) Agree staffing requirements. Arrange accommodation.

(j) Design exhibition layout and evaluate transport and local assembly problems.

(k) Advise exhibition organizers of local labour requirements.

(l) Arrange local availability of chairs, fridges, desks.

(m) Review exhibition literature requirements and other display material and arrange for language translations or new material to be created.

(n) Brief advertising or PR agency if additional local activity envisaged.

(o) Arrange product availability for the exhibition.

(p) Collect all working requirements, literature, note pads, and emergency repair kit for equipment.

(q) Organize shipment to exhibition site.

(r) Issue instructions on store manning dates, personnel responsibilities.

(s) Issue invitations to all potential overseas clients.

(t) Liaise with designer on local assembly.

Maintaining a check-list can prevent major disasters. A firm exhibiting in Switzerland had not checked the duty position with respect to temporary imports of stock and were faced with a £40,000 duty bill at the border. This made it impossible for them to effectively exhibit.

A European manufacturer of hospital equipment found that their power demands on the exhibition site were such that if all its items were switched on, the power system fused.

17. Evaluating exhibition effectiveness. Exhibitions only have value when they achieve a positive end result. The effectiveness of exhibition expenditure is often something companies fail to review. The expenditure should be related back to the original objectives giving due attention to the following:

(a) Sales per £.

(b) Sales leads per £.

In addition the actual expenditure should be compared with

budget to ensure that the planning process is accurately including all costs.

18. Support for exhibitions. Government organizations often provide support for companies exhibiting overseas. The BOTB provides several services:

(*a*) Subsidies for overseas seminars and small exhibitions individual firms will create on their own account.
(*b*) Providing a percentage of the freight costs for samples.
(*c*) Assisting with travel costs.
(*d*) Subsidizing the costs of exhibition space under certain circumstances.

Public relations

19. Definition. Public relations can be defined as the favourable presentation of information concerning the product or the company in media that has not been paid for. It aims to create a climate of opinion that is favourable to the company by drawing attention to its services to the community. It is therefore more diffuse than advertising which may be used when there is a special controversy, as in the case of concern about industrial pollution of the environment or about nuclear power stations, as additional back-up for the public relations effort. A public relations strategy will depend heavily on providing accurate information about the company and what it is doing.

20. Visible and less visible PR. A public relations strategy frequently operates at two levels: visible and less visible. Visible public relations channels include regular press briefings, usually in the form of press releases supplying information about items deemed 'newsworthy': new products, technical innovations, senior executive appointments, penetration of new markets, sponsorship of events and so on. Less visible methods may include lobbying of politicians and government departments – for the overseas firm this will mean the leaders involved in overseas trade, foreign aid, and foreign affairs.

It should be clear from this description that, for the majority of companies, public relations will tend to be secondary to other main promotional tools. As public relations tends to be non-specific in its coverage, the majority of consumers of a specific product will tend to miss public relations coverage.

21. Methods. The methods by which the company operating in the international environment can gain exposure include the following:

(*a*) The placing of information concerning product or company in national media with overseas exposure.

(*b*) The placing of information concerning product or company in foreign media.

(*c*) The creation of a favourable image within the local community if the company has a higher level of investment in the overseas market (*see* Chapter 16).

Access to media available for public relations activity

22. Media with international exposure. Each country will have newspapers and magazines that have a degree of international exposure. Details of new products or services appearing in these will allow a degree of international exposure.

> The *Financial Times* is now printed in New York and Frankfurt as well as London. Details of product innovations will be available to a wide and influential readership.
> The Overseas Service of the BBC and other international radio stations can provide opportunities for new products and processes to gain promotional coverage.

23. Access to foreign media.

(*a*) *Using foreign correspondents in the home market.* Some 800 foreign correspondents maintain an office in London, and similar numbers of foreign correspondents are maintained in other major cities.

(*b*) *Government press offices.* The Central Office of Information (COI) can provide a service to British manufacturers to promote their goods overseas by providing press releases on British goods to international media.

(c) *Access via distributors and agents overseas.* The involvement of agents and distributors overseas in gaining local publicity is often overlooked. Locally organized publicity has three major advantages.

(*i*) As it has a local content, it is far more likely to get media coverage than press releases sent to overseas correspondents who are most likely to be interested in political and social events rather than business.

(*ii*) It can provide a source of motivation to the distributors' staff.

(*iii*) It will often provide material which can be effectively incorporated into sales presentation material.

Public relations for local subsidiaries

24. Special considerations. The local subsidiary of the multinational company faces different problems to the international firm attempting to get products or services established in a foreign market. Because the local subsidiary is an employer of individuals in the community (and often a major one), information concerning the company will have to emphasize the subsidiary's role in the local community.

(*a*) Its record as a good employer.
(*b*) Its financial contribution to the community.
(*c*) Its interest in the historic and cultural factors within the society.
(*d*) The high quality and safety of the products that the company produces.

Much of the interest of the subsidiary will tend to be in keeping the company out of the news – maintaining a low rather than a high profile.

Progress test 18

1. What is sales promotion? (**1**)
2. Why is sales promotion important and what are the implications for organizing a successful campaign overseas? (**2–4**)
3. Describe the advantages and limitations of direct mail as a method of sales promotion overseas. (**8–10**)

198 Marketing Overseas

4. How can the company marketing overseas use international exhibitions to maximum effect? (**11-18**)

5. What approaches are available to the international company wanting to improve its image before the public? (**11-18**)

19
Overseas sales management

The nature of international sales management

1. Sales management in the marketing mix. Personal selling will have a vital role for the majority of companies in developing a presence overseas. It will form one of the most important elements of the way in which the company promotes its products overseas and will be particularly important in certain areas:

(*a*) When the product has a high level of technical content.
(*b*) When the product is highly priced.
(*c*) When the company is a new entrant in a competitive overseas market.

It will often be impossible to persuade buyers overseas of the value of a new product without extensive discussion and personal contact which will be provided by overseas sales management. Such activity is often termed missionary selling.

In all product areas, however, there will be an element of personal selling which will take various forms.

(*a*) Direct sale from the parent company to the end user (*see* chapter 15).
(*b*) The use of intermediaries in the distribution process with a locally based salesforce such as agents and distributors (*see* chapter 15).
(*c*) The establishment of a local sales or production subsidiary with local sales staff directly employed by the parent company (*see* 16:**25**).

200 Marketing Overseas

2. Sales management tasks. The nature of the sales management will vary considerably and will depend on the type of distribution channel used, but it is possible to identify three equivalent sales management tasks:

(*a*) Direct contact with overseas customers.

(*b*) A mainly supervisory role in dealing through agents and other intermediaries.

(*c*) Direct management of an overseas salesforce by an overseas based sales management team.

The role of the sales manager

3. The importance of the overseas sales manager to the international company. The company can view the recruitment of an overseas manager in a number of ways.

(*a*) *As an investment to ensure that its overseas markets remain profitable.* The company will have an interest in measuring the achievements of its export managers against the profitability of the sales achieved in the markets for which they are responsible.

Export managers will be expensive to maintain with the high level of travelling costs and the necessity for them to have language skills. One survey showed that approximately 50 per cent of export managers could speak a foreign language, rising to 66 per cent at director level.

(*b*) *As part of its overall sales strategy.* No company can base its sales strategy soley on the experience of its overseas agents. The company itself must rely on the experience of its export management to take the decisions about the key markets based either on current sales achievement or likely sales potential.

(*c*) *As an essential link* between the company and its agents overseas with a key role in developing the opportunities in the market.

Overseas sales managers provide a key motivational influence for overseas agents and distributors. Their individual presence in the market ensures that the local representative will tend to continue to actively support the supplier in the market.

4. The role of the overseas sales manager in the development

of the company. The export manager will help the development of the company overseas in a number of ways:

(a) *Knowledge.* Experience suggests that companies selling overseas will have sources of information about changing market conditions that are independent of those supplied by agents or distributors. It is only through the overseas sales manager or a similar mechanism that the company can link its own knowledge of its markets to the skills of its agents to develop its business.

(b) *Perception.* In all likelihood, each distributor will have a large product range of which the overseas company's goods is only a small percentage – rarely more than 20 per cent of turnover. The agent in consequence will view his total business operation in a different light to the supplier's export manager and will often miss new business potential as he concentrates on the remaining 80 per cent of his turnover. For example, an agent involved in industrial cleaning might easily concentrate on the design and supply of equipment and product to a new industrial complex while ignoring less significant business for his overall product range which would be available at the local hospital. Should the supplier be more actively involved in the hospital field it would be obvious that concentration on this particular account would yield greater benefits than the industrial complex. This situation might be clear to the overseas sales manager but not necessarily so to the agent.

5. The size of the export salesforce. Certain factors influence the size of the export salesforce:

(a) The size and potential of the markets involved.
(b) The distribution channels that have been chosen.
(c) The nature of the selling task.

Many companies place far too much responsibility on the few overseas sales managers that they employ. A survey in the 1970s showed that in large companies the average turnover for which a national sales manager was responsible, was one fifth of that of the overseas sales manager.

Though it is often difficult to quantify the exact impact that increasing sales management overseas will have on company

202 Marketing Overseas

performance it would appear that the majority of successful exporting companies maintain a high level of investment in overseas sales management.

6. The issues of sales management. Sales management involves the following:

(*a*) The identification of potential customers in markets at home and overseas, in conjunction with the marketing department, and how they should be approached: that is, the sales strategy.

(*b*) Defining the nature of the selling task involved.

(*c*) Determining the numbers and the nature of the salesforce required.

(*d*) Recruiting, training, and supporting the individuals involved.

(*e*) Maintaining information systems to direct the sales task and evaluating the effectiveness of the sales effort.

The national and international sales manager

7. Major differences. Because of the differing nature of the distribution channel used overseas, international sales management will differ from home market management in two major respects:

(*a*) The degree of control exerted in the selling process.

(*b*) The nature of the overseas sales management task.

8. The problem of control of overseas markets. Certain characteristics of the company with overseas markets make its management policy crucial to exercising effective control over those markets.

(*a*) It is at some distance from the market and all that that means: different legal, cultural, and linguistic systems from that at home with the accompanying differences in exchange control, currency, import/export and consumer regulations.

(*b*) In all likelihood the company will have chosen a channel of distribution where its control over the market is limited (*see* Chapter 12).

A survey of British exporters showed the following percentages using agents for distribution (though naturally not in all markets).

Company size (by no. of employees)	Use of Agents (%)
1–100	68
101–500	79
501–1000	85
1001–10,000	85
10,000+	85

These findings are reinforced by a survey of small American and Canadian firms which found that of those exporting 53 per cent used agents and only 4 per cent sold direct.

As a result of channel and geographical diversity, the sales manager will be tending to work intermittently within overseas markets and through a range of intermediaries for whom the manager has no direct authority, in contrast to the home-based sales manager continually operating in a single market with a salesforce for which he has direct responsibility.

The recruitment of home-based export managers to spend time in the market alongside the distributor and his salesforce is the channel most frequently used by companies to secure a measure of control of their overseas markets.

9. The nature of the overseas sales management task. The international sales manager will often have to deal with a range of issues that are not part of the home-based sales manager's responsibility. These will include the following:

(*a*) Maintaining the flow of information to overseas agents and distributors.

(*b*) Involvement in negotiation in overseas markets often at governmental or major industrial level.

(*c*) Having a greater understanding of the technical and maintenance issues involved in a product sale than would be expected in the home market because of the distance separating the markets.

(d) Greater responsibility for the implementation of local promotional activity including an active role in the planning and execution of exhibitions overseas.

(e) More constant involvement in training and motivation of individual salesforce than would occur in the home market.

(f) Greater responsibility for the broader strategic issues that the firm will need to consider in overseas markets.

(g) Fuller understanding of more complex documentation and distribution problems that exist in servicing the overseas market and the ability to cope with local difficulties while in the market.

(h) Greater involvement in the definition of new overseas market opportunities for the international company.

10. The skills of the overseas sales manager. All the differences in the sales task mentioned above imply that the overseas sales manager will need additional skills.

(a) *Language.* Local language skills will be vital for local training and negotiation.

(b) *Cultural understanding.* Dealing with a range of different cultures each with their own distinct problems requires greater understanding and proficiency in dealing with people.

(c) *Organization and administration.* The overseas sales manager will need to develop greater organizational skills to handle the wide range of administrative tasks including the planning and execution of detailed overseas itineraries.

(d) *Analytical skills.* The overseas sales manager will need to develop a greater understanding of the information that is required both to define new market opportunities but also to maintain control over existing markets (*see* Chapters 8 and 9).

Sales strategy and sales management overseas

11. Important factors. Sales strategy will need to parallel marketing strategy to provide the greatest support in the markets with the largest potential. Decisions about key markets and allocation of effort by market, and potential business development will therefore be important aspects of the successful sales strategy.

19. Overseas sales management

Important factors are the complexity of the selling task, key markets and allocation of time, and potential business development.

12. The complexity of the selling task. Where the selling task is complex, sales management will need to concentrate on either long periods of contact with the potential customer or training in the market.

13. Key markets and allocation of time. The analysis of present sales by export management will clearly define the degree of likely importance of each market. It will be vital from such a base to define what expansion of sales could be achieved in the various existing markets. For example, where the company might have a 40 per cent share of a £2 million market it would be unlikely that substantial additional market share could possibly be generated. Compare this with a similar sales value within a larger market: for example, a 5 per cent share of a £16 million market where it would appear that considerable market share gains might be possible. It would be logical for the company's export sales manager to allocate more time to the second market than the first unless there are other factors involved. Should the first market be facing increased competition which is creating serious problems for the agent, or one or other of the markets is limited on profitability or by government intervention, decisions will have to be made about the level of support that the company can realistically provide to each.

Where a company is involved in a geographically large market, it will also be important for the export manager to decide within the parameters set by the company, on the allocation of time and effort by region. In the USA especially, many companies concentrate initially on a limited region to ensure that effort is not too thinly spread.

14. Potential business development. The issue of potential business development within the country or region will be more difficult to evaluate. The time and effort allocated should ideally suit the overall potential of the firm, but this will be qualified by the difficulties inherent within the market. Such problems will include the amount of control that they could exert via the agency agreements, the effect of government legislation on the nature and quantity of goods that could be imported, the degree to which foreign exchange is controlled, and other political and economic factors.

15. Sales management and overseas subsidiaries or sales offices. When the company begins to establish either a branch office or local subsidiary overseas it can either maintain expatriate sales staff or recruit locally. The advantages and disadvantages of such options are similar to other personnel issues within the firm (*see* Chapter 23).

Progress test 19

1. What is the role of sales management in the marketing mix of the international company? (**1**)
2. In what ways will the appointment of overseas sales managers aid the development of the international company? (**3-4**)
3. What tasks will the export salesforce be involved in and how will this differ from the home salesforce? (**6-9**)
4. What additional skills will the export sales manager require? (**10**)

20
Pricing factors in overseas marketing

The pricing environment

1. Key factors. There are a number of key factors that the firm involved in international trade will need to consider:

(*a*) Strategic issues in pricing.
(*b*) The effects of the pricing policy on the distribution channel.
(*c*) The effects of pricing on packaging and product policy.
(*d*) The additional costs of trading in the international environment.
(*e*) Volume and price relationships.
(*f*) Legislation and price controls in the international environment.
(*g*) Effects of currency instability on international pricing.
(*h*) Credit control and cash flow effects of international trade.

Strategic issues

2. Strategic issues in pricing. These include the following:

(*a*) Return on investment.
(*b*) Promotional policy in the market.
(*c*) Effects of competition.
(*d*) Risk factors in the market.

3. Return on investment. Both the speed of return on investment and the level of desired profitability will have an influence on the level of pricing in the market.

A toy company will need to achieve a rapid return on a new line as it will quickly need to be replaced, whereas a company establishing an animal feed factory overseas would envisage a continuing return over a number of years. These considerations will affect the level of pricing in the market. The nature of the strategic goals will have an important influence on price. High returns on investment will demand high volumes and/or high levels of per unit profitability.

Firms will therefore have differing short-term goals, though common long-term objectives – maximum return on capital employed, market share, profit on sales.

4. Effects of promotional expenditure. The speed of return on investment will also be affected by the level of promotional expenditure by the firm, in the market. There are four options available.

(*a*) *High price and high promotional expenditure – market skimming.* This short-term strategy attempts to sell a substantial volume of product at a premium price.

Skateboards are a good world-wide example of market skimming strategies. The product gained rapid acceptance at high prices followed by an equally rapid decline.

(*b*) *Low price and high promotional expenditure.* This is the market penetration policy by which large volumes are sold at either nil or minimal profit.

A significant amount of Japanese overseas trade has been built on the policy of market penetration strategies, including watches, cameras and televisions.

(*c*) *Low price and low promotional expenditure.* This will slowly establish the product in the market place but at a low level of profitability.

(*d*) *High price and low promotional expenditure.* The 'premium' policy will be particularly appropriate for products with a prestige image.

5. The effects of competition. The nature of the competition will naturally determine in part the pricing policy that the firm follows in the market and how it responds to price changes. Response strategies include the following:

(*a*) *Maintaining the original price.* This response may be appropriate where the company occupies a dominant position in the market on image and/or quality (*see below*).
(*b*) *Price reduction.*
(*c*) *Product improvement while maintaining price.* The computer market attempts to maintain the price of their individual products by either adding extra software or extra memory to the unit.
(*d*) *Price maintenance with improved service.* Increasing the length of the guarantees on cars and consumer durables has been one method of maintaining price in the market place for many companies operating in those sectors.

6. Risk. The pricing strategy will also need to consider the financial stability of the market. Where the market is either experiencing rapid inflation or has a high probability of a devaluation, pricing in a major currency will be of obvious benefit to the exporting company.

Consider a country like Brazil with an inflation rate in the 1970s of around 300 per cent. A product sold on 30 days credit in cruzeiros would be worth 25 per cent less to the exporting company at the end of this period. Invoicing in dollars would overcome this problem.

Factors affecting pricing

7. Pricing and product factors. Price will be one of the elements of building the brand image in the market. A high priced product will have quality associations. This will be particularly important in the area of industrial and service products where price is not the predominantly important factor, and issues such as reliability and durability are more crucial.

In a commodity market it will often be difficult to differentiate products which rely on 'image' rather than pure product attributes.

Port is regarded in the United States as a cheap drink, normally bought in plastic containers. Attempts by Portuguese shippers to establish a premium priced and quality imported product in the market have been largely unsuccessful.

8. Pricing and the distribution system. The firm will have to consider the components of the distribution chain in the pricing strategy adopted in the market. Intermediaries in the distribution chain will need to be financially rewarded to achieve maximum co-operation and market coverage, though this will need to be viewed in relation to two factors:

(*a*) The level of service that the intermediaries are expected to provide.

(*b*) The importance of the intermediaries in the distribution chain.

9. Costing international trade. There are additional costs that the firm engaged in international trade will have to either absorb or pass on to overseas customers.

(*a*) *Development costs incurred in overseas markets including the following:*

(*i*) Overseas travel.

(*ii*) Overseas promotion, e.g. exhibitions.

(*iii*) Legal costs – agency agreements, licensing arrangements.

(*iv*) Costs of movement of product from one market to another such as any special manufacturing requirements; special packaging if relevant; documentation charges; insurance costs; transport costs; transport to docks; harbour or airport dues; shipping costs; foreign duties & taxes; overseas delivery costs.

(*b*) *Service costs.*

(*i*) Finance costs including exchange control and extended credit in overseas markets.

(*ii*) Promotional costs.

(*iii*) Provision of spare parts, replacement stock.

(*iv*) Credit costs – the cost of maintaining extended credit to finance overseas trade.

10. Approaches to cost recovery. Companies operating in both

20. Pricing factors

home and overseas markets tend to adopt one of three approaches to recovering both manufacturing and additional costs of distribution and promotion.

(*a*) *Cost orientation.* This involves the addition of a mark-up on each unit produced to achieve an overall acceptable level of gross margin.

(*b*) *Recovery orientation.* This considers the overall level of planned production for the year and sets the necessary level of pricing on this basis to ensure that the firm receives sufficient income to achieve the profit targets set.

(*c*) *Competitor or customer orientation.* This considers that the market is the most important factor in price evaluation providing the basic level of return on capital can be achieved.

Setting price levels by either cost or overhead recovery methods will ensure that the firm meets its overall profit requirement providing the planned volumes are sold. However pricing without reference to the market means that the company may not be maximizing its market potential.

A British biscuit firm found that they could charge substantially more for their product in West Germany than they had been for the last 15 years, and reducing the price below what was suggested by their costing convention enabled them to sell large volumes to Canadian retail outlets.

11. Volume and price relationships. The sales volumes and the profitability that the company achieves will be affected by the pricing policy it adopts in the market. Central to the maximization of profit will be the following issues:

(*a*) The effect of volume on cost (economies of scale).
(*b*) Market pricing structures.
(*c*) Price elasticities.
(*d*) Problems and opportunities for marginal pricing.

12. Volume effects on cost. For every product manufactured there will be an element of fixed cost (factory buildings, heating) and an element of variable cost (raw materials, and labour). As the volume

212 Marketing Overseas

increases the company achieves economies of scale (*see* 1:3(*h*)) which enable it to be more competitive.

For some companies economies of scale will be very important – petrochemicals, cars, and consumer durables are examples. For others, such as clothing and perfume firms, the level of fixed costs will be far less and therefore volume will not greatly affect the cost base.

Setting a price

13. Market pricing structures. The way in which the in-market price is calculated will be determined by the nature of the distribution channel. In consequence different markets will exhibit different patterns in the way in which the final prices are calculated. Part of the management information system that an international firm needs to establish includes the collection of international pricing structures (*see* chapter 8). The following factors will need to be considered for an export operation, with different calculations being applied in the case of local manufacture and joint venture operations.

Cost point	
Ex works price	100
Freight etc. (Ch 21)	10
Landed cost	110
Clearance charges	2
Duty	12
In warehouse cost	124
Agent's margin	45
Cost to wholesaler 1	169
Wholesaler margin	5
Cost to wholesaler 2	174
Wholesaler margin	2
Retailer/end user	176

Pricing structures within the Japanese market will need to take into account the number of wholesalers that will be involved, with primary, secondary and tertiary firms involved in the distribution chain. In contrast distribution of many products in Western Europe will not involve the use of wholesalers but direct sale from distributor to end user or retailer.

14. Price elasticities. Reducing the price of products increases their demand, in other words demand is elastic. The degree to which demand changes with price is the price elasticity that the product shows. Different markets will exhibit differing price elasticities for the same product, influenced by competition, personal disposal income and other factors. Understanding the nature of the price elasticity can help the exporting company in setting the level of market prices that will achieve the best compromise between volume and profit.

15. Sales at marginal cost. For many companies export business can be seen as providing marginal revenue to enable the fixed overheads to be more evenly spread across the product line. Marginal costing of export products (selling at the cost of additional production) can be a viable operation providing the company considers the following factors.

(*a*) The company should be absolutely sure that the product cannot be sold anywhere else at a better price.

(*b*) The sales should be in addition to, and not a replacement for, sales at full price otherwise the effects on budgeting will be severe.

(*c*) The sale should not require any additional financing or extra credit which will further affect the company's overall profitability.

(*d*) The proposed sale should not contravene any existing or potential legal or governmental action (*see* 16:**20**).

(*e*) The sale should not interfere with long-term strategic plans for market development. While it is always easy to reduce price it is much more difficult to increase it; discounts offered to one customer in the market must be offered to others and become an expected part of the pricing structure which erode profitability.

(*f*) The company will need to ensure that it maintains a fair degree of control over the destination of the product, and that it is unlikely to be re-exported back to the home or other major markets.

Legal and governmental aspects of pricing

16. Dumping. The importance of governmental action in controlling price where dumping or 'unfair' competition is taking place has already been discussed. Companies need to avoid, if possible,

214 Marketing Overseas

running counter to the laws on dumping as the action once started will be long-term.

17. Maximum prices. Price controls operate in many markets to establish maximum or ceiling prices. Companies may have to clear any price rise with government bodies and may only be allowed to change prices once a year if at all. West Germany sets the retail price of cigarettes which means that cigarette companies cannot compete on price.

18. Profit margins. Members of the distribution channel may have their profit margins determined by government control. The UK Department of Health sets the levels of profitability of drug manufacturers and wholesalers within the National Health Service.

19. Cartel pricing. The most common way in which monopolies or cartels become established is by agreement over price.

> The Common Market under Article 85 of the Treaty of Rome forbids any trade association which may serve to reduce or distort competition within the Community. Article 86 forbids any company taking advantage of its dominant position in the acquistion of supplies or the charging of raised prices. Up to the mid-1980s there had been little action taken under these articles of European law.
> American legislation on the subject of unfair pricing discrimination is fairly extensive including the Federal Commission establishing a governmental organization to investigate possible cartels, and various items of antitrust legislation such as the Sherman Act of 1890 and the Antimerger Act of 1950. American firms are also forbidden under American law to enter into cartel pricing in overseas markets.
> Japanese legislation on cartel formation is limited, though MITI, the government organization responsible for economic policy, does have extensive powers to re-organize industrial organizations.

20. Transfer pricing. Government legislation may also affect the way in which subsidiary companies can either buy or sell products or services to intermediaries. This is the area known as transfer pricing.

Its effects include the following:

(*a*) The level of taxes that the subsidiary company will pay in the community.

(*b*) The amount of investment that remains within the country which will affect the level of employment in the country.

National governments will therefore be interested in having a role in determining what price subsidiaries of multinationals charge each other for goods and services. The various ways in which transfer pricing can be implemented however (*see* 21:**28**) means that effective control is difficult. Nevertheless, the problem of transfer pricing will be an important factor in multinational inter-company activity.

Currency implications

21. Currency stability and international pricing. The international company has to cope with two ways in which currencies can alter with respect to each other.

(*a*) 'Floating' rates by which the currencies gradually alter in relation to each other.

(*b*) 'Fixed' rates which may mean that there will be periods of stability followed by step changes in exchange rates.

Since the late 1960s there has been an increasing trend towards countries adopting floating exchange rates as the large movements of capital associated with international trade have made supporting fixed exchange rates increasingly difficult.

22. Dealing with currency instability. The firm needs to establish a policy with respect to the effects of changes in the financial environment.

(*a*) At the corporate level.

(*i*) Rather than attempt to predict rapid changes in currency rates the firm should assess what will happen if currency changes occur.

(*ii*) The firm should structure its assets to minimize the effects of changes in the exchange rates.

(*b*) At the local level.

216 Marketing Overseas

The major control at a local level will be whether:

(*i*) to price in local or some major trading currency;
(*ii*) to hold or change prices following changes in the exchange rate either to improve profitability or expand sales.

23. Advantages of quoting in the exporters' currency.

(*a*) Administrative convenience.
(*b*) Minimize foreign exchange problems associated with quotations in multiple overseas currencies.
(*c*) Simplifies planning and forecasting systems.

24. Advantages of pricing in the local currency.

(*a*) Currency gains: for the British exporter pricing in an overseas currency has tended in the long-term to improve profit margins at home as sterling has continued to weaken against such currencies as the German mark.

(*b*) Local currency quotations may help the company to gain access to low-cost finance in the market.

(*c*) Local currency quotations help to convince firms of the overseas company's commitment to the market, and are administratively more convenient as the customer does not have to arrange for large intermittent payments of foreign exchange.

(*d*) Local currency invoicing may often speed the payment of invoices and the remittance overseas as the company's banking arrangements can be set up to handle overseas currency via overseas branches of the home bank.

25. Devaluation policy.
In a rapidly changing international currency environment, the exporting company will often face major devaluations of overseas currencies. The effect of the devaluation will be to reduce the profitability of the market if the company maintains the previous pricing structure, though there may be advantages in so doing. The company should ideally establish a devaluation policy for major markets which determines the way in which prices should be changed if devaluation occurs. Factors that will influence the decision include the following:

(a) Strategic factors such as return on investment, speed of market penetration.

(b) Whether the pricing structure includes the cost of transport to overseas markets or is based on ex-works or FOB (*see* Chapter 21). Dollar movements have been a very important component of pricing where the firm uses air freight, the cost of which moves up and down in line with fuel costs.

(c) How financially stable the market is: where the market is either experiencing rapid inflation or has a high probability of a devaluation, pricing in a major currency will be of obvious benefit to the exporting country.

In small markets the cost of continually changing pricing will be considerable; in larger markets pricing in the local currency may be essential to meet the competitive criteria which will often have a substantial effect on company profitability.

A British company achieving 60 per cent of its turnover in the United States and pricing the product in dollars would have seen the overall level of sterling profit (provided sales remained constant in both countries and the local dollar price was maintained) decline by 20 per cent from 1985 to 1986 because of the movements in the pound relative to the dollar.

Companies can also offset many of the problems of currency movements by buying foreign currency forward – this improves the budgeting process as companies can be sure that some at least of the risk has been removed.

Cash flow implications

26. Exporting and cash flow. Exporting will have consequences for the financial well-being of the company as money will take longer to come back to the organization. Whereas within home markets payment for products will generally be received within 30 days, export payment terms will be lengthened by the following factors:

(a) Delays on shipment.
(b) Length of time in transit.
(c) Length of time clearing customs.

218 Marketing Overseas

(d) Length of credit allowed the overseas buyer.
(e) Delay in remittance from overseas bank.

27. The importance of reviewing overseas arrangements. The international firm will need to carefully review both the nature of the pricing structure for overseas markets and the control systems that are employed.

(a) To ensure that the firm is achieving an adequate return on sales.
(b) To ensure that the company is minimizing delay at each stage of the export process.

One area that companies tend to ignore is the delay in payment from overseas banks to the parent company's account. This can often be more than 15 days. Many banks can provide rapid transfer methods which will substantially improve cash flow for the supplier company.

(c) To ensure that the firm is maintaining an information system that can identify problems and rapidly correct them.

Progress test 20

1. Describe the factors affecting pricing in the international environment. (**1-6**)
2. Explain the role of pricing in (i) market skimming; (ii) market penetration; (iii) a premium policy. (**4**)
3. What costs will the company involved in overseas trade have to budget for and how will it recover them? (**9-10**)
4. Explain the relevance of (i) the volume and cost relationship; (ii) market pricing structures; (iii) price elasticities; (iv) marginal pricing. (**10-15**)
5. How do governments affect pricing? (**16-20**)
6. Describe the currency issues confronting the international firm. (**21-25**)
7. How does exporting affect company cash flow? (**26**)

21
Implementing pricing policy - export terms and conditions

Introduction

1. Structure of international payment systems. Payment for products delivered to, or services provided in the overseas markets can involve a number of factors.

(*a*) Money payment for export shipments, or
(*b*) non-money payment for export shipments (countertrade), or
(*c*) transfer of sums between subsidiaries.

The overseas contract of sale

2. Defining the nature of export shipments.
It is important to realise that export shipments are effectively a contract between the buyer and seller. This includes the following:

(*a*) A contract of sale between buyer and seller.
(*b*) A contract of carriage.
(*c*) A contract of insurance.
(*d*) Bank contract if the payment is to be made via bank draft.

The delivery of the shipping documents will be a vital part of the completion of many of these contracts. The way in which these contracts are structured provides security for both the buyer and seller; ensuring on the seller's behalf that when the goods are shipped payment will be received and on the buyer's behalf that terms and conditions of orders are fulfilled.

220 Marketing Overseas

Documentation

3. The nature of shipping documents.

Item	Contains
Bill of Lading	Contents of shipment/contract between shipper and supplier
Airway bill	As for bill of lading
Certificate of Origin	Notarized documentation by consular authorities on point of manufacture
T form	Shows duty paid on non-EEC goods
Hazardous cargo declaration	Indicates special cargo storage requirements
Customs entry	For export/import statistics
Black List Certificate	Similar to Certificate of Origin – non-Israeli origin Arab League States
TIR Carnet	Applies to container transport overland for intermediate country customs clearance
Standard shipping note	Specifications of goods shipped
EEC Certificate	Details of duty concessions
Export licences	Clearance for goods subject to control

4. Aids to defining documentation needs. SITRO, the Simplification of International Trade Board, partially funded by the BOTB helps British exporters in providing material to standardize export documentation. They have developed a computer package, called SPEX, which helps to produce standard export documentation. SITRO is also involved in the international standardization of export documentation via United Nations trade bodies.

5. Cost of documentation. The amount of time that a firm must spend to ensure that documentation is accurate will be considerable as it will be essential that documentation is exact if payment is achieved by some form of letter of credit (*see below*); otherwise considerable delays on payment will often occur. This will mean that firms will have to either employ individuals with specific skills in these areas or use intermediaries such as freight forwarding agents

21. Export terms and conditions

who have specific skills for particular markets, for example in South America or the Middle East. Either route will incur cost.

The cost of export documentation is much higher than analyses of national distribution costs (*see* Chapter 12) suggest. It has been estimated that compliance with all regulations for an export order can run at 3–4 per cent of total face value.

A shipment of electrical goods from the United Kingdom to Italy required no less than 37 different documents – and this was between countries supposedly in a 'Common' Market.

6. The timescale of documentation. Companies will need to be aware of the length of time that some of the documentation, specifically consular certificates, may take to acquire. Obtaining export licences for certain categories of goods may also be a difficult and time-consuming exercise.

Terms of trade in exporting

7. The terms used. There are a number of ways in which the contract between buyer and seller can be described, and by which the payment for the additional costs involved in the export process can be determined. It is important that any firm involved in the development of international trade has a clear understanding of the nature of the contracts into which it is entering with overseas customers.

The terms of trade include the following, later explained in fuller detail:

(*a*) Ex-works, ex factory.
(*b*) FOT, FOR.
(*c*) FAS, DD.
(*d*) FOB.
(*e*) CF, CIF.

In general terms these provide an ascending scale of service to the overseas customer. Ex-works prices will mean that the seller has minimal responsibility for ensuring that the goods reach their destination, CIF terms the highest. As a corollary, CIF terms ensure that the seller maintains maximum control over the despatch of goods.

8. The importance of terms of trade. The contractual nature of the agreement between buyer and seller makes it essential that both parties are clear as to the obligations of each. Additional and unforseen costs that have to be borne by either party will be a major source of friction.

9. Ex-works. This contract involves the supplier only in making the goods available as specified in the order from the customer and informing the customer of the availability. Though this is the simplest method for the supplier, disputes can arise over the nature of the external packing but this has been reduced by the advent of containerization.

10. Free on rail (FOR): Free on truck (FOT). The supplier is responsible for making sure that the products are loaded onto the railway system at a particular depot, as specified in the contract. Once the goods are loaded the contract has been fulfilled and the remainder of the responsibility rests with the buyer.

11. Free alongside (FAS): Delivered docks or depot (DD). The supplier is responsible for the shipment of products to the port or depot (increasingly important as inland container depots handle increasing amounts of trade). The contract will involve the supplier meeting a particular vessel in a port or a particular deadline at an inland depot. The supplier will have to clearly state the port or depot to which delivery is to be made and whether additional payment in the port is necessary or whether delivery to port warehouse is sufficient.

12. Free on board (FOB). The supplier is responsible for the transport of goods from the factory to meet a specific vessel in a specific port and will meet all port storage and handling charges.

13. Carriage and freight (CF): Carriage insurance freight (CIF). The supplier pays all the charges involved in the transport of the goods from the factory to a designated overseas port. The buyer is then responsible for port charges, duty, and transport to warehouse in the overseas country.

14. Advantages of CF, CIF pricing. There are a number of advantages associated with CF and CIF systems for both buyer and seller.

(*a*) It provides the buyer with a clear price structure which can be clearly understood. To the buyer in Australia, ex-works Huddersfield is not very helpful, whereas CIF Sydney is clear and comprehensive.

(*b*) It provides the supplier company with the maximum amount of control over the destination of the goods as it is the supplier that chooses the vessel by which the product is shipped.

(*c*) It allows the company to price differentially, on a market-by-market basis. Where the potential exists to charge a higher market price (*see* 20:**10**(*c*)) firms should take avantage of it, and the comparison of one CIF price with another requires considerable calculation to ascertain whether the underlying price is in fact different.

15. Disadvantages of CF, CIF pricing. There are however a number of disadvantages of CF and CIF pricing.

(*a*) It involves the company in substantially more administration and will certainly mean that the company will have to employ more personnel in the shipping department.

(*b*) Overseas clients may have particular shipping lines that they wish to use, or insurance companies with which they do business.

(*c*) CF, CIF pricing is practical only with full container loads. Where the company is shipping in consolidated containers to overseas markets the administration becomes too complex.

(*d*) Changes in currency rates will put more pressure on a company operating on CIF terms to re-adjust prices than one offering ex-works terms because of the higher value of the per unit price.

(*e*) Shipping rates (particularly if the supplier is using air freight with the cost tied to the rise and fall in aviation fuel cost) will often vary rapidly and this may require the exporter to minimize the

224 Marketing Overseas

forward risk of export quotation by reducing the length of time for which the quotation holds valid.

16. Shipping terms and the export quotation.

(a) The exact nature of the contract should be clarified, and the obligations of both parties towards the costs involved.

Item	Ex-works	FOB	CIF
Cost of goods	+	+	+
Carriage to port	-	+	+
Handling/storage	-	+	+
Freight costs	-	-	+
Insurance	-	-	+

(b) The quotation should be clearly stated in the currency of choice (see 21:**14**).

(c) The timescale over which the contract operates should also be clearly stated.

(d) Any extra documentation that is required, such as Certificate of Origin, should also be clearly stated on the quotation.

Methods of payment in overseas export sales

17. Payment in advance. This can be either cash with order (CWO) or cash on delivery (COD).

These payment terms are essential where there are major problems with either trading partners or trading countries. This provides the maximum possible level of security over the payment for the goods.

18. Letters of credit. These are guarantees issued by banks to ensure payment once the goods have been received in the overseas country.

There are two types of letter of credit commonly used:

(a) The irrevocable credit drawn on an overseas bank which can only be modified with the agreement of both parties. For many markets this is acceptable, but where there are potential problems with payment or foreign exchange a more certain form of payment is the second option.

(b) A confirmed irrevocable letter of credit drawn on the overseas bank and guaranteed by a bank in the supplier's territory.

A major problem with letters of credit is that the documents must be absolutely accurate as the bank will only pay on presentation of correct documentation. It has been estimated that around 20 per cent of invoices for overseas shipments are inaccurate. Failure to deliver correct documentation naturally invalidates the contractual arrangements that exist between buyer and seller, and buyer and bank.

19. Sight drafts. These are contracts drawn up by the exporter requiring payment at a specified time after the delivery of goods, either immediately or at 30, 60, or 90 days.

20. Open account. In this method the buyer agrees to pay within a certain time of receipt of goods without having the contractual nature of the sight draft. It is common within the EEC as it allows maximum flexibility within a well-organized legal system.

Minimizing risk of default in payments

21. Choices available.

(a) Ensuring that documentation is accurately completed.
(b) Carrying out credit checks on overseas customers either via a bank or the overseas commercial service (*see* 15:**15**(c)).
(c) Insuring against default.

22. Export credit guarantee scheme (ECGD). Export credit is provided by the majority of major trading countries to firms exporting from their territories. The UK scheme run by the BOTB is one such example. It provides cover up to 90 per cent of the total shipment value (for some engineering projects 100 per cent is available). Cover can last up to five years. The insurance is designed to cover a number of eventualities.

(a) Failure of the buyer to pay within six months of the due payment date.

(b) War, revolution, civil disobedience which causes a breakdown in trading conditions.

(c) Government action on foreign exchange, import licences.

(d) Additional transport or insurance costs arising from changes in shipping or freight procedures.

ECGD cover does not include insurance for disagreements between suppliers and buyers on quality of merchandise which underlines the importance of accurately describing the goods in the contract of sale. Furthermore it is in the interests of the company using the ECGD to keep a wary eye on the governmental debt situation in its markets since further ECGD guarantees may be restricted if a seriously indebted government is having difficulty in negotiating with the IMF.

Financing overseas sales

23. Options available. The nature of the overseas sale is such that the company will need to carefully consider the implications on working capital and the way in which it controls its finances (*see* Chapter 20 and 21:**30**).

The options include the following:

(a) Raising money on the strength of the export order (supplier credit).

(b) Raising finance via the transfer of invoices (factoring).

(c) Receiving goods instead of money (counter trading).

(d) Using the overseas agent or distributor as a source of credit (*del credere* agency agreements).

24. Supplier credit.

(a) *By the transfer of insurance policies*. ECGD or similar cover can be used to raise finance through normal commercial banking firms.

(b) *By bill guarantees*. Commercial banks will often allow the exporter to borrow up to the full amount of any insured export sale over an agreed period.

(c) *Credit lines*. Exporters with substantial overseas activity and a good banking record are able to finance export trade via an open credit arrangement with an upper limit.

25. Factoring. This involves a company buying the supplier invoice (debt) for cash at a discount to the full value and then collecting payment from the overseas buyer. There are two main methods of factoring available to the exporting firm:

(*a*) *Irrevocable letter of credit acceptance.* An irrevocable letter of credit can be sold to the accepting bank at a discount before the due date.

(*b*) *Export factoring houses.* A number of large firms (mainly subsidiaries of major clearing banks) will act as finance houses for the exporter, buying the overseas invoices at around 80 per cent of face value, and when the bill is paid, remitting the remainder minus the finance charge.

26. Counter-trading.

(*a*) *Defining counter-trading.* Counter-trade is any payment system that involves the use of goods as payment for other goods.

(*b*) *The importance of counter-trading.* Since the oil price rises of the early 1970s the amount of counter-trading has increased for a number of reasons.

(*i*) Shortage of foreign exchange brought about by heavy overseas borrowing, and poor export earnings in many commodity markets.

(*ii*) The increasing competition of major exporting countries within a slowly growing world economy.

(*iii*) The growth of major trading houses such as those in Japan and Korea that are ideally structured to handle counter-trading. It is now estimated that around 20 per cent of world trade is accounted for by some form of counter-trade.

(*iv*) Increasing Third World indebtedness. Counter-trade or barter provides a mechanism to circumvent IMF attempts to regulate the economic policies of heavily indebted governments.

(*c*) *Types of counter-trade.*

(*i*) *Barter.* This involves the acceptance of product in return for goods or services.

In 1985 Saudi Arabia concluded a major barter deal for the purchase of Tornado fighter aircraft with payment that was to be in the supply of crude oil.

(*ii*) *Switch trading*. This uses a third party to sell the bartered product on the world markets.

The Japanese trading companies Mitsubishi and Sumimoto have developed large scale projects with the People's Republic of China that have involved switch trading of a wide range of industrial commodities in return for machine tools and other industrial equipment.

(*iii*) *Buyback arrangements*. These are often part of industrial co-operation agreements (*see* 16:**3**). In them, the supplier company agrees either to take the entire payment in one particular product or component or part payment in a range of possible commodities (also termed parallel trading).

27. Disadvantages of counter-trading. The nature of counter-trade often involves the acceptance of products for which the small company cannot find markets and which it needs to finance and store. Counter-trading is therefore often the preserve of the large company or one with the support of a well-established international trading company that can act as an intermediary in the disposal of counter-traded products.

Multinational financing

28. Transfer arrangements between multinationals. The problems of transfer pricing between subsidiaries of international firms have already been mentioned (*see* 3:**6**). The way in which funds can be transferred between countries is however broader than transfer pricing. Methods include the following:

(*a*) Transfer pricing.
(*b*) Payment by dividends.
(*c*) Payment on management contracts.
(*d*) Payment on technology transfer (licence fees and royalties).
(*e*) Lending money to either the parent company or the subsidiary.
(*f*) Leasing of equipment either from the parent company or the subsidiary.

The multinational firm therefore has a number of additional methods by which funds can be transferred and needs to develop a structured approach towards producing the best solution to individual subsidiary parent company relationships.

29. Key issues in financial management for multinationals. The company will have to work through the following three stages of evaluation:

(*a*) Should funds be remitted?
  (*i*) To pay for technology.
  (*ii*) To obtain a higher rate of return elsewhere.
  (*iii*) To improve the access of the company to the total assets of the company.
  (*iv*) To minimize risk.
(*b*) How much should be transferred?
  (*i*) Funding requirements of parent company and subsidiary.
  (*ii*) Local and home market taxation systems.
  (*iii*) Cost and availability of funds from other sources.
(*c*) What form should the transfer take?
  (*i*) Tax implications.
  (*ii*) Types of transfer permitted by local government.
  (*iii*) Organization and structure of international firm.

Financing overseas investment

30. Main sources. The company considering increasing investment overseas will be able to derive funds from a number of sources:

(*a*) Retained earnings within the overseas market.
(*b*) Local commercial finance (from banks and other institutions).
(*c*) Local government finance (loans often at very favourable rates for industrial development).
(*d*) Transfers from group funds.
(*e*) Funds from international borrowings (from such sources as the Eurodollar market).
(*f*) Funds from international development organizations such as the World Bank.

230 Marketing Overseas

31. Assessing different sources of funding. The assessment of attractiveness will depend on an evaluation of the following factors:

(*a*) *Cost*. The level of interest will naturally be of predominant concern.

(*b*) *Cash flow*. The speed at which the loan needs to be repaid will often have important implications for the way in which companies' financial operations are structured.

(*c*) *Control*. How much control will the lending institutions demand in the way the investment is directed?

(*d*) *Currency instability*. For many investments the company will need to consider not only the overall cost of borrowing but also the potential problems that may be created in relation to currency instability.

> The Lyons group expanded overseas into Europe and the United States borrowing Swiss francs and dollars to do so. The devaluation of sterling in the late 1960s hit the group extremely hard and eventually was a factor in the takeover by the Allied group.

32. Insuring against investment problems. The ECGD scheme run by the BOTB will also provide insurance against the loss of capital investments in addition to export earnings in many overseas countries providing cover is arranged before the investment is finalized. Similar schemes are in operation in other countries.

Progress test 21

1. What is (*a*) a Bill of Lading; (*b*) an Airway Bill; (*c*) a Certificate of Origin; (*d*) a T form; (*e*) a Hazardous Cargo Declaration; (*f*) a Black List Certificate; (*g*) a TIR Carnet; (*h*) a Standard Shipping Note; (*i*) an EEC Certificate; (*j*) SITRO? (**3–4**)

2. Describe the cost and other factors involved in achieving accurate export documentation. Why are they important? (**5–6**)

3. What is a term of trade? List them and explain their implications for buyers and sellers in overseas markets. (**7–15**)

4. Explain the pricing advantages and disadvantages of CF and CIF. (**14–15**)

21. Export terms and conditions

5. (*a*) What is payment in advance? (*b*) Explain the difference between a Letter of Credit (an Irrevocable Credit) and a Confirmed Irrevocable Letter of Credit. (*c*) What is a Sight Draft? (*d*) What is an open account? (**17**)

6. How can a company ensure that it is paid for the goods or services supplied to customers overseas? (**21–22**)

7. What is (*a*) supplier credit; (*b*) factoring; (*c*) counter-trading; (*d*) *del credere* agency agreement? (**23**)

8. Why has counter-trading increased in importance? Describe the various facets of the issue. (**26–28**)

9. How do multinationals transfer funds? What are the strategic issues involved? (**28–32**)

22
Organizing for overseas marketing

The importance of organization design

1. The nature of organization. Organization refers to the way a company is structured. This will determine a number of important issues in business activity:

(a) The way in which decisions are taken and action formulated.
(b) The way in which activities are grouped and duties allocated among staff.
(c) The way in which authority and responsibility are defined.
(d) The method by which skills and task requirements are combined.

The organization's structure should aim to ensure that organizational goals are achieved with maximum efficiency whether they be return on capital employed, or sales volume expansion.

2. Some basic keys to organization design.

(a) Authority and responsibility should be closely linked. Where groups have the responsibility in certain areas they should also have the authority necessary to ensure that the resources allocated are used to the maximum effect.
(b) The number of links in the chain of authority should be as limited as possible.
(c) Every individual in the organization should be clear as to the line of authority in existence, and there should be a straight line of authority from the top to the bottom of the organization.

22. Organizing for overseas marketing

(d) As many decisions as possible should be taken by the individuals that have to implement the ensuing actions. This involves the decentralization of the decision-making process to the lower levels of the organization.

(e) The degree of supervision within the management structure should relate to the nature of the task; the more complex the task, the shorter the span of control. Thus where there are a large number of individuals carrying out simple tasks, production line assembly for example, the need for supervision will be limited. Where tasks are complex, however, the need for supervision will be greater.

(f) The structure should be responsive to changing company goals and should be able to react flexibly to change in the external environment, such as the changing demands of customers or alterations in the constraints facing the firm (see 6:2(d); 6:18—19).

3. The organizational requirements of international marketing. When a firm expands into the international environment it will be taking on a range of additional functions, but of special importance are the following:

(a) Production and marketing functions.
(b) Transport and shipping (particularly in the area of documentation).
(c) Finance.

The structure of these groups will need to change to reflect their changing roles in the overall company organization as the importance of the international role within the company alters.

Organizational development for overseas markets

4. A series of stages. Though they may all be present in the same company dealing with different aspects of the overseas business one can distinguish an evolution which can be presented in a series of stages.

(a) The use of current company facilities to cope with intermittent export orders.
(b) The development of an export department.

234 Marketing Overseas

(*c*) An international department.
(*d*) The division of the company into sections that can deal with multinational or transnational activities.

The creation of both the export and international departments can be seen as additions to an already existing national structure (Fig. 22.1), whereas the multinational organization requires a more fundamental reorganization (Fig. 22.2).

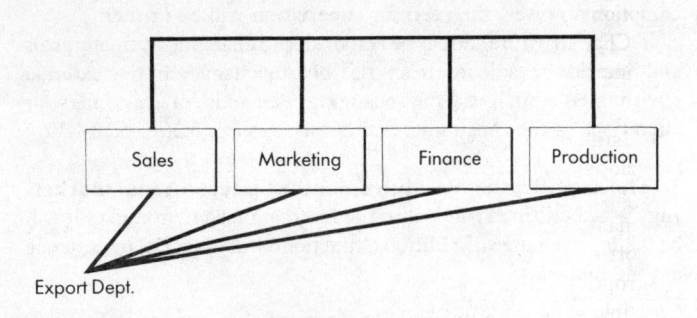

Figure 22.1 *National structure*

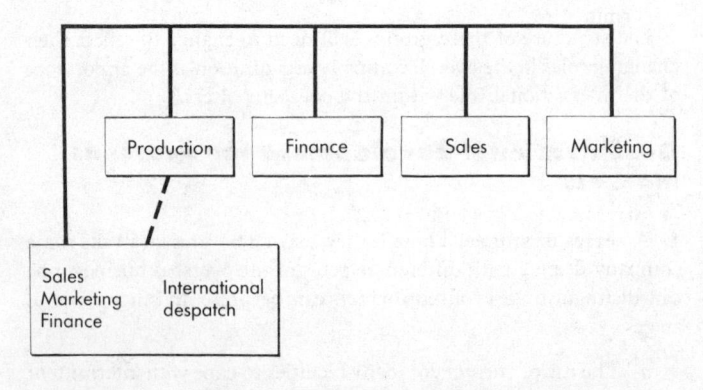

Figure 22.2 *International structure with separate international sales, marketing and finance departments*

22. Organizing for overseas marketing

Each type of operation will require differing levels of knowledge and understanding of overseas market conditions, and it will be essential that the firm is prepared to invest in the necessary training so that staff can meet the demands that overseas development will place upon them.

The need for training is particularly acute in those markets where firms are required to take major initiatives in order to become established overseas. The demands of the overseas environment are such that a firm attempting to become established overseas without additional support such as is provided by the Japanese trading houses (*see* Chapter 14) will need to develop a high level of understanding of the international environment.

5. Using existing company facilities. The early stages of the development of international trade will normally see the home trade despatch department handling the intermittent orders that occur normally, employing freight-forwarding agencies with knowledge of export procedures. This organizational structure will be most appropriate for the small firm which should sub-contract as much as possible of the labour-intensive aspects of export documentation and shipping to specialist agencies (even though the additional costs will be considerable on an order-by-order basis) as the firm will not have to invest in the fixed cost of an additional department for handling intermittent export orders.

6. The export department. An export department will become necessary once the volume of orders has reached the level where it will be cost-effective to employ individuals specifically to handle export matters. Their tasks will include the following:

(*a*) Maintaining a control on the length of time that is required to process orders.

(*b*) Liaising with production to ensure that deadlines are met and special packaging requirements are fulfilled.

(*c*) Ensuring that export quotations and pro-forma invoices are provided as quickly as possible.

(*d*) Controlling the issuing of documentation and checking the nature of the final shipping note.

236 Marketing Overseas

(*e*) Determining shipping procedure and advising the customer of any delay in procedure.

(*f*) Checking payment schedules and advising the finance department of outstanding invoices.

(*g*) Arranging for the packing of containers with the warehouse.

7. The skills of the export department. An export department should bring together certain essential skills:

(*a*) Understanding of all the documentation requirements and contract terms.

(*b*) Ability to answer queries on customs formalities and export licences.

(*c*) Understanding of all shipping possibilities; understanding the role of forwarding agents.

(*d*) Awareness of packaging requirements for overseas markets and how this will affect the production process.

8. Training the export department. Exporting is a complex and changing field, it is therefore essential that the company maintains the expertise at a high level. Far too much export expertise is developed in an ad-hoc fashion. Previous chapters have emphasized both the pitfalls and benefits of exporting procedure and it is unlikely that the company will be able to maintain up-to-date skills in all the necessary areas.

A programme should be developed whereby personnel are continually updated in a number of areas:

(*a*) Transportation and documentation.
(*b*) Legal aspects of the export trade.
(*c*) Cargo insurance.
(*d*) Computerization of the export process.

9. Managing the export department. As Fig. 22.1 shows, the initial reporting structure of the export department will be to the home market sales director. As export business grows the company may see the need to appoint a specialist export director and additional staff to handle administrative issues overseas.

10. The international department. When a company invests

22. Organizing for overseas marketing 237

overseas, the nature of the control that the company needs to exert over its subsidiary will change and the export department will be expanded to cope with a broader range of activities. This structure is often referred to as Type A international management (*see* **16**) where overseas companies report direct to executives in the parent company.

11. The tasks of the international department. The international department will be far more concerned with planning and support functions for the overseas subsidiary. Tasks for the international department will include the following:

(*a*) Creating strategic plans for the overseas company.
(*b*) Providing technical support where necessary.
(*c*) Administering all legal aspects of overseas activity (patents, trade marks etc.).
(*d*) Planning and aiding in the creation and implementation of promotional plans (for example providing print material).
(*e*) Training sales staff and other personnel overseas.

12. The skills of the international department. The tasks that the international department faces will differ considerably from the export department and they will require a different body of knowledge:

(*a*) Selling skills particularly in overseas environments.
(*b*) Knowledge of market research procedures and promotional techniques overseas.
(*c*) Understanding the financing and credit implications of international marketing.
(*d*) Being aware of the nature of the legal system in overseas countries.
(*e*) Language skills to operate in the overseas market.
(*f*) Understanding local distribution and pricing factors.

13. Training the international department. Most important will be the opportunity to visit the overseas market so that conditions can be understood at close hand. Visits from the overseas subsidiary to the parent company can also improve the dialogue. Training in specific technical issues will however be important:

238 Marketing Overseas

(a) Language skills.
(b) Export management accounting.
(c) Export distribution and promotion.
(d) The nature of export markets.
(e) Sales management overseas.

14. Managing the international department. As the international department grows in importance it will tend to compete with other departments for resources, and there will be increasing disagreements on the level of pricing and the cost at which goods are transferred to the international division. The main conflict that arises will be between geographic interests (the overall performance of the overseas subsidiary) and the interests of the individual production units responsible for the world-wide performance of their particular product group. As the international department grows in importance this conflict will need to be resolved and varying structures have been developed by multinational companies which allow the international interests of the company to operate as an independent profit centre rather than as an additional department within the organization.

Training

15. Types of training available. The firm will have a number of options available for developing export skills. These include the following:

(a) Courses arranged internally (if the company has sufficient staff to justify a course).
(b) Courses run by the appropriate institute or Chamber of Commerce, for example, in the UK, the Institute of Export runs courses on many subjects.
(c) Courses run by outside consultancy firms or academic institutions.
(d) Correspondence courses.

Many firms fail to take advantage of the many opportunities that exist to improve the skills of their export personnel at little or no cost to themselves as many governments provide substantial subsidies in these areas.

Multinational organization

16. Major differences between multinationals and other companies. Multinationals will tend to differ in organizational requirements from the international company in a number of respects:

(a) They are substantially bigger in scale.
(b) They cover a wider range of products.
(c) The spread of investment is substantially greater.

As a result, firms with substantial interests overseas tend to divide their activities into either product or geographic units. The range of possible structures is outlined in Fig. 22.3 and comprise the following:

(a) Overall management Type A.
(b) Geographic management Type B.
(c) Product group management Type C.
(d) Matrix management Type D.

		Product			
		A	B	C	D
	A	1	2	3	4
Geographical	B	5	6	7	8
area	C	9	10	11	12
	D	13	14	15	16

Figure 22.3 Product/territory matrix organization

Management

17. Geographical management. This form of management divides the company into geographical operating units, for example Africa, North America, Europe, Asia. It is most appropriate under the following conditions:

(a) Where there is little difference in the range of products sold.

240 Marketing Overseas

(b) Where there is a wide spread of geographical activity.

(c) Where the products require limited R&D investment.

The disadvantage of this system is that there will be little liaison between the operating units which will tend to be sales rather than product led.

Some companies, because of political structures, have created regional subsidiaries with additional responsibilities:

(a) Companies with developmental responsibility outside their home markets. For example a subsidiary in France with responsibility for Belgium and Holland both within the EEC.

(b) Regional supervisory units with either full profit responsibility or the provision of management support services to the local companies.

Though these structures may have advantages in certain conditions, they introduce another management tier between the head office and the operating unit which will often reduce efficiency.

18. Product management. This form of organization implies an international co-ordination between product areas in each overseas country. It has particular advantages under certain conditions:

(a) Where there is a high R&D input.

(b) Where the product has no local variations.

(c) Where the company has a limited number of large product groups.

(d) Where the company concentrates its activity into a number of key markets.

The disadvantages exist mainly at the subsidiary level as priorities between the various product groups will be difficult to define.

19. Matrix management. This management structure requires a combination of product and geographic reporting systems which are able to combine the advantages of both systems providing the level of management expertise is high and the individuals within the company have a clear, common company objective.

The disadvantage of the matrix management system is that it often encourages the continued increases in the number of individuals

22. Organizing for overseas marketing

employed in staff functions within the head office which can often lead to overlapping zones of responsibility and duplication of effort.

20. New product development in multinational companies. The way in which the company is organized will have a considerable effect on the level of innovation and the speed at which new developments are introduced. The most successful companies for product introductions will be those with product-based organization structures. The introduction of the concept of the world product mandate (*see* 10:**17**) is an attempt by companies with other organization structures to improve the innovatory potential of subsidiaries.

21. Training multinational management. As the level of sophistication within the company increases, management of multinational organizations will need to acquire additional skills in certain areas:

(*a*) Language skills.
(*b*) Strategic analytical techniques.
(*c*) Financial control of multinational product divisions.

22. Decentralization v centralization in decision-making. With the advent of fast communication systems and a vast increase in data-processing capacity there has been a tendency in multinational companies towards increasing centralization of control. Head offices are increasingly demanding more and more information concerning financial and planning matters from their subsidiary units.

Progress test 22

1. Describe the steps in the organizational development of an expanding company active in overseas markets. (**4–6**)
2. What are the staffing implications for the company expanding overseas? (**1–15**)
3. What differences are there between the tasks associated with an export department and those of an international department? (**6–15**)
4. Comment on multinational organization for export. (**14–21**)

23
Staffing the international firm

Introduction

As the international firm becomes more complex, it will rely more and more heavily on a large management team to direct and control a range of activities in a number of overseas countries. General Motors with an international workforce of 800,000 has manufacturing plants throughout America, Europe, Africa and Asia.

1. Staffing policy options. The international firm will need to develop a staffing policy to cope with the expansion and complexities of running a series of overseas operations. These are some of the options available:

(*a*) The employment of individuals from the parent company in overseas posts (the expatriate route).

(*b*) The employment of third-country nationals, individuals working in an overseas subsidiary who are not nationals of the parent company's country.

(*c*) The employment of local nationals to run the operations in their own countries.

(*d*) The formation of an international team of executives that will be drawn from any country, but mainly from the countries within which the company operates.

23. Staffing the international firm 243

Employing expatriates

2. The advantages of employing expatriates.

(a) The company can ensure that it maintains a high level of expertise in overseas companies.

(b) The employment of expatriates improves the control that the international company maintains abroad as the individual links that managers have will be with the home country and not overseas. Issues such as high levels of inter-company transfer pricing will be much easier to control with expatriate management. This will be particularly important when the management team is out of contact with the head office or is involved in highly complex decisions involving major company investment.

(c) The employment of expatriates allows the international company maximum flexibility – management can be moved from country to country and from operation to operation. Japanese management do not normally spend large periods of time overseas before being transferred back to Japan.

(d) The company can ensure that management has a common approach to problem-solving by extensive training before posting overseas.

(e) The employment of expatriate staff will overcome any language problem that might exist within the firm (though obviously not in its outside contacts), as all internal documentation and information structuring will have a common base.

(f) In some countries even though local management of sufficient expertise exists, recruiting may still be difficult.

> Overseas companies have found recruitment of Japanese management for local subsidiaries in Japan a very difficult task. The explanation that is provided for this phenomenon is that historically Japanese management looked for lifetime employment in an organization and that overseas firms did not provide a congenial working environment.

Commonly, the use of expatriate management is most pronounced during the early phases of company expansion into overseas markets and in particular key areas of operation which are most sensitive, such as finance and marketing.

3. Disadvantages of employing expatriates.

(*a*) Expatriate staffing is extremely expensive. The contracts offered to expatriates will have to include some or all of the following:

(*i*) Payment of all local housing expenses.

(*ii*) Provision of a car (often with driver).

(*iii*) Payment of additional local allowances for servants, cost of living.

(*iv*) Payment for annual flights back to domicile for the entire family.

(*v*) Extended periods of leave.

(*vi*) Education expenses for children.

The costs involved can be very considerable. The annual cost to the company of establishing an expatriate sales manager in the Middle East could be as follows:

Item	Cost (£)
Salary	22000
Housing	15000
Allowance for servants	3000
Car	3000
Education for children	5000
Transport for family	7000
Miscellaneous (pension, clubs)	3500
Total	58500

This calculation still ignores the costs of supervision by line management at home including market visits.

(*b*) Expatriate staff will tend to have a limited understanding of the local market, language, and business conditions.

(*c*) They will have limited access to the decision-making process in government.

(*d*) The government will often place limitations on the length of time that they can be employed or the overall numbers that are permissible.

(*e*) The employment of expatriates at any level of the firm emphasizes the 'foreign-ness' of the operation, which may in the long term cause political problems.

(f) Promoting managers to expatriate posts may cause problems when they return to the parent company as they will expect similar positions in what may be a much larger concern. There may be problems associated with salary and benefits when they return home.

(g) The employment of expatriates at the most senior levels within the overseas subsidiaries may often cause resentment amongst the national workforce who rapidly become aware of the barriers that exist to recruitment and the lack of access to decision-making.

Employing local nationals

4. The advantages of employing local nationals. For many countries the employment of local nationals will be an essential part of the company's staffing policy. This is because of the advantages that employing local nationals will bring.

(a) Substantially lower cost in many countries. This is not always the case – it will be often cheaper for a European firm to employ an expatriate manager in the United States than to engage local management with much higher salary expectations.

(b) It often allows the firm access to the political decision-making process.

(c) It may be essential under the current legislation in the overseas country.

(d) It will substantially improve the company's understanding of the local market, language and business customs.

(e) It will minimize the problems that exist with promotion paths within the overall organization.

(f) It will reduce the 'foreign-ness' of the firm as leaders of the business community will be in contact solely with their own countrymen.

(g) Employing local nationals may have the effect of improving the overall morale of the firm as individuals can see that there is a clear path to top management.

(h) Employing a high percentage of local staff ensures that the company can emphasize its contribution to the local economy as part of its public relations campaign (*see* Chapter 18).

5. Disadvantages of employing local nationals.

(a) In many countries there may be a shortage of skills (particularly in specialized areas such as electronic engineering and computer-aided manufacturing processes).

(b) It will often be difficult to develop a common approach to the development of the business.

(c) Local nationals may be less willing to implement policies that they regard as contrary to host-country wishes (for example, reduction in employment in the local manufacturing plant).

(d) The barrier to further advancement within the company beyond the local subsidiary may serve as a demotivating force and mean that the more able individuals will seek work elsewhere.

Employing third-country nationals

6. The advantages and disadvantages.
This is seen as a half-way house between employing expatriates and local nationals and as such it has some of the benefits and some of the disadvantages. European firms engaged in management contracts to run hospitals in the Middle East often recruited Egyptian doctors.

Though the recruitment of third-country nationals can do much to reduce the salary costs and improve understanding of local conditions (for example, language ability and religion are prime factors), they will still suffer from some of the drawbacks of expatriate employment and in rare instances will be even less acceptable than expatriates who are regarded as divorced from potential rivalry.

American companies have in many instances used a pool of South American management to staff Southern Hemisphere operations. However, political disputes throughout the region, such as the rivalries between Argentina and Chile, Argentina and Paraguay, Guatemala and Belize, often create problems in implementing this policy.

Creating an international management team

7. Definition.
Some transnational companies have moved towards

the creation of an international management group by which individuals are recruited from all overseas countries in which the company operates and then moved to appropriate posts.

8. Advantages of an international management team.

(*a*) It provides the company with management expertise in depth on the problems and opportunities of international trade. Management at senior level within any country will tend to take a more international view because they will have had experience of other markets and take the 'international' rather than 'national' view of any new product or service proposal.

(*b*) It provides a powerful recruitment tool and method of retaining management who are able to see a promotion path extending beyond the local subsidiary.

(*c*) It will have the effect of creating a similar management philosophy and firm individual links within what may be a far-flung industrial organization.

9. Disadvantages of an international management team.

(*a*) It will be very difficult to harmonize payment and benefit structures on a world-wide basis, especially where an international management group is only part of a national pay structure.

Company cars are part of the British business scene. Year-end bonuses are common in Germany and France, but rare in other overseas countries. Pension and schooling provision vary from nation to nation.

(*b*) The creation of an international management team will require the company to maintain a detailed and comprehensive personnel function at head office which may be seen as interfering with local subsidiary activities.

(*c*) The management turnover caused by the response of individuals to continual changes in location may have the effect of reducing management diversity – a single type will survive (*homo agminis* – moving man). This effect is felt most in the upper middle to senior management grades within any multinational organization – individuals who are the most important in implementing a central corporate strategy.

Factors influencing the choice of staffing system

10. The most important factors.

(*a*) Importance of the investment: the international firm will naturally try to employ the best available individuals where there is an important investment. This is especially true in certain areas:

   (*i*) New product development.

   (*ii*) Major sources of profit for the company.

(*b*) The nature of the organization structure (*see* Chapter 22).

(*c*) Local market conditions including the following:

   (*i*) Labour laws.

   (*ii*) The availability of local management of a sufficient level of expertise.

   (*iii*) Political stability and nationalistic tendencies, including the likelihood of nationalization or expropriation.

   (*iv*) Cost of employing local nationals.

   (*v*) Communications: the ability of the head office to communicate effectively with the subsidiary will affect the nature of the individuals employed. For example, isolated operations may demand more senior personnel than those that are easily monitored.

(*d*) Management style: the way in which the company regards its international subsidiaries will have a central role in the way in which they are staffed, regardless of the degree of centralization or decentralization that is present within the organization structure.

> Harold Geneen, the President of International Telephone and Telegraph, had a fundamental effect on the nature of the management that were recruited for one of the most diverse and widespread transnationals. Loyalty to the company became a vital promotion criteria.

(*e*) The length of time that the subsidiary has been established: there is a tendency, as previously mentioned, for the management structure to change as the subsidiary becomes well established with the recruitment of more local staff.

(*f*) The nature of ownership of the foreign subsidiary: different policies may be followed where the company is involved in a joint

23. Staffing the international firm

venture or where there is a substantial local shareholding. Most multinationals, however, appear not to regard this as being of major importance if the management control (whether by management contract or equity) remains vested in them.

(*g*) International links: where the overseas subsidiary is acting as a manufacturing centre for overseas markets it will be important for the overseas company to employ individuals that have international rather than national experience.

(*h*) Complexity of product. Where the product has a high percentage of technical content it will be important for the overseas company to ensure that the standards of production are maintained by employing individuals who have a high degree of knowledge of the production process.

(*i*) The nature of the industry: certain industries are much more likely to experience the transfer of management between countries than others. Service industries with their need to provide a high personnel element (*see* Chapter 24) will tend to require a higher level of local personnel purely as a result of the business in which they are operating.

11. Staffing and company strategy. Many major companies will develop a personnel strategy as a fundamental part of their overseas development. By recruiting local staff and training them as part of their international investment programme companies can further develop their image as a major contributor to the wealth and skills of the overseas market in which they invest.

> IBM has for many years followed the tradition of maintaining full employment within their workforce, and not laying off staff or closing factories on a world-wide basis. This policy has helped them to become a more acceptable employer in many overseas markets, even though this policy was under threat in the mid-1980s.

12. Future trends in staffing the multinational company. Rapid developments in communications and data-processing capability are likely to mean that international companies will rely increasingly on local management for the vast majority of their staffing requirements, with a very small percentage of senior management being moved internationally between one subsidiary and another.

Progress test 23

1. List the alternative staffing policies available to the international firm and give the advantages and disadvantages of each. (**1–6**)
2. What is an international management team? How does it operate? (**7–9**)
3. What factors influence the choice of staffing policy? (**10–12**)

24
Marketing overseas for the service company

Introduction

1. The importance of services in international trade. A significant proportion of international trade consists of payments for services rather than goods. The United Kingdom balance of payments depends heavily on 'invisible' overseas earnings which are obtained from the main sources indicated below (excluding tourism). The decline in the contribution of the UK manufacturing sector to the share of world trade since the late 1970s has strengthened the importance of the service sector to the economy.

Service	Net receipts 1984 £ million
Shipping	1000
Airlines	400
Construction overseas	1100
Entertainment	160
Insurance, banking	5500

Other countries such as Japan and West Germany run substantial deficits on service trading – in other words they tend to import services rather than export them. For the United Kingdom therefore the overseas earnings of the service sector are becoming increasingly important with new sectors such as advertising starting to make a contribution.

Factors affecting the development of international service companies

2. Encouraging factors. Many of the features of the world econmy mentioned earlier in the book are encouraging the growth of the international service organization.

(a) *Growth requirements.* Many companies in the service sector as well as the industrial sector have reached the stage where they cannot achieve satisfactory levels of growth in their home markets either because of dominant market positions or the possibility of anti-monopoly action.

(b) *The expansion in the numbers of multinationals.* The growth in the number of multinationals has meant there has been a corresponding increase in the demand for world-wide service provision.

The strategy of the advertising agency Saatchi and Saatchi has been to develop a world-wide network to provide a global advertising service to the multinational companies such as Procter and Gamble. DHL, the air courier firm, has grown rapidly by meeting the need for rapid and secure document transfer between international firms.

(c) *The development of common information systems.* The standardization of information systems and their importance in many areas of the economy has led to a continuing increase in demand for international systems.

Business Information Systems (BIS), provides banking information systems which have world-wide applications, with over 400 sites in Europe, the Middle and Far East and North America.

(d) *Reduction in trade barriers.* The steady increase in the level of world-wide trading has meant that the number of companies able to provide global banking and financial services has increased.

(e) *Minimal distribution and ownership problems.* As a service company operates from fixed premises or provides a mobile service unit, international service companies face few distribution problems providing they can become established. Similarly, as the service cannot be patented, product infringement is not an issue that the service company will need to consider, though trade mark protection will still be important.

(f) *Reduction in cultural barriers.* The increasing harmonization in products that is occurring world wide is also reflected in an expanding market for standard international services.

The market for hire cars is an example of such a market. Hertz and Avis are two companies that have managed to exploit the worldwide business and private market for hire cars.

(g) *Increasing affluence.* The steady growth in disposable income in many of the world's economies has meant that there is more demand for travel and entertainment, much of which will be provided on an international basis.

Kuoni, the Swiss-based travel company, has developed an international market for premium-priced holidays with, for example, tours of Northern China and Venezuela.

(h) *Changing age structures.* The increasing number of elderly people throughout the world has meant an expanded demand for services such as health care.

3. Special problems in the development of international service companies. The service company, as has already been mentioned (*see* Chapter 1), faces additional problems in the definition of the marketing mix.

In addition to the main issues of price, promotion, product, and distribution, the service company has to consider carefully the implications of:

(a) People – the staff needed by the company to carry out the service.
(b) Physical – the place in which the service is provided.
(c) Process – how the service is carried out.

The interaction of all these factors can be best illustrated by the highly successful McDonald's chain. The way in which the staff operate, with rapid service and a pleasant manner, the clean and bright nature of the restaurants and the way in which the company manages the smooth production of large quantities of food, keeping

Marketing Overseas

it fresh and hot, are all elements in the company's international success.

Problems for service companies

4. Personnel issues (people) for the international service company. For the majority of service companies it will be necessary to employ a large number of local nationals when they become established overseas.

> A Hilton hotel may employ over 400 people. Of these perhaps five will be supplied as part of the management contract, the others will be largely recruited locally.

Because of this large local element, the company will have to consider the following factors:

(*a*) *Language.* Language barriers may exist that make the application of identical techniques used in the home market difficult to apply.

(*b*) *Education.* The educational qualifications of the local employees will have an effect on the skills they bring to the execution of the service.

> Familiarity with technology is an obvious example. Many services, particularly those in the financial services sector, operate via sophisticated electronic systems, which may be difficult to handle without lengthy training.

(*c*) *Attitudes towards service tasks.* Different groups will regard certain tasks as unacceptable, and this may affect the way in which the service is organized.

(*d*) *Legislation.* In common with full-scale manufacturing investment, service companies will have to implement all local legislation concerning the employment of large numbers of local nationals and this may affect manning and operating the service.

> The EEC rules on road haulage would mean that an overseas company establishing a local subsidiary would have to design depot locations and manning levels to take account of them.
> Legislation may also affect the way in which companies can operate. Safety laws in Norway allow the employees a direct

24. The service company

control over working conditions in which they operate, with employees able to halt the firm's activity.

(e) *Male/female roles in society.* In many countries the nature of the tasks that men and women can perform are different; for example, whether it is acceptable for a woman to serve at a counter may vary according to the culture.

(f) *Working conditions.* Both legislation, the cost of space, and climatic conditions will affect the nature of the working conditions that the company will need to provide.

(g) *Motivation.* The way in which the employees can be directed and encouraged will also vary from country to country.

Good service awards and badges, part of the American service sector philosophy of promoting individual performance, are not so suitable in a society such as Japan where group effort is more important.

5. Environmental (physical) factors in service development overseas.

Obviously the importance of the environment will be far greater for companies wishing to run retailing operations in overseas locations but there are a number of general issues that any service company will need to consider:

(a) *Dimensions.* The service will have to consider the issue of how it should lay out the physical environment in which the service takes place.

Hotel rooms in Japan tend to be smaller than in the United States; ceilings of retail outlets tend to be higher in France than in the United Kingdom.

(b) *Facilities.* For services involved with the consumer the nature of the facilities offered will often be adapted to meet cultural preferences.

American hotel chains began to offer rooms specially designed for the female executive in the 1980s. Similar facilities would not be appropriate in the Middle East.

(c) *Legislation.* Different countries will have different legislative control on building design in a number of areas.

(i) *Access for the disabled.* Most Western European and North American countries now specify how buildings should be designed for access.

(ii) *Safety.* Different rules will exist from country to country on provision of safety equipment and how buildings should be designed.

(d) *Availability* – hours of opening. The hours that service centres can be open will vary from country to country and often from city to city. A service can only be 'consumed' when the service is open to the public. It is in the interests of the service company to have the longest possible opening hours.

(e) *Climate.* The type of climatic conditions prevailing in the overseas market will have a considerable effect on the nature of the service offered.

> Drive-in cinemas and restaurants are common features of American and Australian leisure activity. Climatic conditions in other parts of the world make such concepts unlikely to succeed.

(f) *Sound.* Certain cultures will find background music or high levels of noise acceptable; in others the level of acceptable noise will be much lower and attempts may have to be made to minimize it by special equipment or building insulation.

(g) *Colour.* The differences in perception of colour on a country-by-country basis have already been commented on in relation to the packaging of consumer goods. Similar problems exist for the service organization that has significant contact with the public – the design of service areas will have to be carefully reviewed in relation to consumer perceptions.

(h) *Scent.* The use of scent or fragrances will also be affected by consumer attitudes which will vary from country to country.

6. Differences in the way the overseas service is carried out (process).

(a) *Acceptability of automation.* Some cultures will find the use of automated procedures acceptable (indeed for many it will be preferred). In others the ability of the service organization to apply automation will be far more limited.

Vending machines for coffee are common features of offices in the

24. The service company 257

United Kingdom and North America. They are rare in France and other countries in continental Europe.

(*b*) *Payment methods.* Different countries will have different payment systems – some relying more heavily on cash, others on credit cards and so on. This will affect the way in which the service is organized in different countries to a certain extent – for example, it will demand that a credit reference system be evolved in countries where credit sales make up a large part of overall turnover.

> Hire-purchase schemes are not common for car purchase in France and therefore do not form part of finance and bank marketing mixes in that country in contrast to the UK market where a substantial number of cars are sold by this method.

(*c*) *Acceptability of pre-packaging.* For services involving the sale of food the degree of acceptability of pre-packaging or early preparation will vary from country to country.

(*d*) *Ethical standards.* Different communities will have different views of the acceptability of certain practices which may alter the nature of the service company overseas.

> Japanese advertising agencies such as Dentsu will often represent a number of competitive accounts within the same advertising agency. In North America and Western Europe this is not considered acceptable and agencies have to resign competitive accounts after take-overs or mergers.

7. Additional barriers to entry for the service company in the international market. Apart from the problems of adapting the service to international conditions which have been discussed above, the service company operating abroad has to take account of a number of additional factors:

(*a*) *Investment and risk.* The development of a service organization overseas will demand a higher level of investment than the normal industrial or consumer goods organization. A small manufacturer of products can 'test the water' by some low-risk export method (*see* Chapter 14) thereby evaluating the problems that it is likely to encounter in the overseas market. The service organization in contrast generally faces the need to employ considerable numbers of people overseas often in expensive accomodation.

(b) *Acceptability*. Because a service is by its very nature not a unique product – it cannot be patented or protected in any way – governments are less likely to consider a foreign service company as providing a particularly valuable form of investment in the country, and are likely to apply especial constraints on their development and/or the transfer of profit out of the country.

Banking regulations in many countries prevent foreign companies from establishing more than single branches in major cities, and there are strict controls on the way in which these branches can operate.

(c) *Fluctuations in demand*. Service companies face the problem of having to cope with fluctuations in demand in all markets. Where an international network is established to provide a service the various constituent parts may suffer greater fluctuations in demand than a national system.

Airlines with international networks face particular problems of this nature. They need to ensure that the national network that they run in the home market has a capacity closely related to the demands of the international network.

Solutions for service companies

8. Minimizing the problems of expansion overseas.

(a) Training: comprehensive and standard training procedures should be introduced to ensure that all employees maintain a common level of achievement throughout the international network.

(b) Planning and information systems: the international service company by maintaining sophisticated information systems will be more able to deal with fluctuations in demand.

(c) Maximizing the use of technology: replacing personnel functions with those provided by equipment will minimize the degree of variability in the level of service provided.

(d) Maximizing the return from management expertise: service companies can exploit most effectively the concept of the management contract and the use of franchising in overseas markets (*see* Chapter 16) to minimize the total investment overseas.

It is estimated that one in three new retail outlets in the United States is now a franchised operation. This trend is likely to gather momentum throughout the major developed world markets.

(*e*) Concentrating on key physical features which can easily be adapted within widely varying international locations.

Laura Ashley has successfully developed store groups both in Europe and North America. Their store design concentrates on emphasizing the nature of the product rather than producing an overall Laura Ashley store 'image'.

Progress test 24

1. How important is the international service sector for the UK economy? (**1**)
2. Account for the development of international service organizations. (**2**)
3. What are the particular problems concerning the development of overseas service companies? (**3–7**)
4. How can the international service company minimize the problems of international expansion? (**8**)

Appendix 1
Case studies

1. BIS in Scandinavia

Background. The nature of the world-wide banking industry is rapidly changing, bringing with it both problems and opportunities.

Since the early 1970s the emphasis has been on de-regulation, reducing the role of governments in the banking area. The result of this is that there has been a steady increase in the amount of competition that banks face from overseas branches opening in their home markets, and banks have also started to compete in other areas in their home markets such as the savings, personal loans and securities markets.

The growth of competition, entry into new fields, and the steady growth in world trade (opening up other opportunities for funding and money market activities) has led to a continuing expansion in information transfer not only between different operating areas of a single bank but also between banks in different countries.

As a result of this expansion in data transfer there has been a dramatic growth in the need for computers and computer technology to handle the increased data requirements which has spawned a new industry, that of banking support services.

Within this market BIS (Business Intelligence Services) has developed a world-wide depth of experience for supplying software for a range of banking needs.

The market. The data processing demands of the banks depend largely on their size and complexity of operation.

Three sectors can be discerned as currently existing:

(1) *Small business volume.* Banks with limited range of operations and/or low profit margins where sophisticated software is not considered a cost effective investment.

(2) *Medium business volume.* This comprises the head offices of medium-sized banks with some international exposure. Sophisticated control systems are vital for accurate control of day-to-day operations.

(3) *Large international banks.* These are the major international banks with very large national networks and extensive overseas exposure. Because of the complexity of the operations these organizations will tend to develop their own computer systems.

In total there are estimated to be 6000 banks world-wide that would fall into these three categories. The main companies supplying these three sectors include:

(a) *Small banks*: NCR, Burroughs, ICL, Wang, Nixdorf with a range of micro-and minicomputer-based systems.

(b) *Medium banks*: Italian International Bank, KAPITI, ARBAT, BIS, with DEC and IBM minicomputer-based systems.

(c) *Large international banks*: Mantech, Hogan, Internet largely IBM mainframe based.

The price of each system was complex. Though suppliers offered standard packages for both small- and medium-sized banking operations, the configuration of the hardware in each case meant that pricing varied from contract to contract.

BIS, while well-established with 400 installed sites spread worldwide (200 in Europe and the Middle East, 100 in North and South America and 100 in the Pacific region), faces competition from the lower end of the market with the increasing power and sophistication of microcomputer systems and from the application programmes on mainframe systems falling in price as the development costs are written off.

Continued international development is a central part of the BIS strategy along with product development, and new market opportunities are investigated as and when they occur. Of the market opportunities that presented themselves in the early 1980s the Scandinavian market was one of the most interesting.

Scandinavia

The Scandinavian market (Finland, Norway, Denmark, Sweden) up until the early 1980s was rigorously controlled with few overseas banks allowed to set up branches. The pace of de-regulation and overseas banking penetration varied on a market-to-market basis.

Finland

Population: 4.8 million.
Urbanization: 60%.
Commercial language: English.

Local banks: 3 controlling 90% of commercial banking.
Foreign banks: 5 overseas banks have limited representation.
Degree of regulation: Still fairly high.
Specific banking regulations: Limited.

Denmark

Population: 5.1 million.
Urbanization: 98%.
Commercial language: English.

Local banks: 3 controlling 60% of commercial banking, 5 others of smaller size. There is a large savings bank sector (similar to the UK building society movement).
Foreign banks: 9 overseas banks have expanding local representation.
Degree of regulation: Decreasing since 1975.
Specific banking regulations: Limited.

Norway

Population: 4.1 million.
Urbanization: 55%.
Commercial language: English.

Local banks: 21 of which the three largest deal internationally.
Foreign banks: 9 foreign banks represented with slow introduction of more branches.
Degree of regulation: Considerably reduced since 1984 which allowed the entry of foreign banks into the exchange and securities sector.
Specific banking regulations: Limited.

Sweden
Population: 8.3 million.
Urbanization: 90%
Commercial language: Swedish.

Local banks: 8 major Swedish banks but 20 smaller operations, and well developed savings and loan institutions.
Foreign banks: None currently established.
Degree of regulation: Legislation passed in 1985 permitted the establishment of overseas bank subsidiaries in Sweden.
Specific banking regulations: Currently fairly extensive but likely to be increasingly liberalized.

The problem facing BIS was to determine whether there existed sufficient business to justify further market investigation and where activity should be concentrated for market development.

2. DLW and the USA

Background. DLW is the largest flooring manufacturer in West Germany, with overall sales of around £200 million of which 77% were domestic sales and 23% were achieved overseas. Turnover had stagnated from 1978 to 1983. Its product range included tufted carpets which made up around 20% of total turnover, non-textile floorings including PVC and linoleum which accounted for 70% of group sales, and rubber flooring, accessories and artificial leather making up the remainder. DLW is the brand leader throughout Europe in two particular sectors, linoleum with 60% market share, and vinyl both cushioned and hard, with around 20% of the market.

DLW operated in both main segments of the market – the contract market which involves the sale of large quantities of floor covering (more than 1000 sq. metres) to housing projects, schools and other institutions, and the retail market where maximum sales were of the order of 500 sq. metres.

Within the European market overall demand for floor coverings remains static though there has been slow growth in certain areas, such as linoleum which is becoming more acceptable for contract flooring projects. In order to increase sales and profitability DLW were actively seeking overseas business especially in growth markets such as the USA.

The flooring market in the USA

(1) *Trends*. The total market in the USA for textile flooring products was around $5 billion in 1984, with retail comprising 55% of the total and contract 45%, with an estimated sale of 1.070 million sq. yards of flooring, or approximately 350 sq. miles per year. Large-scale investment in machinery had made the USA the leading world textile carpet manufacturer with impressive economies of scale. The main change in the market was the considerable expansion of the carpet tile market which by 1985 accounted for 15% of the total contract market, as the importance of flexibility in under-floor electrical and fibre optic ducting becomes more and more important in the office environment.

The market for non-textile products was smaller at around $1.3 billion, with an estimated 75% going to the contract market and 25% to the domestic market: 75% of the sales are in rolls and 25% in tiles. The steady increase in the use of computers was also having an impact in this sector with a growing demand for non-conductive tiles. Little if any linoleum was sold though it was possible that the increasing attraction of 'natural' products might lead to wider scale development. The market is highly competitive and only two companies – Armstrong and Congoleum – are profitable due to their concentration on the retail market and heavy advertising budgets. The contract market, as might be expected, was highly competitive on price. The retail market had shown volume growth of 23% since 1981; the contract market of 37%.

(2) *Structure*. Due to the wide geographical area of the United States the market can be split into six main sectors, as shown on p. 265.

The geographical division of the United States is also reflected in the nature of the distribution network. There are very few national distributors of flooring materials, especially in the contract market. Retailers with national coverage such as Sears and Penny's operate to an extent in the contract market, and together with specialist carpet retailers provide a measure of national distribution in the retail sector.

Area	Centre	Percentage of market
North East	New York	20%
South East	Atlanta	10%
South	Houston	5%
West	Los Angeles	10%
Central I	Chicago	20%
Central II	Cleveland	20%

Trade fairs and permanent exhibition sites in the main centres were seen by some of the major manufacturers as crucial to becoming established in the market.

DLW Strategy. DLW decided that they would attack the US market by:

(1) Appointing agents rather than setting up their own operation. They appointed 13 agents throughout the USA.

(2) Supplying to order and not maintaining stock within the mainland USA. The demands of the US market meant that they had to introduce new colours and patterns.

(3) Concentrating on PVC and linoleum products particularly in the contract sector.

(4) Establishing a premium price position in the market at 50% above the competition to provide a high level of promotional support for the distributors.

(5) Concentrating on personal trade contact rather than investing in large-scale advertising expenditure.

DLW progress

Year	Index of sales	%US market
1981	100	0.00092
1982	306	0.00272
1983	373	0.00312
1984	884	0.00659

80% of sales comprised PVC rolls; 17% linoleum. Progress was however significantly below expectations at around 30% of forecast.

Re-assessment. By 1984 DLW were considering what changes they needed to consider for their international marketing policy.

3. A tale of two companies

Hemichem. Hemichem is a small, UK-based chemical manufacturer specializing in diagnostic laboratory chemicals for the medical market. It currently has two offices: a head office in Norfolk, and a sales office in London because of the necessary contact with the main Department of Health and Social Security offices. Even though it is still a very young company – it has only been in existence five years – and it operates with very few staff, the company believed that the uniqueness of its major product, a range of diagnostic kits for simple testing of problems in the blood, would open up potentially lucrative markets overseas.

Hemichem has therefore appointed an overseas sales manager, Jeffrey Saunders, who conforms with the company's tight staffing policy by working without back-up support most of the time. Nevertheless, important successes were achieved, with the establishment of markets in Ireland, Holland, Denmark and Germany: all markets where language posed no problems, for Saunders speaks only English. Attendance at medical exhibitions was seen as a key element in this early success and Saunders had to depend on support from the Hemichem UK staff at these events. This approach had worked reasonably well however, and it was duly applied early in 1985 at a major exhibition near Marseilles. Here a medical services group, Services Medicales, placed an initial order for the Hemichem range and expressed an interest in acting as distributor for the product in France. Saunders promised that he would supply a full and comprehensive briefing document to Services Medicales on his return to the United Kingdom.

Services Medicales. Based near Orange in Southern France, Services Medicales was a small operation, managed by its owner and founder M. Bouvier who spoke little or no English. His main customers and interests were independent clinics in the South of France but he was also developing substantial business in the north of Italy and had a brother-in-law that ran a similar company in French-speaking Switzerland. Within the South of France his contacts were very wide. So although the initial order for Hemichem was small, potentially substantial business could be developed through Services Medicales. However, to date Services Medicales had little experience of dealing with companies based outside France.

Events following the Marseilles exhibition. To M. Bouvier's surprise he heard no more from Hemichem following the placement of his order at the Marseilles exhibition. The promised full documentation and a price list had not arrived since Saunders' return to the UK. Six weeks later, M. Bouvier wrote to Hemichem in French. Receiving no reply he telephoned on five occasions but was either unable to get any reply from the London office (his sole address for contact with the company) or was connected with an assistant who spoke no French and failed to take a message. Finally he decided to approach the local Chamber of Commerce for assistance.

Two telexes were sent to Hemichem by the Chamber of Commerce. A reply came one month later, apologizing for the delay caused by the absence of Jeffrey Saunders abroad and the need to redirect all telexes from the Hemichem sales office in London – where the telex was located – to the head office in Norfolk.

Two more telexes were despatched on behalf of M. Bouvier finalizing the Services Medicales order, requesting the detailed documentation promised at the earlier exhibition and inviting the Hemichem export manager to France for a meeting. Again there was no reply and the Chamber of Commerce duly phoned the UK company. An acutely embarassed Saunders promised to despatch the goods within a week. Two weeks later the company had still failed to find a freight forwarder that could handle the products to the South of France and were forced to approach the company that transported goods for Services Medicales, which had a UK associate. The additional cost involved was substantial. Further difficulties then arose when the transporter informed Services Medicales that Hemichem had been unable to release the goods on their first appearance at the head office.

Documentation delays. On arrival at Calais the goods were refused entry into France as the appropriate EEC forms for the shipment of medical goods had not all been included and those that were had not been translated into French. Hemichem were eventually able to find a clearing agent via the freight-forwarding company that would be able to gain the release of the products providing that the company was prepared to indemnify the freight-forwarder against possible import violations. This was eventually agreed and the goods received clearance.

Banking delays. Hemichem's standard payment procedure for new accounts – accepted by Services Medicales – was by irrevocable letter of credit at 30 days. The small branch of the Credit Agricole, with which Services Medicales dealt, decided to pay by bank guarantee instead of letter of credit. There was in fact little difference in the two methods of payment except that UK banks are more familiar with the latter and, in addition, Credit Agricole had omitted the correct interbank verification code. Its only English speaker was on maternity leave.

Banking created other delays since all telexes from the French bank had to be sent from Southampton via London for verification as the Hemichem banker, a branch of one of the major clearing banks, was without a telex. By now Services Medicales was becoming increasingly anxious to take delivery of the goods. A further telex about the urgency of the problem was now sent but three days later the UK clearing bank claimed not to have received it. Refusing to look further into the matter, the UK bank maintained that it was the responsibility of the buyer.

Conclusion. Both Hemichem and Services Medicales began to accuse each other of bad faith. The goods remained in a warehouse in Orange and due to their short shelf life eventually had to be destroyed. There was no insurance.

Appendix 2
Examination technique

Revision

1. Introduction. All students have their own methods of revising and you will certainly have yours. It is likely, however, that you will benefit by spending a few minutes reading this short guide to revision.

Your revision should have three main aims:

(*a*) complete understanding of the subject;
(*b*) retention and recall of the subject;
(*c*) the ability to explain and apply the subject.

Understanding is the key to both the learning and use of a subject. Thus it is understanding which is crucial to examination success and your revision should be designed above all to reinforce understanding. No matter how much a subject may interest you when you actually study it, learning it for an examination can at best be tedious and at worst boring. You must try to lessen this effect.

2. Revision programme. Tedium in revision is caused mainly by reading the same original notes over and over again. This is also unproductive. It is far better to adopt a *positive revision* programme, one which uses your time profitably and enables you to teach yourself. Your Handbook is the perfect basis for such a programme.

Revision should be done a chapter at a time. Try adopting the following sequence.

(*a*) *Re-read* the chapter thoroughly.
(*b*) *Make revision notes*. These can consist of no more than the headings in the text with a very brief note about important principles.

270 Appendix 2

Take each note in turn and try to recall and explain the subject matter. If you can, proceed to the next; if you cannot, look in your Handbook. By doing this, you will revise, test your knowledge and spend your time profitably by concentrating your revision on those aspects of the subject with which you are least familiar. In addition, you will have an excellent last-minute revision aid.

(c) Construct a chart for each topic using the headings in your Handbook. Many people respond well to diagrammatic explanations and summaries which provide an extremely quick and efficient means of revision. You need to think how best to construct them and in doing so you teach yourself and better understand the subject.

Two tips: do not try to include too much on each diagram; and do not try to economize on paper. The impact and usefulness of a diagram depends very much on its visual simplicity. The same applies to revision notes.

(d) Prepare concise explanations of key principles that you are likely to need so that during the examination you do not have to think about how to explain something which you probably know well but cannot easily put into words there and then.

(e) Answer the progress tests again. You should find a significant improvement in the number of questions that you can answer immediately. This exercise will primarily test your ability to recall and explain facts.

(f) Plan answers to the specimen examination questions in the Handbook and any others set by the relevant examining body. Planning answers is often a more useful exercise than actually writing the answer out in full. In planning you have in effect answered the question and writing it out is a largely mechanical exercise. If, however, you feel that you need the practice in essay writing, answer some fully.

Read the notes on answering questions (*see* **3** below) before planning any answers.

The examination

3. Examination technique.

(a) Read the examination instructions carefully.

(b) Read through the questions and provisionally mark which ones to answer. Take care over your choice. An apparently simple question might have a hidden twist – do not get caught out.

Similarly, never decide to answer a question which is in two or more parts on the strength of the first part alone. Make sure that you can answer *all* parts.

(c) Make sure you have selected the right number of questions – you get no extra marks for answering more!

(d) Remember that the first 50 per cent of the marks for any question is the easier to earn. Unless you are working in complete ignorance, you will always earn more marks per minute while answering a new question than while continuing to answer one that is more than half done. So you can earn many more marks by half-completing two answers than by completing either one individually.

(e) Concentrate on displaying your knowledge. There is almost always one question that you are not happy about but nevertheless need to attempt. In answer to such a question put down all you *do* know, and then devote the unused time to improving some other answer. Certainly you will not get full marks by doing this, but nor will you if you fill your page with nonsense. By spending the saved time on another answer you will at least be gaining the odd mark or so.

(f) Plan all your answers – this is absolutely vital.

(g) If time is running out put down your answer in the form of notes, making sure that every part of the question has some answer – no matter how short – that summarizes the key elements. Don't worry about shortage of time: it is more often a sign of knowing too much than too little.

(h) Check through your answers. A few minutes doing this can eliminate many minor errors and give a final 'polish' to your answers.

4. Specific issues for Marketing Overseas.

(a) Nature of the questions. Some questions will be of a 'general' nature, requiring broad comment about a range of issues, while others will be more detailed and require specific answers on a limited area (*see* Appendix 3). You *must* identify in your answer plan the range of issues involved in each question.

(b) Use of up-to-date material. The international environment is changing continually and you should follow issues in such publications as the *Economist*, the *Financial Times* and the *Wall Street Journal* so as to be able to provide up-to-date examples in the examination.

Appendix 3
Examination questions

Chapter 1
1. What do you think are the key differences between national and international marketing? Which are the most important?
2. 'Marketing is all about defining opportunities.' Comment on the advantages and disadvantages of the international marketplace in the light of this statement.
3. How important is the distinction between export trading, export marketing and international marketing?
4. What is the marketing mix? How will the international environment alter the emphasis placed by the company on different elements?

Chapter 2
1. 'International institutions have greatly helped the development of world trade'. Comment on the importance of their activities for the multinational company.
2. What issues underline the trends in UK international trade and what implications do they have for international marketing?
3. Discuss how government assistance can help the international company. For a named country discuss how assistance is provided and how in your opinion it could be improved.

Chapter 3
1. 'Globalization is a much over-rated concept.' Discuss.
2. The major world markets are becoming increasingly the preserve of big players. How will this affect the new company expanding overseas?

3. Discuss the implications of international industrial concentration on the marketing policies of small, high-technology firms.

Chapter 4
1. 'Multinationals have too much influence on world trade.' Do you think that this is the case? What action should be taken to minimize their influence?
2. Compare and contrast the marketing problems of the multinational with those of the national company.
3. What global trends have influenced the development of multinationals? Which are still most relevant?

Chapter 5
1. 'Segmentation is the key to marketing success both at home and overseas.' Discuss the relevance of this statement for (*a*) the manufacturer of ball bearings; and (*b*) the perfume house.
2. 'Cultural barriers pose few problems for the international marketeer.' Discuss.
3. Which do you consider the most effective way of segmenting overseas markets and why?
4. There is too much emphasis on economic differences between markets as a means of defining international market opportunity and not enough on social and cultural differences. Do you agree?

Chapter 6
1. 'Too many strategies are simplistic.' Evaluate the complications of international strategic development.
2. What are the essential components of an international strategic plan?
3. What are barriers to entry? Why are they important to strategic planning and how would they be likely to affect (*a*) a bank; (*b*) a pharmaceutical firm?
4. Concentration of activity in key markets is an essential part of overseas strategic development. How accurate do you find this statement to be?

Chapter 7
1. How useful are strategic models to the international firm as an aid to investment decision-making?

2. Compare the risks faced by a firm such as IBM in investing overseas with those of a shoe manufacturer such as Bata. How would this affect their international manufacturing policy?
3. World-wide a company manufactures: (a) vending machines; (b) sophisticated machine tools; (c) industrial lubricants. What risk factors will each of these products have associated with them and how would they affect the options on market development?
4. South Africa and Argentina have both suffered from political problems in the 1980s. Compare and contrast these countries in terms of risk evaluation for overseas investment.

Chapter 8
1. A company manufacturing measuring equipment with a turnover of £5 million is considering overseas expansion. What are the key issues it should consider and how should it collect information to make the appropriate decisions?
2. What are the main shortcomings of statistical data available to the firm planning overseas expansion and how can the problems thus caused be minimized?
3. Why is information crucial to the international marketeer?
4. Comment on the problems of carrying out market research overseas. How can the many pitfalls best be circumvented?

Chapter 9
1. How should a company maintain a marketing information system? What are the key differences between the national and international company?
2. What are the most serious limitations of forecasting systems for the international company? Discuss the advantages and disadvantages of the available forecasting techniques.
3. 'Information for short-term action, rather than long-term planning, is the most important feature of the information system in established international companies.' How will this affect the marketing department?

Chapter 10
1. Product improvement, adaptation, or diversification. What problems relating to product change face the international firm?

2. What are the advantages and disadvantages of product standardization for the international firm?
3. How will the international firm be able to develop new products effectively?

Chapter 11
1. Outline the problems faced by the international firm in packaging its goods. How can they best be overcome?
2. Patent and trade mark protection pose many problems for the international firm. Describe the problems.
3. How will servicing and guarantee issues affect international product policy?

Chapter 12
1. 'The total distribution concept is a vital element in overseas marketing.' Do you agree?
2. Why is the motivation of intermediaries so important in international marketing and how can it best be achieved?
3. What are the strategic issues in distribution channel design? How would they affect: (*a*) an international market research agency; and (*b*) a manufacturer of furniture?
4. Overseas distribution is a compromise between cost and control. Discuss.

Chapter 13
1. How does the nature of physical distribution relate to international market strategy? Identify the key issues.
2. How should an international firm evaluate its physical distribution systems?
3. Discuss the developing role of freeports in the development of international trade. How should overseas countries develop the freeport concept to help in trade development?

Chapter 14
1. Why has the role of export houses declined in the 1980s? Evaluate where they might be used in the development of international trade.
2. What is a buying house? For what type of manufacturer would

they be most important as a channel for overseas development and what factors would they need to consider?

3. Discuss the advantages and disadvantages of different methods of indirect exporting.

4. Co-operative exporting is a little-used technique. What are the advantages and disadvantages of this method compared with other distribution channels?

Chapter 15

1. Defining the exact role of overseas principals is a vital part of the overseas distribution process. Discuss.

2. Direct selling is too little used in overseas distribution. Do you agree?

3. In certain Western European markets your distributors of children's toys are continuing to lose market share. What alternative distribution methods should you consider and what implications would they have for marketing policy?

4. Technological expertise is an increasingly saleable commodity in the world market. What issues confront the firm in maintaining control while maximizing the rate of return?

Chapter 16

1. Do you consider that the role of joint ventures has been overstated in international marketing? Comment on the advantages and disadvantages of joint venture operations.

2. The nature of the investment reflects market conditions. Relate the role of joint ventures, industrial co-operation arrangements and wholly-owned subsidiaries to strategic issues.

3. One in three new businesses in the United States is franchised. To what extent will franchising be important for the future of international trade development and what do you think are its limitations?

4. You as a manufacturer of bulk chemicals are approached by a major industrial company in a Third World country (in which you currently do no business) with a local manufacture proposal. What factors would you need to consider and what is likely to be the best arrangement?

Examination questions 277

Chapter 17
1. Standardization of media campaigns is one of the most difficult issues in international marketing. Discuss.
2. Strategic issues in promotional planning must be reflected in the nature of the promotional material used. Evaluate this statement for the computer company developing overseas.
3. A firm sells both industrial batteries and processed food overseas. What implications would the differing products have on the type of promotional technique employed?

Chapter 18
1. The importance of public relations in the development of the overseas company is often overstated. Evaluate the role of public relations for both the small and the large company and determine its overall importance in the communications process.
2. Exhibitions are crucial for many business enterprises overseas. Assess their importance and comment on the nature of the pitfalls that exist and how they may be overcome.
3. You are offered a number of possible in-store promotional deals over the next twelve months. Due to budget restrictions you are unable to take up more than two out of the six offered. How will you choose between the options available?

Chapter 19
1. 'Linguists with bags of samples.' Discuss the key differences between selling in the home market to selling overseas.
2. In what specific areas of company activity and for what products will the role of the export sales manager be most important?
3. How should the international company determine the number of sales managers to carry out the overseas sales activity?

Chapter 20
1. Why is an understanding of pricing strategy crucial to the profitable development of international business? What issues need to be considered?
2. Government action is crucial to price setting, particularly for the multinational company. Discuss the role of government policy in the development of a pricing strategy.

3. What is a differential pricing policy? Why should firms adopt it and what implications does it have for international development?

Chapter 21
1. Why is an understanding of terms of trade so important to the international company? Discuss their role in the development of trade.
2. The importance of counter-trading has steadily expanded. Explain why this should be so and what implications this trend has for the international company.
3. International financial control is vital in the development of multinational companies. Explain how this is achieved and how it will affect the international trading position of the multinationals.

Chapter 22
1. Good organizational structure is essential for the implementation of marketing policies. Discuss.
2. A company manufactures both photocopiers and cameras worldwide. What implications would this diverse product range have for organizational planning?
3. Decentralization or centralization? What are the advantages or disadvantages of the two approaches for the international company?

Chapter 23
1. The costs of manning the international firm can be a major overhead expense. Discuss the issues involved.
2. How will the company strategy and the nature of its products affect the way it recruits staff internationally?
3. What do you think is the key role of the international management team?

Chapter 24
1. Benetton, the Italian fashion wear retailer, has successfully expanded overseas. What limitations facing the development of services overseas will it have overcome?
2. It has often been considered that the 4 Ps of marketing – price, promotion, place and product – are inadequate to define the marketing issues of a service company. How accurate is this statement in relation to the international service company?

Examination questions

3. Service companies are becoming increasingly international. Discuss the ways in which they can effectively expand overseas and the features of international trade that are leading to this growth.

Appendix 4
Major world economies and turnovers of multinationals, 1984

Country	GNP $ billion (excluding oil)	Company	Nationality	£000 million
USA	3628	Exxon (Esso)	USA	83.6
Japan	1233	Shell	UK/Neth	61
Germany	616	General Motors	USA	55
France	496	AT&T	USA	51
UK	426	Mitsubishi	Japan	46
Italy	352	Mitsui	Japan	44
Canada	334	Mobil	USA	43
Australia	172	Itoh	Japan	39
Spain	160	BP	UK	38
Brazil	160	Marubeni	Japan	36
Netherlands	123	Sumimoto	Japan	35
Sweden	96	Ford	USA	33
Switzerland	92	IBM	USA	32
Belgium	76	Texaco	USA	29
Austria	65	Sears	USA	26.5
Norway	55	Dupont	USA	26
Denmark	55	Nissho	Japan	25
India	55	Chevron	USA	21
South Korea	50	Gulf	USA	21
Greece	39	Standard Oil	USA	20
Turkey	35	GEC	USA	20
Finland	22	Atlantic/ Richfield	USA	19
Mexico	18	ENI	Italy	18
Eire	17	Toyota	Japan	15
Saudi Arabia	17	IRI	Italy	14
New Zealand	15	Occidental	USA	14
Indonesia	15	K-Mart	USA	14

Index

advertising agency, 184
   selection of, 185–6
agents (*see* also export agencies),
   types of, 140
   advantages of, 141
   disadvantages of, 141–2

BCG strategic model, 65
branding, 104–5

cash flow, *see* pricing
communication
   definition, 173
   distribution, 173
   issues in, 174–6
   standardization, 180–3
   strategy, 176–7
contract manufacture 167–8

direct export, *see* export (direct)
direct mail, 153–4
direct sales, 152–3
distribution channels (*see* also export agencies,
    export (direct), licensing, franchising,
    communication),
   definition, 111
   importance of, 112–5
   intermediaries in, 115–6
   international, 111–2

282 Index

    maintaining, 118-9
    strategies and, 117-8
distribution (physical),
    packaging for, 122-3
    total concept, 121-2
    stock control, 129-30
    warehousing 128-9
    transport and, 123-8
distributors (*see also* export agencies),
    advantages, 142-3
    disadvantages, 143
    motivating, 150-2

export agencies,
    advantages of, 132-3
    buying offices, 134-5
    confirming houses, 134
    cooperative ventures, 136-8
    disadvantages of, 133-4
    international trading companies, 136
    importance of, 132
    specialist, 135-6
    types of, 131-2
    wholesalers, 134
export (direct),
    agreements with agents and distributors, 148-50
    contact with agents and distributors, 146-8
    defining requirements, 144-5
    evaluation of agents and distributors, 146
    finding agents and distributors, 143-6
    distribution issues, 138-9

forecasting, 83-6 (*see also* marketing strategy),
    qualitative, 86-9
franchising, 160-2

GEC strategic model, 66-7
globalization, 22 (*see also* international environment,
    international trade, product standardization,
    communication standardization)
    implications of, 30-31
    and international industrial concentration, 24-9

reasons for, 29–30

industrial co-operation, 156
information,
  choosing research, 78–9
  defining requirements, 70
  external, 75–6
  importance of, 69
  shortcomings in, 76
  specific research, 77
  structures, 72–3
international activity,
  development of, 6–8
international environment,
  importance of, 2–6
  problems of, 6
international marketing,
  definition, 6
international trade (see also UK trade, globalization),
  developed world and, 11
  developing countries and, 10–11
  foreign investment and, 4, 23–4
  GNP, 11
  illegal, 17–18
  nature of, 12
  structure, 13–17
  trends in, 10

joint ventures, 163–4

licensing,
  advantages of, 158
  disadvantages of, 159
  distribution channel, 159–60
  issues in, 157–8

management contracts, 162
market research, see information
marketing,
  definition, 1 (see also international marketing)
  mix, 1, 199–200
  role of, 1

marketing strategy,
  constraints on, 51–9
  objectives of, 50
  options, 61
  production and, 67–8
  risk and, 61–3
  strategic decisions, 49
  strategic models, 61–3
multinationals (*see also* export agencies – international trading companies)
  controls on, 36–8
  definition, 32
  development of, 33–4
  financing, 228–30
  future of, 38
  organization, *see* organization
  types of, 32–3

organization,
  basic features, 232–3
  importance of, 232
  multinational, 239–41
  stages in, 233–9
overseas local assembly, 168
overseas manufacture, 170–1

packaging, 101–4 (*see also* distribution (physical))
pricing,
  cash flow, 217–18
  currency aspects, 215–17
  factors affecting, 209–12
  legal aspects, 213–15
  strategy, 202–8
product life cycle, 63
products,
  abandonment, 92–4
  development, 97
  extension, 97
  new product development, 99–100
  options for, 91–4
  protection, 105–7
  standardization, 94–6

Index

    warranties, 107–9
promotion, *see* sales promotion
public relations, *see* sales promotion

sales management,
    marketing mix, 199–200 (*see also* services)
    role of manager, 200–203
    size of salesforce, 201–2
    skills, 204
sales promotion
    definition, 188
    importance, 188
    implementation, 189
    couponing, 190–1
    exhibitions, 191–5
    public relations, 195–7
segmentation,
    approaches to, 45–8
    definition, 39
    importance of, 39–40
    in different markets, 43–4
    problems of, 41–2
services (*see also* franchising),
    importance, 251
    development of, 252–3
    problems in, 253–8
staffing,
    expatriate, 242–5
    factors affecting, 247–9
    international management team, 246–7
    local nationals, 245–6
    third country nationals, 246–7
standardization, *see* globalization, product, communication, packaging
strategy, *see* marketing strategy, pricing, communication

UK trade, 18–20

M&E Handbooks

Law

'A' Level Law/B Jones
Basic Law/L B Curzon
Cases in Banking Law/P A Gheerbrant, D Palfreman
Cases in Company Law/M C Oliver
Cases in Contract Law/W T Major
Commercial and Industrial Law/A R Ruff
Company Law/M C Oliver, E Marshall
Constitutional and Administrative Law/I N Stevens
Consumer Law/M J Leder
Conveyancing Law/P H Kenny, C Bevan
Criminal Law/L B Curzon
English Legal History/L B Curzon
Equity and Trusts/L B Curzon
Family Law/P J Pace
General Principles of English Law/P W D Redmond, J Price, I N Stevens
Jurisprudence/L B Curzon
Labour Law/M Wright, C J Carr
Land Law/L B Curzon
Landlord and Tenant/J M Male
Law of Banking/D Palfreman
Law of Evidence/L B Curzon
Law of Torts/J G M Tyas
Law of Trusts/L B Curzon
Meetings: Their Law and Practice/L Hall, P Lawton, E Rigby
Mercantile Law/P W D Redmond, R G Lawson
Private International Law/A W Scott
Sale of Goods/W T Major
The Law of Contract/W T Major
Town and Country Planning Law/A M Williams

Business and Management

Advanced Economics/G L Thirkettle
Advertising/F Jefkins
Applied Economics/E Seddon, J D S Appleton
Basic Economics/G L Thirkettle
Business Administration/L Hall
Business and Financial Management/B K R Watts
Business Organisation/R R Pitfield
Business Mathematics/L W T Stafford
Business Systems/R G Anderson
Business Typewriting/S F Parks
Computer Science/J K Atkin
Data Processing Vol 1: Principles and Practice/R G Anderson
Data Processing Vol 2: Information Systems and Technology/R G Anderson
Economics for 'O' Level/L B Curzon
Elements of Commerce/C O'Connor
Human Resources Management/H T Graham
Industrial Administration/J C Denyer, J Batty
International Marketing/L S Walsh
Management, Planning and Control/R G Anderson
Management – Theory and Principles/T Proctor
Managerial Economics/J R Davies, S Hughes
Marketing/G B Giles
Marketing Overseas/A West
Marketing Research/T Proctor, M A Stone
Microcomputing/R G Anderson
Modern Commercial Knowledge/L W T Stafford
Modern Marketing/F Jefkins
Office Administration/J C Denyer, A L Mugridge
Operational Research/W M Harper, H C Lim
Organisation and Methods/R G Anderson
Production Management/H A Harding
Public Administration/M Barber, R Stacey
Public Relations/F Jefkins
Purchasing/C K Lysons
Sales and Sales Management/P Allen
Statistics/W M Harper
Stores Management/R J Carter

Accounting and Finance

Auditing/L R Howard
Basic Accounting/J O Magee
Basic Book-keeping/J O Magee
Capital Gains Tax/V Di Palma
Company Accounts/J O Magee
Company Secretarial Practice/L Hall, G M Thom
Cost and Management Accounting – Vols 1 & 2/W M Harper
Elements of Banking/D P Whiting
Elements of Finance for Managers/B K R Watts
Elements of Insurance/D S Hansell
Finance of Foreign Trade/D P Whiting
Investment: A Practical Approach/D Kerridge
Practice of Banking/E P Doyle, J E Kelly
Principles of Accounts/E F Castle, N P Owens
Taxation/H Toch

Humanities and Science

Biology Advanced Level/P T Marshall
British Government and Politics/F Randall
Chemistry for 'O' Level/G Usher
Economic Geography/H Robinson
European History 1789–1914/C A Leeds
Geology/A W R Potter, H Robinson
Introduction to Ecology/J C Emberlin
Land Surveying/R J P Wilson
Modern Economic History/E Seddon
Political Studies/C A Leeds
Sociology 'O' Level/F Randall
Twentieth Century History 1900–45/C A Leeds
World History: 1900 to the Present Day/C A Leeds